PROGRAMMING
FORTRAN 77

J. Ashcroft
R. H. Eldridge
R. W. Paulson
G. A. Wilson

Department of Mathematics,
University of Salford

COLLINS
8 Grafton Street, London W1

Collins Professional and Technical Books
William Collins Sons & Co. Ltd
8 Grafton Street, London W1X 3LA

First published in Great Britain by
Granada Publishing 1981
Reprinted 1982, 1983, 1984
Reprinted by Collins Professional and Technical Books 1986

Distributed in the United States of America
by Sheridan House, Inc.

Copyright © 1981 J. Ashcroft, R. H. Eldridge, R. W. Paulson and G. A. Wilson

ISBN 0–00–383392–5
(Previous ISBN 0–246–11573–4)

Printed and bound in Great Britain by
Mackays of Chatham, Kent

CONTENTS

PREFACE

The aim of this book is to teach a person with little or no knowledge
of computing how to write FORTRAN 77 programs. There are always two
stages in using a computer to solve a problem. The first is to
analyse the problem and develop a strategy (or algorithm) which will
produce the answer. The algorithm must be broken down into an
ordered sequence of simple operations and attention must be paid to
any special cases that might arise and appropriate measures taken.
The second stage is that of writing a program which will carry out
the operations required to produce the solution. Whilst this book is
primarily concerned with the second stage and describes how to write
programs in FORTRAN 77, it has been recognised that the first stage
is important, and often more difficult. Because of this, care has
been taken to describe, where appropriate, the analysis of the
problems considered and the way in which the solution is broken down
into suitable steps for programming.

The authors have not endeavoured to give an exhaustive description
of every part of the FORTRAN 77 language. In chapter 1 a brief
historical account of the development of computers is given, together
with an introduction to some of the basic ideas and terminology used
in computing. Chapters 2 to 9 give a detailed description of what
the authors believe to be main features of the language, which will
be sufficient for general programming. Most of the remaining
features are described briefly in chapter 10. The full definition of
FORTRAN 77 is contained in the report

    American National Standard Programming Language FORTRAN
    (A.N.S.I. X3.9 - 1978), published by the American National
    Standards Institute inc., 1430 Broadway, New York, U.S.A.
This is referred to later in the book as the ANSI Standard. The
beginner should understand that this report is probably only useful
as a reference work for experienced programmers.

A feature of the book is the numerous example programs which are given in the text. These have all been tested on an ICL 1904S computer using the FORTRAN 77 compiler which has been written at the University of Salford by Mr. D. M. Vallance and Dr. D. Bailey. The implementation is described in the manual

The Salford University FORTRAN 77 compiler, available from
the Computer Centre, University of Salford, Salford M5 4WT

The example programs are broadly of two types. The first are simple programs written to illustrate particular features of FORTRAN 77 at the time that they are introduced. The second type are longer and more demanding, being intended to show how programs are developed and to illustrate something of the range of problems that FORTRAN 77 can be used to solve. A number of programming exercises are given at the end of most of the chapters in the book, but it is anticipated that many readers will wish to supplement these with exercises which are relevant to their own discipline. For the most part, the standard of the exercises is below that of the harder examples in the text.

Since FORTRAN was originally developed for scientific and engineering work, most of the problems which it is used to solve are numeric; and this, to a large extent, is reflected in the book. Readers are advised to skip over any part of the book which uses a technique or a term with which they are unfamiliar.

Readers will notice that, at various points in the text, reference is made to features which are described later in the book. When this occurs, it is not intended that the reader should immediately look ahead, but simply that a mental note should be made that this is a point which will be discussed more fully later.

The order of the material presented in this book has been carefully structured to enable a variety of different types of computing course to be studied. In addition it gives valuable insight into the construction of computer programs and will serve as a reference text for details of the language.

A basic short computing course would require the material in chapters 1 to 4 inclusive and in addition sections 5.1 to 5.6 of chapter 5. If time permitted, sections 6.1 to 6.4 on formatted output from chapter 6 and some of the example programs from section 6.6 could be included.

An intermediate course would contain the material from chapters 1 to 6 and most of chapter 7, perhaps omitting section 7.6 on common blocks and BLOCK DATA subprograms. In addition, the basic material on character variables from sections 8.1 and 8.2 of chapter 8 would be useful.

Chapters 8 and 9 are intended to be self-contained. They contain material of interest to those whose problems require large amounts of data in a variety of formats. This would probably form part of a more advanced course.

A variety of additional features are described in chapter 10 in largely self-contained sections which can be picked out and studied in isolation as required. The choice of what items to relegate to chapter 10 rather than include in the main body of the text is open to discussion. However, it is the opinion of the authors that these features, although often very useful, are required less frequently than those described in earlier chapters, and that they should therefore be studied when the need arises.

It would be impossible and undesirable to cover in detail every minute feature of FORTRAN 77 in a teaching book of this size. For this, the ANSI Standard must be studied. However, it is the belief of the authors that no significant feature of the language has been omitted and that anyone acquainted with all the material in this book should be capable of setting almost any algorithm into a working FORTRAN 77 program.

The appendices are intended for reference purposes. Appendix 1 gives details of all the intrinsic functions available within the language. A much more detailed account of the mechanism used to access array elements in the computer store and the association between dummy and actual array and character arguments of subprograms is presented in appendix 2. Appendix 3 classifies the executable and non-executable statements of FORTRAN 77 and indicates the restrictions on the order in which the various statements may appear in a program unit. In addition, it gives details of the construction of all FORTRAN 77 statements. In appendix 4, the main differences between FORTRAN 77 and its predecessor (FORTRAN 66) are described. Before FORTRAN 77 was published, most compilers incorporated extensions to FORTRAN 66, but since these varied from implementation to implementation, it was felt that it would be preferable to relate FORTRAN 77 to FORTRAN 66 rather than to any particular implementation.

Finally, the authors would like to express their gratitude to the University of Salford, particularly the Department of Mathematics, for providing the facilities and environment which has made this book possible. The authors also wish to take this opportunity to thank all their colleagues at the University who have helped in the preparation of the book. In particular, thanks are due to Ernest Wilde for all the help and encouragement which he has freely given us at all times; to Dave Vallance and Dave Bailey of the University's Computing Laboratory for writing the compiler and for discussing abstruse points about the language with us; to Jim Cowie for his patient assistance with the preparation of the text; and to all those in the Mathematics Department and the Computing Laboratory who have read and commented upon the text.

J.A.
R.H.E.
R.W.P.
G.A.W.

CHAPTER 1
INTRODUCTION

This chapter describes some of the basic features of a computer and how it may be used to solve problems.

1.1 BASIC PRINCIPLES

A COMPUTER is a machine that processes data. It is a tool which man has invented, and is developing, in order to help him to solve problems. A computer has no personality of its own; anything that it does is as a result of human instruction. It has a limited repertoire of simple instructions which it obeys slavishly. The machine has no way of knowing whether the instructions it is obeying are what was really intended. It can go on obeying the same group of instructions indefinitely, since it does not have the intelligence to realise that this is obviously incorrect. In spite of this, computers are used increasingly because of their speed and accuracy in performing repetitive calculations or operations. A computer can add two numbers together within a microsecond (one millionth of a second) and get the correct result!

Because of its speed of operation, the machine is not given its instructions one by one. If this were done, it would be inactive for relatively long periods while instructions were being given to it. Instead, the computer stores all the instructions needed to complete a particular task. This complete set of instructions is called a COMPUTER PROGRAM. It then carries out the whole set of instructions automatically in the sequence laid down by the person who has written the program, and who is called the PROGRAMMER. The sequence of steps necessary to perform a particular computation is called an ALGORITHM.

The program controls operations which are carried out on DATA stored in the computer. The operations performed by a computer are of an elementary nature. Typically they are simple arithmetic operations, such as addition and multiplication, and the comparison

of numbers.   Since   characters other than numbers are coded
numerically by the computer, these operations can be extended to the
comparison and manipulation of characters.

A computer itself consists of a system of electronic circuitry and
mechanical devices.   This is called the HARDWARE of the computer.
The SOFTWARE consists of the programs necessary to operate the
hardware and to provide the solution to a particular problem.
Although this book is concerned with the writing of software, a basic
knowledge of the hardware makes a proper understanding of the
software much easier to grasp.

1.2 HISTORICAL BACKGROUND

Down through the ages man has sought to increase the speed and
accuracy of his calculations.   Forms of ABACUS, such as pebbles in a
sand tray or beads on a counting frame, were in widespread use
throughout the Mediterranean and the Eastern world well before 1000
BC.   Over the years the abacus was refined and techniques for its use
improved but no new form of calculator was produced until the end of
the sixteenth century AD.   About 1594, John   Napier   invented
logarithms and a form of calculator using logarithms, known as
NAPIER´S BONES, was developed. A few years later, William Oughtred
realised   that calculations could be performed by sliding two
logarithmic scales together and the SLIDE RULE was   invented.
Mechanical machines using gears were also developed at this time with
Pascal producing an adding machine in 1642 and Leibnitz extending the
capability to include multiplication about 40 years later.

None of these devices and machines were automatic because they
required the continuous intervention of a human operator.   This
prompted the question of whether it was possible to devise a fully
automatic calculating machine capable of carrying out extensive
calculations without human intervention.   The first man to put
forward detailed proposals for such a machine was Charles Babbage in
1834. He never built his machine, which was called an Analytical
Engine,   because   it   was   impossible to achieve the precision
engineering it required, but his ideas provided the foundation on
which computers were eventually built. Babbage proposed to control
his machine by punched cards containing instructions for the required
operations, which was similar to the way that punched cards were used
to control the patterns on Jacquard looms, which had been invented
around 1800.   These cards formed what would now be called the
program. The idea of using punched cards was taken up by Hollerith,
who mechanised the processing of information for the United States
Census Bureau around 1890, and this led to the development of office

machines for sorting and counting.

The first fully automatic calculating machine, designed by Aiken in association with IBM, was produced in 1944. It was called ASCC (Automatic Sequence Controlled Calculator) and was purely electro-mechanical, consisting of about 750,000 component parts. It was extremely slow by modern standards, taking about 4 seconds for a multiplication. The first completely electronic computer was called ENIAC (Electronic Numerical Integrator and Calculator). Designed by Eckert and Mauchly, it was completed in the United States in 1946. It was about 1000 times faster than ASCC but maintaining its 18,000 valves in working order for long periods of time was difficult. In its original form it was programmed by plugging interconnecting wires into a board in the appropriate positions. This made changing programs a very slow and tedious process. At this time, Von Neumann proposed the use of a stored program, the sequence of instructions to control the machine being held internally in the store of the machine and being capable of alteration and manipulation just like data. ENIAC was later modified to partially implement this idea. Already the next computer, EDVAC, was being designed to incorporate features such as a stored program and much larger internal store. It became operational in 1951. However, it was preceded in 1949 by EDSAC, which was built at Cambridge University by a team headed by Wilkes and which was the first practical-sized stored program computer.

In the early 1950's, the invention of the transistor and magnetic core storage had a profound effect on computer technology, extending computer speed and capacity enormously. Computers incorporating these advances became known as SECOND GENERATION machines to distinguish them from earlier types. Progress continued to accelerate with the use of integrated circuits which, together with the development of operating systems which allow several users to access the one computer simultaneously, produced the THIRD GENERATION machines from the middle 1960's. Now, with the advent of silicon chip technology, it is possible to have a reasonably powerful minicomputer the size of a television set; and a microcomputer, which can be connected to appropriate mechanisms for getting information in and out, on a single silicon chip.

1.3 BASIC HARDWARE ELEMENTS

There are five basic elements to a computer system. Their use is illustrated by the following example.

Suppose that the length "Z" of the hypotenuse of a right angled triangle is to be calculated from the lengths, "X" and "Y", of the other sides by a slave who cannot think for himself but who will obey a set of instructions exactly. He has a desk with an "in-tray" in which is placed a slip of paper containing the values of "X" and "Y" and an "out-tray" in which he will eventually put a slip of paper containing the value of "Z". He is also provided with a calculation sheet which contains the set of instructions he is to obey and space for writing down values of quantities, and a calculator to assist with arithmetic. Assuming that "Z" is given by Pythagoras' formula

$$Z = \sqrt{X^2 + Y^2}$$

the calculation sheet is as shown below

CALCULATION SHEET	
Instructions	X
(1) Take the slip of paper from the in-tray, read the values and write them in the boxes labelled X and Y.	Y
(2) Calculate X^2 and Y^2 and write their values on the scrap pad.	Z
(3) Add these values together.	scrap
(4) Calculate the square root of this sum.	pad
(5) Record this value in the box labelled Z.	
(6) Write this value on a slip of paper and place it in the out-tray.	

The slave performs the calculation by obeying the instructions on the calculation sheet. He does not need any intelligence, since this is provided within the instructions. Thus the slave can be made redundant and the process automated.

The five basic elements that are required for the computer are an INPUT DEVICE (in-tray) and OUTPUT DEVICE (out-tray) for communication with the outside world, a STORE (calculation sheet) containing the set of instructions to be obeyed and space for storage of data and results, an ARITHMETIC UNIT (calculator) for doing the arithmetic and a CONTROL UNIT (the slave) to interpret the instructions and perform the appropriate operations.

The part of the computer system which carries out the processing of programs consists of the MAIN STORE and CENTRAL PROCESSOR UNIT, or CPU, which contains the ARITHMETIC UNIT, and the CONTROL UNIT. Other devices, such as those for input and output, are connected to these and are usually referred to as PERIPHERAL UNITS (or PERIPHERALS).

The main store contains a large number of memory locations, or storage locations, each containing one computer WORD consisting of a fixed number of symbols. The important feature about the symbols is that they are represented by electrical phenomena which have only two distinguishable states. For this reason, the fundamental components of a word are often referred to as BINARY DIGITS, or BITS, and the WORD LENGTH is equal to the number of bits contained in a storage location. A group of eight bits is called a BYTE. A byte may be used to represent letters of the English alphabet, decimal digits, punctuation marks and certain other characters used in everyday scientific work, each eight-bit pattern representing a different character. For this, one of a number of standard codes is followed, examples of which are EBCDIC (Extended Binary Coded Decimal Interchange Code) and ASCII (American Standard Code for Information Interchange). Because the word length of one machine may be different from that of another, storage capacities are usually measured in numbers of bytes. The size of the store is normally given in terms of KILOBYTES, where a kilobyte is a thousand bytes.

The content of a word need not represent a number or a sequence of characters, it can represent any information that is comprehensible to the hardware. For example, it can represent a computer instruction that will be decoded by the CPU. An instruction has to indicate the operation to be performed and the storage locations that contain the data to be used. A storage location is referenced by its ADDRESS, which is a binary number. The VALUE of a given storage location is determined by the content of that location. Thus each storage location has two distinct properties, its address and its content (or value). The content of a location does not alter until a new value is inserted into that location, and the address of the location never alters.

Most computers have to store more information, both programs and data, than there is space available in the main store. This need is met by supplementing the main store with auxiliary storage, called BACKING STORE, usually consisting of MAGNETIC DISC UNITS, MAGNETIC TAPE UNITS and MAGNETIC DRUMS. A magnetic disc is shaped like a gramophone record and groups of magnetic discs are assembled into DISC PACKS. The surface of each disc possesses a number of identifiable tracks in which the information is stored as a pattern of bits. A FLOPPY DISC is a flexible form of magnetic disc. Magnetic tape is a ribbon of plastic with a coating of magnetic oxide on which the information is stored. A magnetic drum is a rotating cylinder on whose surface the information is stored. In each case, the data stored is transferred to the main store when it is required for processing.

Magnetic tape units are sometimes called SEQUENTIAL ACCESS DEVICES. This is because the information on a magnetic tape can only be accessed in the same sequence as it was originally written to the

tape. If information is required from a point halfway through the
tape, the whole of the first half of the tape must pass the reading
mechanism before the required information can be read. In the case
of a magnetic disc, which is commonly called a RANDOM ACCESS DEVICE
or DIRECT ACCESS DEVICE, it is possible to move the read/write
mechanism directly from one part of the disc to another, so that
information may be read from any sector of the disc without having to
read any other information from the disc first.

The computer communicates with the outside world through INPUT
PERIPHERALS and OUTPUT PERIPHERALS. An input peripheral accepts data
in some suitable form and translates it into sequences of electronic
impulses for input to the CPU. An output peripheral carries out the
reverse process. Clearly, a magnetic disc unit or magnetic tape unit
may be used as either an input peripheral or an output peripheral.

Another common input device is the CARD READER. A CARD PUNCH is
used to prepare 80-column cards, in which each character is
represented by a column with holes punched in it.   The card reader
interprets different combinations of holes as different characters.
When computers were first developed, programs and data were normally
submitted on cards, and this has acted as a constraint on many
programming languages, including FORTRAN.

The LINE PRINTER is the most common output peripheral. This device
prints information from the computer's store one line at a time.   The
maximum number of characters that can be printed on a line of output
depends on the equipment being used, the commonest value for this
maximum being 132 characters.

A COMPUTER TERMINAL is a peripheral which can be used for both
input and output. In most commercial installations, it has replaced
punched cards as the main method of submitting programs and data.   A
terminal consists of a KEYBOARD, which is used to communicate with
the computer, and a DISPLAY, which shows the computer's response.
The display output may be on paper or it may be on a television
screen, in which case the terminal is called a VISUAL DISPLAY UNIT,
or VDU.

1.4 THE FORTRAN LANGUAGE

In the last section, it was stated that a computer sees instructions
given to it as strings of binary digits.   This is normally termed
MACHINE LANGUAGE.   Clearly, it is difficult for normal human beings
to write programs in machine language without making large numbers of
errors.   Programming languages avoid this problem by enabling
programmers to write programs in terms with which they are familiar,
then to call in a special program called a COMPILER which translates

their programs into machine language. The process of translation is
called COMPILATION.

The most efficient programming language is one which   gives
precisely one instruction for every machine language instruction.
This is called a LOW-LEVEL PROGRAMMING LANGUAGE, or ASSEMBLER
LANGUAGE.   Each instruction will have a specific name and storage
locations will probably be referred to by SYMBOLIC NAMES which are
associated by the compiler with distinct addresses in the store. As
an example of assembler language programming, consider the following
instruction

"Add together the contents of storage locations called FRED and
BERT, storing the result in the storage location called ANDY"
This could require three assembler language instructions of the form:

    LOAD FRED
    ADD BERT
    STORE ANDY

The effect of these instructions is to transfer a copy of the
contents of the storage location named FRED to the CPU; then to add
to this number a copy of the number from the storage location named
BERT; and finally to store the result in the storage location named
ANDY. The similarity with the use of a pocket calculator should be
noted.   As low-level languages are usually too abstruse for the
general programmer, programs are not normally written in assembler
language except by computing specialists.

The development of HIGH-LEVEL PROGRAMMING LANGUAGES dates from   the
middle 1950´s.   The aim was to make it possible for people who were
not computing specialists to write their own programs.

The fundamental idea of every high-level language is that
programmers should write programs in terms with which they are
familiar.   The earliest high-level language to be widely used was
FORTRAN, which is an acronym for FORmula TRANslation.   FORTRAN was
originally designed to be used for scientific and engineering work
and it remains the most widely-used language for this purpose. Other
languages were developed for different purposes, the most widely-used
being COBOL (COmmon Business Orientated Language) and BASIC
(Beginners All-purpose Symbolic Instruction Code), which is designed
for elementary educational work.   The format of each of these
languages reflects the purpose for which it was originally designed.
FORTRAN has a pseudo-algebraic format which reflects its engineering
origins; while COBOL, being designed for business work, is intended
to be as close to English as possible.

It should be noted that one high-level language instruction
normally corresponds to more than one machine language instruction.
For example, the FORTRAN version of the instruction given earlier in

this section is
        ANDY=FRED+BERT
In this example, one high-level instruction corresponds to three assembler instructions.

As more and more facilities became available, FORTRAN developed to take full advantage of them. Manufacturers normally implemented their own version of the language, which was tailored to their own machines. The result was that a number of different "dialects" of FORTRAN were developed which had a central core common to most, but with different facilities being available in the different versions. This meant that if a program was written to be used on one machine, it normally needed a number of changes to make it work on a different machine. This caused a considerable waste of time and effort if a company changed its computer, or if a program was run on a different machine within the company.

The result was a demand for a standard form of the language; that is, a definition of FORTRAN which would result in a program working correctly no matter which machine was used to run it. Accordingly, in 1966 the American National Standards Institute (ANSI) defined a standard form for the language which has become known as ANSI FORTRAN or STANDARD FORTRAN. In essence, this was a subset of the various dialects of FORTRAN which were then available. A program written in ANSI FORTRAN is PORTABLE, which means that it could be used on any "FORTRAN-speaking" computer with a minimum of alterations. The definition of a standard for the language also means that there is a basis for comparison between a particular implementation of FORTRAN and ANSI FORTRAN. A programmer having a knowledge of ANSI FORTRAN could expect to be provided with a list of points where a particular compiler differed from the Standard.

This version of FORTRAN was rather limited in the facilities which it made available, even by 1966 standards. It was rarely implemented precisely as laid down by the Standard, since most implementors included commonly accepted additional features in their implementation. A widely accepted version of the language is called FORTRAN IV, which is based on the Standard but which includes extra facilities.

The many developments in computing since 1966 have made it necessary to revise the Standard. Accordingly, an expanded version of the Standard called FORTRAN 77 (FORTRAN - 1977 version) was published in 1978. The 1966 Standard has come to be known as FORTRAN 66. For almost all purposes, FORTRAN 66 is a subset of FORTRAN 77, so that virtually all programs which conform to the old Standard will also conform to the new. FORTRAN 77 contains many new features which make it possible to tackle a wider range of problems than FORTRAN 66 allowed; and which also make writing programs much easier. The complete definition of FORTRAN 77 is contained in the ANSI Standard reference document, details of which are given in the preface of this book.

1.5 DATA CHARACTERISTICS

The basic unit of information, or DATA, is the CHARACTER. As was seen in section 1.3, computers work in terms of bits, but characters are coded as various combinations of bits. Any character which is allowed by the computer can be used as data. However, since some characters may be allowed by one computer but not by another, it is advisable to limit the characters used as data to those which can be used in a FORTRAN 77 program. These are

A - Z	the letters
0 - 9	the digits
+	the plus sign
-	the minus sign, hyphen or dash
*	the asterisk
/	the slash or oblique character
=	the equals sign
(	the opening bracket, or left parenthesis
)	the closing bracket, or right parenthesis
,	the comma
.	the decimal point, full stop, or dot
	the space, or blank character
:	the colon
'	the apostrophe, or quote sign
£ or $	the currency symbol

Note that the currency symbol is dependent on the computer being used. It is usually a pound sign or a dollar sign, but any other symbol is allowed.

The only constraints which FORTRAN 77 puts on the method of coding for the characters given above are that each letter should be coded by a smaller value than the code for a letter which comes after it in the alphabet, and that a similar constraint should apply to the coding of the digits. Thus the coding for A must be less than the coding for B, which must be less than the coding for C, and so on. Likewise, the coding for 0 must be less than the coding for 1, which must be less than the coding for 2, and so on. No rule is laid down as to the relative sizes of the coding for any of the other characters; nor indeed for the size of the coding for the digits compared to that of the coding for the characters, except that all letters must either precede or follow all numbers in the coding sequence.

Groups of one or more characters together form a FIELD. The characters within a field normally have a particular relationship to each other. For example, they may be all part of a number, or all part of a name.

One or more fields may be grouped to form a RECORD. This may be thought of as the amount of data that can be transferred to or from the memory by one statement in a FORTRAN 77 program. An example of an INPUT RECORD or DATA RECORD is a standard 80 column card, which contains data to be read into the computer. An example of an OUTPUT RECORD is a line of line-printer output. Both of the above are examples of FIXED-LENGTH RECORDS. When using other input and output media, records of any length are allowed.

Two more names which are commonly used to describe data are FILE and DATABASE. A FILE is a collection of one or more records which normally have common characteristics. For example, the records in a company's personnel file may have the name of an employee in positions 1 to 25 of the record, the employee's room number in positions 26 to 30, the employee's telephone extension in positions 31 to 35, and so on. The data contained in each of these fields will vary from record to record, but each record in the file contains the same fields in the same relative positions. The method of accessing the records in a file will be described in chapter 9. A DATABASE is a collection of interrelated data which supports the operations of an organisation. It has a number of characteristics, including a requirement that it should be stored without unnecessary or harmful redundancy and that it should be independent of the multiple programs which use it. The data should also be structured in such a way as to allow for future application development. There is no facility built into FORTRAN 77 for accessing databases. This requires an extended version of the language which uses statements that do not form part of the Standard.

1.6 COMPILATION, LOADING AND EXECUTION OF FORTRAN 77 PROGRAMS

When a program is run on the computer, it normally passes through three stages, which are termed "compilation", "loading" and "execution". In order to run a program, it is necessary for commands to be given to the operating system of the computer. The method of doing this varies from machine to machine depending on what facilities the computer manager has made available.

Errors in the program can be recognised by the computer at any of the three stages. They will normally be signalled by an ERROR MESSAGE, which gives the point in the program at which the error

occurred and also a diagnosis of the fault. The helpfulness of the
error message will vary from compiler to compiler since, in general,
the more checks that are carried out, the less efficient it will be.
When an error occurs, the rest of the three stages mentioned earlier
are normally aborted.

As stated in earlier sections, the FORTRAN 77 program is translated
into machine language at the COMPILATION stage, which is the first
stage in running a program. The compiler checks the syntax of the
FORTRAN 77 program and gives a COMPILER ERROR MESSAGE if any
grammatical mistakes are detected. Because of typing mistakes, it is
unusual for a program to compile correctly on its first run, even
when it is written by an experienced programmer. The result is that
programmers soon become familiar with the messages generated because
of their mistakes. Unfortunately, it often happens that an error in
one instruction in the program will make another part of that
instruction or a different instruction appear incorrect to the
compiler. This means that two error messages will be printed, one
referring to the genuine error and the other to the spurious error.

The LOADING stage, which is also known as CONSOLIDATION, is the
second stage in running a program, where any routines required by the
program are incorporated into it. A ROUTINE is a special set of
instructions designed to carry out a particular task. The routines
which are incorporated may be systems routines, such as those which
cause data to be read or printed; or intrinsic functions, which will
be described in chapter 3; or subprograms supplied by the programmer,
which will be described in chapter 7. The most common LOADER ERROR
MESSAGES arise as a result of misspelling the name of a subprogram or
an intrinsic function.

The third and final stage of running a program is the EXECUTION
stage.   This is when the instructions in the program are actually
obeyed by the computer. EXECUTION (or RUN-TIME) ERROR MESSAGES arise
when the computer is asked to obey a valid instruction with invalid
data.   This can arise if, for example, the instruction is to divide
by a number from a particular location when that number is zero; or
the instruction is to take the square root of the number in a
location when that number is negative.

It sometimes happens that a program passes through all three stages
and then gives results which are incorrect. This may be because of
faults in the program logic or simply because an incorrect formula
has been used.   Accordingly, a new program should be tested using
data that gives known results. If this is not done, any results from
the program should be regarded with suspicion. It should be noted
that, except for very simple programs, it is not normally sufficient
to test the program with only one set of data. A proper test makes

sure that every path in the program logic is followed, which normally means a number of runs of the program with different sets of data. Not testing programs in this way is a common fault of beginners, who frequently produce programs which give correct results for a particular set of test data, but which fail or give incorrect results when run using another set of data.

Especially in longer or more complicated programs than those discussed in this book, a program may sometimes give results that are incorrect and the programmer cannot find the fault in the program logic that has caused the error. When this happens, it is a good idea to insert extra instructions into the program to cause the program to print intermediate results. If this is done judiciously, it is usually possible to trace the error quite easily.

Finally, beginners should be aware that there is no such thing as a unique "correct" computer program for solving a particular problem. It is normally possible to say that one program is easier to follow than another, or that one is more efficient than another, although this may depend to some extent on the computer on which the program is run. In this book, numerous example programs are given. They have been written as specimens, to be studied and evaluated by the student. Normally, there are improvements that could be made to the programs, such as incorporating extra checks on input data. Doing this in the text would have lengthened the programs, thereby confusing the reader, so the appropriate comments are normally made in the accompanying text. The notes in the text are at least as important as the programs. They should be read carefully, as they sometimes indicate deficiencies in the program being considered as well as giving supplementary explanation.

CHAPTER 2
LIST-DIRECTED INPUT AND OUTPUT
AND SIMPLE ASSIGNMENTS

This chapter describes how numbers can be read into the store of the computer, and also how numbers and character strings are printed. The basic construction of a FORTRAN 77 program and a number of specification statements are also described.

2.1 THE BASIC LAYOUT OF A FORTRAN 77 PROGRAM

Consider the simple FORTRAN 77 program

```
^^^^^^PROGRAM EX21
^^^^^^READ *,A,B,I
^^^^^^PRINT *,A,B,I
^^^^^^END
```

Where a space character is essential in this program, it is denoted by ^; the other space characters are optional. The effect of the program is to read two real numbers and one integer from a data record into locations in the store of the computer which are referred to later in the program by the names A, B and I. The contents of the locations named A, B and I are then printed on the line printer.

The data supplied to the program consists of two real numbers and an integer. They are supplied on a data record, and are separated by one or more space characters. Hence the data supplied to the program could be

3.14159^-0.0005^^^^^2240

In order to run the program, commands must be given to the computer which tell it where to find the program, to compile, load and execute the program, and where to find the data required by the program. How this is done depends on the computer system being used. The necessary instructions are given in the JOB CONTROL LANGUAGE (J.C.L.) of the computer.

When this program was run at Salford, the results were

    3.141590   −5.000000E−04   2240

It should be noted that the layout of these results will probably vary, depending on the compiler being used.

Every computer program consists of a sequence of instructions to the computer. These instructions are called STATEMENTS. The example program contains four statements. These are a PROGRAM statement, a READ statement, a PRINT statement and an END statement. Details of how these statements are constructed are given in section 2.3. Statements are either EXECUTABLE or NON-EXECUTABLE.

An EXECUTABLE STATEMENT specifies an action to be taken by the computer, such as reading numbers into its store, storing the result of an arithmetic calculation, or checking whether or not a condition is true. Executable statements are obeyed in the order in which they appear in the program unless a control statement (to be described in chapter 4) alters this sequence. Thus the first executable statement in the program will be obeyed first, then the second, then the third, and so on provided no control statement alters this sequence. The executable statements used in the example program are the READ statement, which specifies that three numbers are to be read from a data record; the PRINT statement, which specifies that three numbers are to be printed on the line printer; and the END statement, which specifies the physical end of the program.

Any statement which does not specify an action to be taken is called a NON-EXECUTABLE STATEMENT. Non-executable statements may specify characteristics or arrangements, such as the type of data that a storage location is to hold, or the number of storage locations to be grouped together as an array. Such statements are called SPECIFICATION STATEMENTS, which appear before any executable statements in a program. Other non-executable statements specify names for programs, set initial values to storage locations, or specify the form in which quantities are arranged on output. The only non-executable statement used in the example program is the PROGRAM statement, which names the program EX21. Appendix 3 details the rules which govern the order of statements in a program.

FORTRAN was originally defined in the expectation that programs would be submitted on eighty-column cards. Although this mode of communication with the computer is now the exception rather than the rule, the layout of a FORTRAN 77 program still conforms to this arrangement. Accordingly, a line in a FORTRAN 77 program contains 72 characters, since the last eight columns of the card were normally used to identify the program and the position of the card in the

program   deck.   For   similar historical reasons, the character
positions in a program line are often called columns.

Each   statement   in   a FORTRAN 77 program must start on a new line,
and it must be written between positions 7 and 72 of the line.   Thus,
in the example program, the P of PROGRAM, the R of READ, the P of
PRINT and the E of END must all appear in or after position 7 of the
line.   No such limitation applies to data, which can be placed
between positions 1 and 6 or beyond position 72 on the data record.

Positions 1 to 6 of the line have special significance.   It may be
that the statement contains too many characters to fit into one line.
When this happens, the statement may be "continued" on the next line
provided the first five characters of the line are blank and a
character other than blank or zero is in position six of the line.
The first line of the statement is called the INITIAL LINE and any
line on which the statement is continued is called a CONTINUATION
LINE. The character which appears in position six of a continuation
line is not part of the statement. It serves no purpose other than to
indicate that the line is a continuation line. The effect is as if
the character in position seven of the first continuation line
appears in position 73 of the initial line, the character in position
eight of the continuation line appears in position 74 of the initial
line, and so on. Note that an initial line must have a blank or zero
character in position six and that a continuation line must have
blank characters in positions one to five. An initial line can have
more than one continuation line if required, but there is an upper
limit of 19 continuation lines for any one statement.

Any line in a program which has a C or an asterisk in position one
is called a COMMENT LINE. Such a line is ignored by the compiler.
This means that it does not affect the program in any way, so that it
can be used to provide documentation for the program.   Comment lines
may appear at any point in the program: they may even appear between
an initial line and a continuation line.

Positions one to five of the initial line of any FORTRAN 77
statement can contain a LABEL.   The use of this feature of the
language will be described more fully in chapter 4, but it is defined
here for the sake of completeness. A label is an unsigned non-zero
integer, and it provides a means of referring to a particular
statement from elsewhere in the program. It is normal practice that
the only statements in a program which carry labels are those which
other statements reference.

Finally, it should be noted that a blank character within a program
has no significance except when it appears in a character constant,
as will be described in section 2.2.   It follows that blank
characters can be used to improve the layout of a program.

2.2 CONSTANTS AND VARIABLES

A FORTRAN 77 program normally contains constants and variables. The difference between the two is that the value of a constant cannot be changed by the program, whereas the value of a variable may.

A CONSTANT is a quantity which does not vary, either during the run of the program or for different runs of the program. There are three main types of constant: character constants, integer constants and real constants.

A CHARACTER CONSTANT, or character string, is a string of characters preceded and followed by an apostrophe.   Examples of character constants are

　　′DERBY^COUNTY′

a character string of length twelve characters;

　　′2+2=4′

a character string of length five characters; and

　　′^^^′

a character string of length three characters. Note that the space character, or blank character (often denoted in this book by ^) is significant in a character string.   If it is necessary for an apostrophe itself to be one of the characters in a character string, a pair of consecutive apostrophes (with no intervening space character) is used to represent the single apostrophe in the string. For example, the character constant

　　′BOB′′S′

represents the characters BOB′S. The length of this character string is five characters.

An INTEGER CONSTANT consists of a string of digits, optionally preceded by a sign. Examples are

　　21　　　　0　　　　　　-5678　　　　+1 000002

Integer constants are held with complete accuracy by the computer provided they are not too large for the machine to accommodate.

A REAL CONSTANT is the compiler′s approximation to a real number. In FORTRAN 77, real numbers can be normal decimals consisting of an optional sign, an integer part, a decimal point and a fractional part. Examples are

　　1.0　　-3.2　　3.14159　　0.0　　+0.000001

If real numbers are very large or very small, it is common arithmetic practice to represent them as the product of a decimal number and ten raised to an appropriate power.   For example, 0.0000716 could be represented as the product of 7.16 and 10 raised to the power -5; and 7160000 as the product of 7.16 and 10 raised to the sixth power. In a similar way, these numbers can be represented in FORTRAN 77 by

7.16E-5 and 7.16E6 respectively. It should be noted that this form does <u>not</u> contain a multiplication sign, and also that the number before the E is essential. If this number is not present, it will be assumed that a variable name or an arithmetic expression is intended. For example, normal arithmetic practice allows the number 0.01 to be written as

$$10^{-2}$$

In FORTRAN 77, however, this number may not be written as
   E-2
since this is an arithmetic expression whose value is two less than that of the variable E. Instead it should be written as
   1.0E-2   or   1E-2
or their equivalent.

It should be noted that real numbers can be stored with only a limited precision by the computer. The process of converting a real decimal number to its equivalent binary form frequently produces a recurring sequence of bits for the fractional part, only a limited number of which can be stored. For example, the binary equivalent of 0.2 is
   0.001100110011...
and a particular computer might be capable of storing only the first 16 bits, thus introducing a ROUNDING ERROR into the value stored. The precision with which real constants can be stored depends on the machine used and typically varies between the equivalent of 7 to 14 decimal digits.

A VARIABLE is an entity whose value may change in the course of running the program. A particular location in the store of the computer may be given a name by the programmer. Using this name, the location can be referenced at various points in the program. For example, a number may be stored in that location, or a copy of the number from that location may be used in a calculation. The name given to the location is called a VARIABLE NAME. Note that a variable name is the name given to a variable. The term does not imply that the name itself can be changed, but that the contents of the location which has been associated with the name may change as a result of obeying statements in the program as it is being run. In program EX21 considered in the last section, three variables named A, B and I were used.

If a location has no number stored in it at a particular point in a program, it is said to be UNDEFINED at that point. At the start of a program all variables are normally undefined. The variables become defined as the statements in the program cause numbers to be put into the storage locations, perhaps as a result of reading values from a

data record or as a result of a calculation. For example, in program
EX21 the variables A, B and I are undefined at the start of the
program. They become defined as a result of reading values from the
data record when the READ statement is obeyed.

Variable names can be chosen, subject to a few simple rules, at the
programmer's discretion. This means that the programmer can choose
names which relate in a meaningful way to the physical variables of
the problem. For example, a program that involves the calculation of
the root of an equation could use a variable named ROOT to hold the
root; or the calculation of the sum of a number of quantities could
have the result sent to SUM; or the calculation of the value added
tax on a transaction could be held by a variable named VAT.

Variable names are required to consist of up to six letters and
digits, starting with a letter. They must contain no characters
other than letters and digits. The following are examples of valid
variable names.

A BILL I251 PI X4X9Z K9 SQUARE LIMIT

The following are examples of invalid variable names.

27   - does not start with a letter
*5   - does not start with a letter, and also contains a
            character other than a letter or digit
AVERAGE   - contains too many characters
K-9   - contains a character other than a letter or digit
E.G.   - contains characters other than letters or digits
JOHN'S   - contains a character other than a letter or digit

Note, however, that PI^BY^20 is a valid variable name. In this
context the space characters, shown here as ^, are not significant
and the compiler interprets the name as PIBY20.

As with constants, there are a number of different types of
variable. For the present, only INTEGER VARIABLES and REAL VARIABLES
are considered. These are used to hold integer numbers and real
numbers respectively. For these variables, there is a standard
convention in FORTRAN 77. This is that any variable name which
starts with one of the letters I, J, K, L, M or N is the name of an
integer variable; while all other variable names are the names of
real variables. For example, the names

A   BILL   PI   X4X9Z   SQUARE

are real variable names, while the names

I251   K9   LIMIT

are integer variable names. Hence, in program EX21, A and B are real
variable names and I is an integer variable name.

The convention can be overridden by declaring all the variable
names which do not follow the convention in special statements at the
start of the program, as will be described in section 2.5.

2.3 CONSTRUCTION OF THE PROGRAM, READ, PRINT AND END STATEMENTS

In this section, the construction of the statements used in program
EX21 is described.

2.3.1 The PROGRAM Statement

This statement gives a name to the program. It can be omitted
without affecting the program, but it is useful for documentation
purposes. Every program given as an example in this book is named.

 The program name (EX21 in the example program) must be chosen in
the same way as a variable name, as was described in section 2.2.
This means that it must consist of up to six letters and digits,
starting with a letter.

 If the PROGRAM statement appears in the program, it must be the
first statement in the program. The program name should not be used
for any other purpose by the program. Note that, since the space
character is not significant in FORTRAN 77 apart from when it appears
in a character string, it can be used to improve the layout of the
program. Hence the statements

^^^^^^PROGRAM EX21

and

^^^^^^   PROGRAM   EX   2   1

are equivalent. It may or may not be felt that the second form is
preferable to the first.

2.3.2 The READ Statement

In the example program, the statement

^^^^^^READ *,A,B,I

causes two real numbers and one integer to be read from a data record
and stored in locations which the program names A, B and I. A, B and
I are variables and their names are chosen by the programmer subject
to the rules described in section 2.2. Hence A and B are real
variables and I is an integer variable.

 The asterisk indicates that LIST-DIRECTED INPUT is to be used.
Each number on the data record is separated from the next by a
SEPARATOR. This is usually one or more space characters. Care must
be taken to make sure that the types of the numbers in the data are
compatible with the types of the variables. If this is not done, a
run time fault may occur. For example, if the data

3.14159 -0.0005 2240.0

had been supplied to program EX21, the computer should object because

of the attempt to read the real number 2240.0 into the integer
location I.   No such problem arises, however, if an integer is read
into a real location. For example, if the data

    3.14159 -5 2240

is supplied to program EX21, the value given to the real variable B
is -5.0.

  The general form of the READ statement is

    ^^^^^^READ *,list

where "list" is a list of variables, each separated from the next by
a comma.

A program can contain as many READ statements as a programmer
wishes.   Each READ statement in the program starts reading from a
fresh data record, even though the previous data record may contain
data which has not been read.

  As an example, consider what happens when the program

    ^^^^^^PROGRAM EX22
    ^^^^^^READ *,A,B
    ^^^^^^READ *,I
    ^^^^^^PRINT *,A,B,I
    ^^^^^^END

was run using the data

    3.14159 -0.0005 78
    2240

The output was the same as for program EX21. The integer 78 is not
read into the store of the computer. This is because the first READ
statement stores 3.14159 in A and -0.0005 in B. There are no more
variables in the list, so the rest of the first data record is
ignored.   The second READ statement reads from a new data record, so
as a result 2240 is read into I.

  If the numbers read from a data record are not sufficient to fill
all the list of variables in a READ statement, then numbers are read
from the next data record. For example, when program EX22 was run
using the data

    3.14159
    -0.0005
    2240

the output was the same as that for program EX21.

2.3.3 The PRINT Statement

In programs EX21 and EX22, the statement

    ^^^^^^PRINT *,A,B,I

causes copies of the contents of the locations named A, B and I to be printed on the line printer, first the contents of A, then the contents of B, then the contents of I. As with the READ statement, the asterisk signifies LIST-DIRECTED OUTPUT. In the case of the PRINT statement, this means that the compiler defines the way in which the numbers are to be arranged on output. In other words, the compiler imposes the number of positions of the output line which are to be occupied by the number; it imposes the number of decimal places or significant digits which are to be printed; and, if the number is real, it imposes whether it is to be printed in exponential or decimal form. This may or may not meet the requirements of the programmer. In any case, the form chosen for list-directed output will vary from compiler to compiler, which means that the results are likely to have different layouts when different compilers are used.

The general form of the list-directed PRINT statement is

          PRINT *,list

where "list" is a list of constants and/or variables, each separated from the next by a comma. The term "list-directed" is used because the list of variables and/or constants is used to direct the layout of the quantities to be printed. Note that the statement

          PRINT *,A,22.7,B

is valid, since constants are allowed in the "list" of a PRINT statement. The output as a result of this statement is the value of A followed by the number 22.7 and the value of B.

A program can contain as many PRINT statements as a programmer wishes. Each PRINT statement starts a fresh line of output. Note that the statement

          PRINT *

causes a blank line to be output.

2.3.4 The END Statement

Every FORTRAN 77 program must terminate with an END statement, which indicates that the end of the sequence of instructions and comments which constitutes the program has been reached. When it is encountered, execution of the program is terminated.

2.4 OUTPUT OF TEXT

In most programs, the simple printing of numbers is not very informative without some form of description to go with them. This can be achieved by including character constants, as described in section 2.2, among the list of items to be output by means of a PRINT statement.

2.4.1 Example Program

The following FORTRAN 77 program is a simpler version of program
EX21. It reads two real numbers and produces a description of the
data in its output.

```
      PROGRAM EX23
      READ *,A,B
      PRINT *,´ONE NUMBER IS ´,A,´ AND THE ´,
     1    ´OTHER IS ´,B
      END
```

Note that from this point in the book, the six space characters which
normally appear at the start of a program line will not be indicated
explicitly by the symbol ^.
  When this program was run using
    3.14159 −0.0005
as data, the results were

```
ONE NUMBER IS     3.141590    AND THE OTHER IS     −5.000000E−04
```

Note the use of a continuation line in this example program.   The
presence of a character in position six of line four of the program
indicates that it is a continuation of the previous line, as was
described in section 2.1.   The spaces between the 1 and the ´
character on the continuation line are present solely to improve the
layout of the program. As was mentioned in section 2.1, they will be
ignored by the compiler because they are not part of a character
string. Notice also that the character string
    ´ AND THE OTHER IS ´
has been split into two parts by the statement to make the program
line shorter. The result of
    ´ AND THE ´,´OTHER IS ´
is precisely the same as the result of
    ´ AND THE OTHER IS ´
Note that the statement
```
        PRINT *,´ONE NUMBER IS ´,A,´ AND THE
     1    OTHER IS ´,B
```
is correct FORTRAN 77, but the mode of operation of the continuation
line causes a large number of space characters to be printed between
THE and OTHER. This is because the second character string has not
been terminated on the initial line, so that all the space characters
up to and including position 72 of the initial line are taken as part
of the string, as are the space characters between 1 and OTHER on the

continuation line.

It is important to distinguish between the output of a character
string and the output of the contents of a location. For example,
the statement

          PRINT *,´A´

will print the character A; while the statement

          PRINT *,A

will print the contents of the location named A.   Care must also be
taken to make sure that the apostrophes which start and terminate the
character string are both present.   For example, the statement

          PRINT *,´A = ´,A,´ B = ´,B

will result in

    A = a B = b

where "a" and "b" represent the contents of   A   and   B   respectively;
whereas

          PRINT *,´A = ,A, B = ´,B

will result in

    A = ,A, B = b

that is, the character string "A = ,A, B = " followed by the
contents of B.

2.5 TYPE STATEMENTS

In section 2.2, it was seen that FORTRAN 77 has a type convention
which states that any variable name starting with I, J, K, L, M or N
is an integer variable name; while a variable name starting with any
other letter is a real variable name.   To make variable names more
meaningful, a programmer may sometimes wish to override this
convention.   For example, if a program involves the use of a Mach
number, it is clearly sensible to define a variable named MACH to
hold this quantity.   The Mach number is a real quantity, so it is
desirable to override the type convention to make MACH a real
variable name.   Similarly, if a program involves counting in some
sense, a programmer may wish to use a variable named COUNT to hold
the integer value of the count at a particular point in the program.

The type convention can be overridden by putting a TYPE STATEMENT
after the PROGRAM statement at the start of the program.   Type
statements are non-executable statements, and the two which are
defined in this section are the REAL statement and the INTEGER
statement.

The general form of the REAL statement is

          REAL list

The effect is that all the variables named in the list are treated by
the program as real variables.   For example,

```
        REAL MACH,ITEM,K9
```
defines MACH, ITEM and K9 to be real variables.
  The general form of the INTEGER statement is
```
        INTEGER list
```
The effect is that all the variables named in the list are treated by
the program as integer variables. For example,
```
        INTEGER COUNT,THREE,FRED
```
defines COUNT, THREE and FRED to be integer variables.
  Any variables used which are not declared in the type statements
follow the normal convention.

2.5.1 Example Program

The following program reads in three currency rates and then prints
them with suitable descriptive text.

```
        PROGRAM EX24
  CCCC   CURRENCY CONVERSION RATE PROGRAM
        REAL MARK
        PRINT *,´CURRENCY CONVERSION RATES´
        PRINT *
        READ *,FRANC,MARK,DOLLAR
        PRINT *,´ONE POUND STERLING IS WORTH´
        PRINT *,FRANC,´ FRANCS´
        PRINT *,MARK,´ MARKS´
        PRINT *,DOLLAR,´ DOLLARS´
        END
```

When this program was run using the data
```
    9.31 3.975 2.272
```
the results

```
  CURRENCY CONVERSION RATES

  ONE POUND STERLING IS WORTH
        9.310000      FRANCS
        3.975000      MARKS
        2.272000      DOLLARS
```

were obtained. In the program, the second line is a comment line.
This is because of the C in position one of the line, as described in
section 2.1. It would have been equally valid to use an asterisk
instead of a C in position one to indicate that the statement is to
be ignored by the compiler.

The third line of the program is used to override the normal FORTRAN 77 type convention. Normally, MARK holds integer quantities, since it starts with an M, but for the purposes of this program, it is required to be a real variable. Note that two PRINT statements occur in the program before any values have been read in. This is allowable, but of course the computer should object if it were asked to print the contents of MARK, DOLLAR and FRANC before any numbers had been read into them. The second PRINT statement does not have a list following it. The effect is to print a blank line, which is often useful to improve the appearance of the output.

2.6 SIMPLE ASSIGNMENT STATEMENTS

In earlier sections, the method of reading numbers from data records into the store of the computer has been described. It is also possible to put numbers into the computer´s store directly by means of an assignment statement. The two simplest forms of this statement are

        variable = constant
and
        variable = variable

The effect is that the variable on the left-hand side of the = is given a value equal to the constant or variable on the right-hand side. The = is called the ASSIGNMENT SYMBOL. Conceptually, this means that the number on the right-hand side of the assignment symbol is stored in the storage location whose name appears on the left-hand side. Any number stored in this location before the assignment statement is obeyed is overwritten (that is destroyed), so that it cannot be recalled.

   Examples of assignment statements are
        A=1.0
        PI=3.14159265
        I=-273
        SMALL=1.0E-8
        K=I
        B=PI

It should be noted that, when an assignment statement involves numeric data, it is not necessary for the type of the quantity which appears on the right-hand side of the assignment symbol in the statement to agree with the type of the variable which appears on the left-hand side. For example, assuming the normal type convention,
        A=1
results in the real variable A being given the real value 1.0; while
        I=3.14159265

and

I=3.74862

both result in the integer variable I being given the integer value
3. Note that, in both cases, the real number is TRUNCATED, which
means that only the whole number part is stored, the fractional part
being ignored by the statement. This is equally true if the number
is negative. For example,

I=-2.783

results in the integer variable I being given the integer value -2.

2.6.1 Example Program

The following program reads two numbers from a data record into
locations named A and B. The two numbers are then interchanged, so
that the number which had been read into A is stored in B and the
number which had been read into B is stored in A. The new contents
of A and B are then printed.

```
      PROGRAM EX25
CCCC  INTERCHANGE THE VALUES OF TWO VARIABLES
      READ *,A,B
      C=A
      A=B
      B=C
      PRINT *,A,B
      END
```

Running the program using the data
   1.0 2.0
gave the following results

      2.000000   1.000000

   The method of interchanging the values of A and B should be noted,
since this technique appears in a number of applications. It is not
sufficient to use the two statements

A=B
B=A

The reason can be seen from the following table.

	VALUE OF A	VALUE OF B
Initial values	1.0	2.0
Values as a result of A=B	2.0	2.0
Values as a result of B=A	2.0	2.0

It will be seen from this that the initial value of A has been destroyed.   The following table shows the effect of introducing the third variable, as in program EX25.

	VALUE OF A	VALUE OF B	VALUE OF C
Initial values	1.0	2.0	undefined
Values as a result of C=A	1.0	2.0	1.0
Values as a result of A=B	2.0	2.0	1.0
Values as a result of B=C	2.0	1.0	1.0

The importance of the statements being in the correct order should be noted.   It would be instructive for the reader to carry out an analysis of the effect of interchanging the statements A=B and C=A in the program.

2.7 THE PARAMETER STATEMENT

A constant can be given a name, called a SYMBOLIC NAME, by means of a PARAMETER statement.   This non-executable statement must appear before any executable statements in the program. It is frequently used when a complicated constant, such as 3.14159265, is to be used at a number of places in the program. There is a smaller probability of typing error if a symbolic name, such as PI, is used instead.

The general form of the PARAMETER statement is

          PARAMETER (name=constant, name=constant, ...)

The symbolic names defined by the PARAMETER statement must be different one from the other, and they must be different from any other variable name used by the program. They must obey the rules which govern the choice of names for variables, which were described in section 2.2. If the normal type conventions are overridden, the appropriate REAL or INTEGER statement must appear in the program before the PARAMETER statement in which the symbolic name is defined. It should be noted that the symbolic names defined in the PARAMETER statement are the names of constant quantities. It follows that symbolic names cannot be used as variables in the program.   Thus they must not appear in the "list" of a READ statement or on the left-hand side of an assignment statement.

As an example of a PARAMETER statement, consider

          PARAMETER (PI=3.14159265, E=2.71828183, LIGHT=186000)

This gives the name PI to the real number 3.14159265; the name E to the real number 2.71828183; and the name LIGHT to the integer number 186000.   These names may be referenced later in the program, for example in assignment statements or PRINT statements such as

          A=PI
          PRINT *,´THE SPEED OF LIGHT IS ´,LIGHT,
       1   ´ MILES PER SECOND.´

The difference between PI as used here and PI given a value by means of an assignment statement as in section 2.6 should be noted. The value of the variable PI can be altered by the program, whereas the constant with the symbolic name PI cannot.

2.8 THE DATA STATEMENT

So far in this chapter, two methods of giving values to variables have been described. The first was to use a READ statement as described in section 2.3.2, which causes values to be read from a data record. This statement is used when the values are to change from one run of the program to the next. The second method was to use an assignment statement, as described in section 2.6, which assigns values within the program.

When variables are to be assigned particular values at the start of a program, and the <u>same</u> values are to be assigned for <u>every</u> run of the program, a DATA statement offers an efficient alternative to an assignment statement. This is because values are assigned prior to runtime as a result of a DATA statement, whereas the values are assigned at runtime by an assignment statement. It should be noted that a DATA statement can only be used to set <u>initial</u> values for variables, in other words, values which the variables have at the start of a program. The values can be changed later in the program when necessary.

As a simple example of a DATA statement, suppose that a program starts with the statements

```
PROGRAM EX26
REAL I,J
INTEGER SPEED
PARAMETER (PI=3.14159265, SPEED=186000)
DATA I,A1,A2,A3,A4,J,B2,K/-8.689,4*1.0,2*PI,SPEED/
    ...
```

The result of these statements is that I and J are defined to be real by the REAL statement; then SPEED is defined to be integer by the INTEGER statement. The PARAMETER statement gives the name PI to the constant 3.14159265 and the name SPEED to the integer 186000. As a result of the DATA statement, the real variable I is given a value −8.689 which it will hold at the start of the program. As with any other variable, this value can be changed as the program runs. The variables A1, A2, A3 and A4 are all given the initial value 1.0. Note that in the above DATA statement,

    4*1.0

is equivalent to

1.0,1.0,1.0,1.0

and that this type of abbreviation can only be used in a DATA statement. Similarly, the real variables J and B2 are given initial values 3.14159265, since the PARAMETER statement has given the symbolic name PI to this number, and the integer variable K is given the initial value 186000, which is the value of the constant SPEED.

The start of program EX26 could also have been written (less efficiently) as

```
PROGRAM EX26
REAL I,J
INTEGER SPEED
PARAMETER (PI=3.14159265, SPEED=186000)
I=-8.689
A1=1.0
A2=1.0
A3=1.0
A4=1.0
J=PI
B2=PI
K=SPEED
    ...
```

The simplest general form of the DATA statement is

DATA variable list / constant list /

It is a non-executable statement which must appear after any specification or PARAMETER statements in a program. It is normal practice for DATA statements to be placed before any executable statements in the program, as this makes it easier to follow the logic of the program. Full details of where a DATA statement may appear in a program are given in appendix 3. Its purpose is to give initial values to the variables in the list; the initial values being specified, in order, by the constants or symbolic names in the constant list. Thus the first variable in the variable list is given an initial value equal to the first constant in the constant list; the second variable is given a value equal to the second constant; and so on. It follows that there must be precisely the same number of constants in the constant list as there are variables in the variable list.

A more general form of the DATA statement is

DATA variable list / constant list /, variable list /
1   constant list /, variable list / constant list /, ...

Note that the commas after each slash character in this statement may be omitted if the programmer wishes. The commas between each item in

the various lists are essential, however. This form is useful when
it is necessary to give initial values to a large number of
variables, since it is easier in this case to break the lists into
shorter ones.

   Example programs which use the DATA statement are given later in
the book.

2.9 EXERCISES

1. Run program EX21 using −0.0000678, 4513641.36 and −67 as the data.

2. Modify program EX21 to print the integer between the two reals.

3. Modify program EX21 to print the numbers under one another.

4. Modify program EX21 so that the output is

   INITIAL DATA
   ******* ****

   A = ...
   B = ...
   I = ...

5. Write a computer program which reads values into locations named
FIRST, SECOND and THIRD. These values are then rearranged so that
the value which was read into FIRST is given to SECOND, the value
which was read into SECOND is given to THIRD, and the value which was
read into THIRD is given to FIRST. The values of FIRST, SECOND and
THIRD are then printed.

6. Modify the program for exercise 5 so that initial values are given
to FIRST, SECOND and THIRD by means of a DATA statement instead of by
reading the values from a data record.

CHAPTER 3
ARITHMETIC STATEMENTS AND
INTRINSIC FUNCTIONS

In the previous chapter consideration was given to reading numbers into the computer, storing them and printing them out again. This chapter describes the manipulation of numbers using basic arithmetic operations and the use of standard mathematical functions such as square root.

3.1 A SIMPLE PROGRAM WHICH USES ARITHMETIC OPERATIONS

Consider the problem of reading three numbers (to be stored in locations A,B,C) and finding their sum and average. A simple program which does this is given below:

```
      PROGRAM EX31
CCCC  PROGRAM TO FIND THE SUM AND AVERAGE OF 3 NUMBERS
      READ *,A,B,C
      SUM=A+B+C
      AVRGE=SUM/3.0
      PRINT *,´SUM AND AVERAGE PROGRAM´
      PRINT *,´A = ´,A,´ B = ´,B,´ C = ´,C
      PRINT *,´SUM = ´,SUM
      PRINT *,´AVERAGE = ´,AVRGE
      END
```

This program, when used with a data record containing the values
```
   2.0    3.462   -1.27
```
produced the results shown below:

```
SUM AND AVERAGE PROGRAM
A =     2.000000      B =     3.462000     C =     -1.270000
SUM =     4.192000
AVERAGE =    1.397333
```

All types of statement in this program have been mentioned in chapter 2. However, two of the statements are a more general form of assignment statement called an ARITHMETIC ASSIGNMENT STATEMENT (usually abbreviated to ARITHMETIC STATEMENT). They are

    SUM=A+B+C

    AVRGE=SUM/3.0

In these statements, SUM and AVRGE are variables referring to storage locations in which are placed the values resulting from the evaluation of the ARITHMETIC EXPRESSIONS on the right-hand side of the "=" symbol. The general form of an arithmetic statement is

    variable = arithmetic expression

Naturally, for the arithmetic expression A+B+C to make sense, the variables A, B and C must have previously been given values. This is done in program EX31 by means of the READ statement.

In the first arithmetic statement in the program, that is

    SUM=A+B+C

copies of the numbers held in A, B and C are transferred to the arithmetic unit of the computer where they are added together, as described in chapter 1. The result is ASSIGNED (an operation represented by the "=" symbol) to the storage location SUM where it is stored, destroying any previous value held in SUM. Similarly, the arithmetic statement

    AVRGE=SUM/3.0

transfers a copy of the value held in SUM to the arithmetic unit where it is divided by the constant 3.0 and the result assigned to the storage location AVRGE. Notice that when a number is transferred from a storage location to the arithmetic unit, it is only a copy that is transferred and the storage location still holds the original number. In contrast, when a number is assigned to a storage location, any previous number held there is lost when it is replaced by the new number.

The two arithmetic statements that have been considered look very similar to ordinary algebraic expressions in mathematics. This is no coincidence since FORTRAN 77 has been designed to enable program instructions to resemble ordinary algebra as closely as possible, which is of considerable benefit to the programmer. An examination of arithmetic expressions and assignment statements follows.

3.2   ARITHMETIC EXPRESSIONS

An ARITHMETIC EXPRESSION is any algebraically sensible sequence of constants, variables, operators, brackets and functions. Constants and variables have already been described in section 2.2. Operators and brackets are considered in the next two sections and functions are considered at the end of this chapter and in chapter 7.

3.2.1   Arithmetic Operators

In ordinary algebra there are six basic operations:
(i)   addition
          represented by + as in a+b,
(ii)   change sign
          represented by — as in —a,
(iii) subtraction
          represented by — as in a—b,
(iv)   multiplication
          represented by x as in a x b or implied as in ab,
(v)   division
          represented by ÷ or / as in a÷ b, a/b or implied
          as in $\frac{a}{b}$,
(vi)   exponentiation (raising to a power)
          represented by position as in a^2 or a^y.

In FORTRAN 77, each operation must be represented explicitly by the appropriate symbol. Examples of the basic operations as they must be written are given in the table below:

operation	symbol	examples			
addition	+	A+B	A+2.56	I+J	K+1
change sign	—	—A	—2.5	—1	—K
subtraction	—	A—B	2.5—A	I—J	K—4
multiplication	*	A*B	A*2.32	2*I	I*J
division	/	A/B	SUM/3.0	I/2	J/K
exponentiation	**	X**2	T**1.4	Y**X	2**K

It should be noted that the multiplication operator may not be omitted, since AB will always be interpreted as a name and not as A multiplied by B.

Also, any operation which implies division by zero (or a number so small that the computer cannot distinguish it from zero) will obviously cause a runtime failure.

3.2.2   Compound Expressions

In ordinary algebra, compound expressions are produced by combining numbers and symbols with the standard arithmetic operations   such   as

A+BxC. However, this expression is ambiguous unless a convention is adopted to specify which of the operations, "+" or "x", is implemented first. Most people will automatically apply the "x" operation first, which is the standard algebraic convention. Thus if A=2, B=3 and C=4 then the value 14 (and not 20) will be obtained. If the "+" operation is required to be implemented first, then the expression is altered, by the use of brackets, to read (A+B)xC. The purpose of the brackets is to force the expression inside them to be evaluated first.

This convention is built into FORTRAN 77. A certain amount of freedom has been allowed to the compiler writer in the manner in which the convention should be implemented, which means that different compilers may treat a given expression in different, mathematically equivalent, ways. The following rules describe one method of implementing the convention and should enable the programmer to interpret any given arithmetic expression.

The various operators are given a level of precedence indicated in the table below:

operator	level of precedence
**	level 1
* and /	level 2
+ and -	level 3

The following rules are then applied:

(a) Expressions (or sub-expressions) without brackets

Under normal circumstances all level 1 operations are performed first, in order from left to right; the two exceptions to this rule being noted below. After that, all level 2 operations are performed in order from left to right. Finally, all level 3 operations are performed in order from left to right.

As an example, consider the expression

4+3*6/2-4**2/8+4*3**3

where integers are used for simplicity. When evaluating this expression, the level 1 operations 4**2=16 and 3**3=27 are performed first so that the expression is simplified to

4+3*6/2-16/8+4*27

Next, the level 2 operations 3*6=18, 18/2=9, 16/8=2 and 4*27=108 are performed so that the expression is simplified further to

4+9-2+108

Finally all level 3 operations are performed to give the result 119.

The exceptions to the rule stated above are:

(i) When two or more consecutive operators are level 1, for example A**B**C, then the operations are performed from <u>right to left</u>. The equivalent algebraic expression is

$$a^{b^c}, \text{ that is, } a^{\left(b^c\right)} \text{ and not } \left(a^b\right)^c = a^{bc}.$$

(ii) Brackets may be inserted to force the sub-expressions contained inside the brackets to be evaluated first, for example, (A+B)/(C+D) causes A+B and C+D to be evaluated before the division. A more detailed examination of the effect of brackets will now be made.

(b) Expressions containing brackets.

In this case, the sub-expression contained in the innermost set of brackets is evaluated first. The complete expression is scanned from left to right until the first closing bracket ")" is found and this is then matched with the nearest opening bracket "(" to the left of it. The sub-expression contained between these brackets is then evaluated according to the rules given in (a) above, and the complete sub-expression (and its brackets) is replaced by the value obtained. Scanning then continues to the right to locate the next closing bracket and the whole process is repeated until all brackets have been removed. Clearly for this process to work, the number of opening and closing brackets in an expression must match and a failure will be produced if they do not!

As an example consider the expression

((-4+3)*6-4**2)/(8+3)*3**3

The first closing bracket in the expression occurs at the end of the sub-expression (-4+3), which is evaluated as -1 and inserted to yield

(-1*6-4**2)/(8+3)*3**3

The next closing bracket occurs at the end of the sub-expression (-1*6-4**2), which is evaluated as (-6-16)=-22 and inserted to yield

-22/(8+3)*3**3

The last closing bracket occurs at the end of the sub-expression (8+3), which is evaluated as 11 and inserted to yield

-22/11*3**3

This expression does not contain brackets and is evaluated as

-22/11*27 = -2*27 = -54

The following general points should be noted

(i) Since the rule for consecutive level 1 operations is slightly different from the general rule, it is recommended that expressions like A**B**C are not used and that brackets are inserted in order to avoid any confusion on the part of the programmer. Thus, either

A**(B**C) or (A**B)**C should be used as appropriate.

(ii) Since the operator ** is level 1 and the operator - is level 3, the expression -3**2 has the value -9. The expression would have to be written as (-3)**2 to yield the value +9.

These general rules look very complicated at first sight when written formally, but it should be noted that they are the standard rules for ordinary algebra. If there is any doubt about the order of evaluation when writing an expression, extra brackets may be inserted to force the order of evaluation to that required.

Some examples of algebraic expressions and their FORTRAN 77 equivalents are given in the table below.

Algebraic Expression	FORTRAN 77 Arithmetic Expression
$a + \dfrac{b}{c}$	A+B/C
$\dfrac{a+b}{c}$	(A+B)/C
$\dfrac{ab}{c}$	A*B/C or A/C*B
$\dfrac{a}{b+c}$	A/(B+C)
$\dfrac{a}{bc}$	A/(B*C) or A/B/C
$b^2 - 4ac$	B**2-4.0*A*C
$\dfrac{x}{x^2 + y^2}$	X/(X**2+Y**2)
$\dfrac{a(1-r^n)}{1-r}$	A*(1.0-R**N)/(1.0-R)
$\dfrac{s(s-a)}{(s-b)(s-c)}$	S*(S-A)/((S-B)*(S-C))
$(a+b-c)^2 - \dfrac{3ab}{2c}$	(A+B-C)**2-3.0*A*B/(2.0*C)

Finally, it should be noted that two operators must not appear adjacent to each other. For example, 2 raised to the power −3 must be written as 2**(−3), not as 2**−3.

3.2.3 The Type (Real or Integer) of an Arithmetic Expression

An arithmetic expression involving real and/or integer values will be of type real or integer depending upon the component parts of the expression. The type of the final answer is important because real and integer numbers are stored by the computer in different ways. As a first step, the type of a simple operation between two numbers is defined.

(a) Operations between two real quantities

When the two quantities involved in an operation are real, the result is real. Thus

A*B   2.5−A   1.0/X   A**1.4   X+4.03

all produce real answers.

(b) Operations between two integer quantities

When the two quantities involved in an operation are integer, the result is integer. Thus

I+J   2−I   J/2   I**N   5*MAX

all produce integer answers.

In all cases, integer arithmetic is used and the result produced is exact in the sense that, since integers can be stored and handled exactly, there will be no rounding error in the final answer. Unfortunately, this rule leads to two peculiarities which can cause problems for the unwary.

(i) Integer division

When a division operation is performed between two integers, the result is defined to be an integer, even when the true mathematical answer contains a fractional part. What happens is that the whole number part of the mathematical answer is retained and the fractional part is ignored. This process is known as TRUNCATION (or rounding towards zero) and is quite different from rounding to the nearest integer. The process is best illustrated by examples, as in the table on the next page.

The following example illustrates an interesting result arising from this process. The expression I/J*J−I is identically zero in ordinary algebra. However, in FORTRAN 77 it leads to the following:

if I=6 and J=3

I/J=2 , I/J*J = 2*3 = 6 and I/J*J−I = 6−6 = 0

if   I=6 and J=4

I/J=1 ,   I/J*J = 1*4 = 4   and   I/J*J-I = 4-6 = -2

In fact the expression has a zero value only when I is a multiple of J and so it can be used to test whether J is a factor of I.

Operation	Mathematical Result	FORTRAN 77 Result
3/2	1.5	1
3/4	0.75	0
-5/3	-1.66666	-1
-6/5	-1.2	-1

(ii) Exponentiation to a negative integer power

An expression like   2**(-3)   is interpreted as 1/(2**3).   This implies integer division and hence is subject to the peculiarities mentioned in note (i), so that 2**(-3)=0. In fact, any non-zero integer (other than 1 or -1) raised to a negative integer power produces the answer zero.

(c) Operations between a real and an integer quantity

When the two quantities involved in an operation are of mixed type (one real and one integer), the result is real. For example,

X+1   A-I   2**X   A/I   I/A   A**N   2**0.25

all yield real answers. In most cases, the integer quantity is converted to the equivalent real quantity and real arithmetic is used to produce a real result.

There is one important exception to the general rule which involves exponentiation to an integer power, such as A**N. In this case the power is not converted to a real number, instead the calculation is performed by multiplying A by itself N times. Thus, if N=3, A**N is equivalent to A*A*A.

(d) Mixed-mode arithmetic

When an arithmetic expression contains a mixture of real and integer quantities, the term MIXED-MODE ARITHMETIC is often used to describe the operation.   It can be seen from the rules stated in (a) to (c) that any arithmetic expression involving real numbers will produce a real result.   An integer result will only be produced from an expression consisting entirely of integers.

When writing an integer constant in a mixed-mode expression, it is probably preferable to use the equivalent real number.   Thus 1/x should be programmed as 1.0/X rather than 1/X. This avoids the computer having to convert the integer 1 into the real number 1.0.

The following points should be noted

(i) When an integer or real number is raised to a real power, for example I**X or A**X, then the operation is accomplished by multiplying the logarithm of I (or A) by X and then taking the exponential of the result. This is obviously a relatively time consuming process, so it is usually more efficient to program x^2 as X**2 (which is calculated by repeated multiplication) rather than as X**2.0.

This also means that in expressions like I**X or A**X, the variables I or A may not be negative, since the logarithm of a negative number is not defined for real numbers. On the other hand, a negative number can be raised to an integer power without any problems.

(ii) The peculiarities of integer division can lead to unexpected results in mixed-mode expressions. Consider the expressions

A+L/M*B   and   A+B*L/M

which are mathematically identical. If A=1.1, L=2, M=3 and B=3.0, applying the rules of precedence detailed in section 3.2.2 yields the results:

A+L/M*B = A + 2/3*B = A + 0*3.0 = 1.1 + 0.0 = 1.1
A+B*L/M = A + 3.0*2/M = A + 6.0/3 = 1.1 + 2.0 = 3.1

The difference occurs because in the first expression there is an integer division (L/M); whereas in the second expression, B*L yields a real result and so the subsequent division by M is real.

It can be seen that mixed-mode arithmetic should be used with extreme care. It is best avoided where possible, with the exception of raising a real variable to an integer power.

3.2.4 Arithmetic Expressions in a PARAMETER Statement

In section 2.7, the PARAMETER statement was defined. It was stated that items in the parameter list should be of the form

          name = constant

In fact, the items in the list may be of the slightly more general form

          name = constant expression

where a constant expression is an arithmetic expression involving constants. These can be either arithmetic constants or the symbolic names of constants which have been defined previously in this or an earlier PARAMETER statement. The following example illustrates this:

          PARAMETER (PI=3.14159265,TWOPI=2.0*PI,PIBY2=PI/2.0,K=2**9)

Note that a value has had to be assigned to the symbolic name PI before the value for TWOPI can be defined in terms of PI. Thus it would be incorrect to reverse the order of the first two entries in the list.

It might be inferred that a similar generalisation would be possible in the DATA statement but this is not the case. Indeed, an expression like 2*PI in a DATA statement is interpreted as two consecutive references to the value given to the symbolic name PI (see program EX26 in section 2.8) and an expression like 2.0*PI would cause a failure! Thus the constant list in a DATA statement must not contain constant expressions.

3.3 ARITHMETIC ASSIGNMENT STATEMENTS

In section 3.1, the expression

SUM=A+B+C

was considered and defined to be an ARITHMETIC ASSIGNMENT STATEMENT. The arithmetic expression on the right hand side of the assignment symbol "=" is evaluated according to the rules considered in section 3.2 and this value is assigned to the storage location referred to as SUM, overwriting any previous value held there. A simple form of this type of statement has already been discussed in section 2.6. It should be noted that assignment is very different from the mathematical concept of equality even though the symbol "=" is used.

When an assignment occurs, if the variable and the arithmetic expression are both of the same type (both integer or both real), the value from the arithmetic expression is simply stored in the designated location. However, when there is a difference in type, a conversion has to take place as described in section 2.6.

The table below shows the effect of various assignments, assuming that I=3, J=5, A=2.35 and B=1.8.

Assignment Statement	Value Stored
C=A+B/I	2.95
K=A+B/I	2
C=(I+4)/J	1.0
I=I+J	8

The following points should be noted:

(i) It is inefficient to calculate the same expression more than once in a program. Thus, whilst in program EX31 it would be possible to write the statements

```
          SUM=A+B+C
          AVRGE=(A+B+C)/3.0
```
this would be inefficient and not good programming practice.

(ii) It is permissible to include arithmetic expressions within the list of a PRINT statement, such as

```
          PRINT *,A,B,A+B
```
However, it is recommended that this feature is restricted to simple expressions.

3.4 INTRINSIC FUNCTIONS

Many mathematical formulae contain standard mathematical functions such as sine and square root. In order to make program writing easier, most of the common mathematical functions are provided as part of FORTRAN 77 and are known technically as INTRINSIC FUNCTIONS. An example of the use of an intrinsic function follows, after which some of the more commonly used intrinsic functions are described.

3.4.1 Example Program using an Intrinsic Function

It is well known that the period T (the time taken for a complete swing) of a simple pendulum of length L is given by the formula

$$T = 2\pi\sqrt{L/g}$$

where "g" is the gravitational acceleration.

The program listed below is designed to read values for L and g, calculate T and print values of L, g and T.

```
          PROGRAM EX32
    CCCC  SIMPLE PENDULUM PROGRAM
          PARAMETER (PI=3.14159265)
          REAL L
          READ *,L,G
          T=2.0*PI*SQRT(L/G)
          PRINT *,'SIMPLE PENDULUM PROGRAM'
          PRINT *
          PRINT *,'LENGTH = ',L
          PRINT *,'GRAVITATIONAL ACCELERATION G = ',G
          PRINT *,'PERIOD OF PENDULUM = ',T
          END
```

This program when used with the data record
```
     2.6   32.2
```

produced the results shown below.

    SIMPLE PENDULUM PROGRAM

    LENGTH =   2.600000
    GRAVITATIONAL ACCELERATION G =   32.20000
    PERIOD OF PENDULUM =   1.785413

The following points are worth noting about this program:

(i)   The variable L would normally be treated as an integer but the type statement REAL L ensures that it becomes a real variable.

(ii)   The value of π is not automatically built into the computer (as it is in most calculators) and so has to be specified. However, since it is a constant and will not change from one run of the program to another, it is not necessary to read it in as part of the data. Hence, the PARAMETER statement is used to give the constant 3.14159265 the symbolic name PI. It is also possible to calculate the value of π inside the program by using the intrinsic function ATAN, as described later in section 3.4.2.

(iii) The values of L and g will probably change for different runs of the program; the value of g depends on the units used for measuring L. Hence these values should be read in as data to make the program versatile.

(iv)   The new feature illustrated by this program is the use of the expression
    SQRT(L/G)
Here, the INTRINSIC FUNCTION SQRT (which is part of the language) has been used to calculate the square root of L/G. The expression inside the brackets after the name of the function is called the ARGUMENT of the function. In this case, the argument is the expression L/G.

(v) It is common practice to run a program several times with different data. This means that it is important to print details of the data used as part of the results, so that it is readily apparent which set of data produced a given set of results. It is good programming practice to print suitable text to indicate which quantities the various numbers represent. These features are incorporated in program EX32 by means of the five PRINT statements.

3.4.2 Commonly used Intrinsic Functions

In this section, only the simplest forms of the most commonly used intrinsic functions are considered. For example, where a particular function is described in this section as having a real argument, it may also be possible to use a complex argument. A complete list of all intrinsic functions and more technical details are given in appendix 1.

(a) The Square Root Function (SQRT)

This was used in program EX32. Its argument (the value whose square root is to be found) may be any real constant, real variable or real expression and the value produced will be a positive real number. Examples are:

SQRT(2.0)   SQRT(X)   SQRT(A+B/C)

The following points should be noted:

(i) The SQRT function will not accept an integer constant, integer variable or integer expression as its argument. For example, the use of SQRT(2) in a program will produce a failure.

(ii) The square root of a negative number is not a real value and so a negative argument for SQRT will produce a failure.

(iii) The value produced by SQRT(X) is known as the PRINCIPAL VALUE of $\sqrt{x}$, that is, the positive real number whose square is x.

(iv) It is possible to produce the same effect as SQRT by raising to the power 0.5, thus SQRT(X) and X**0.5 will produce the same value. However, it is very much more efficient to use SQRT rather than exponentiation, which involves evaluating EXP(0.5*LOG(X)).

(b) The Trigonometric Functions (SIN, COS, TAN)

The standard trigonometric functions sine, cosine and tangent are provided in FORTRAN 77. The argument should be a real constant, real variable or real expression which represents the angle in RADIANS. The value produced is a real number. Examples are

SIN(0.5)   COS(X)   TAN(A**2+B**2)

The following points should be noted:

(i) The conversion factor from degrees to radians is $\pi/180$. For example, $23^\circ = 23 \times \pi/180$ radians, so that the FORTRAN 77 expression for sin 23° is SIN(23.0*PI/180.0). If a number of angles have to be converted from degrees to radians, it is clearly more efficient to calculate the conversion factor PI/180.0 once and store its value, rather than recalculate it each time an angle has to be converted.

(ii) The argument for SIN, COS and TAN may not be an integer constant, integer variable or integer expression.

(c) The Inverse Trigonometric Functions (ASIN, ACOS, ATAN)

The inverse trigonometric functions $\sin^{-1}$, $\cos^{-1}$, $\tan^{-1}$ (also called arcsin, arccos, arctan) are provided in FORTRAN 77 and named ASIN, ACOS, ATAN respectively. They accept as argument any real constant, real variable or real expression and produce a real number which is the PRINCIPAL VALUE of the angle in radians.

It should be remembered that there is an infinite family of angles all of which have the same sine, for example

$$\sin(x), \sin(x+2\pi), \sin(x+4\pi), \ldots, \sin(x+2n\pi), \ldots$$

all have the same value. A similar result is true for cos and tan. The principal values of the inverse trigonometric functions are defined in the following way:

$\sin^{-1} x$ — the principal value A is the angle (in radians) such that $\sin A = x$ and $-\pi/2 \leq A \leq +\pi/2$

$\cos^{-1} x$ — the principal value A is the angle (in radians) such that $\cos A = x$ and $0 \leq A \leq \pi$

$\tan^{-1} x$ — the principal value A is the angle (in radians) such that $\tan A = x$ and $-\pi/2 < A < +\pi/2$

Examples of the use of these functions are

ASIN(0.35), ACOS(X), ATAN(X+2.0*Y).

The following points should be noted:

(i) The argument for ASIN, ACOS and ATAN may <u>not</u> be an integer constant, integer variable or integer expression.

(ii) Since the value of sine or cosine always lies in the range (-1.0,+1.0), the argument for ASIN and ACOS must also lie in this range, otherwise an error will occur. The argument for ATAN may be any finite value within the range of values acceptable to the computer.

(iii) The trigonometric result $\tan(\pi/4) = 1$ is well known. Thus the arithmetic statement PI=4.0*ATAN(1.0) is a convenient way to generate the value of π. Hence, the conversion factor from degrees to radians may be written as ATAN(1.0)/45.0.

(d) <u>The Logarithm and Exponential Functions</u> (LOG, LOG10, EXP)

The mathematical functions

$$\log_e x, \log_{10} x \text{ and } e^x$$

are provided in FORTRAN 77 and are called LOG, LOG10 and EXP respectively. The argument should be any real constant, real variable or real expression and a real number is produced. Examples are

LOG(1.2), LOG10(X), EXP(-X**2).

The following points should be noted:

(i) The argument for LOG, LOG10 and EXP may <u>not</u> be an integer constant, integer variable or integer expression.

(ii) The logarithm of a negative number is not a real value and so a negative argument for LOG or LOG10 is not permitted.

(e) The Hyperbolic Functions (SINH, COSH, TANH)

The mathematical functions

$$\sinh x = 0.5(e^x - e^{-x}) \qquad \cosh x = 0.5(e^x + e^{-x})$$
$$\tanh x = \sinh x / \cosh x$$

are provided in FORTRAN 77 and are called SINH, COSH and TANH respectively. The argument should be a real constant, real variable or real expression and a real number is produced.

(f) The Absolute Value Function (ABS)

When x is a real number, the notation $|x|$ is used to denote the absolute value of x (its numerical value when the sign is ignored). Examples are $|2| = 2$, $|-2| = 2$.

The FORTRAN 77 version of this function is called ABS. It will accept as argument any real constant, real variable or real expression and will return a real number as its value. It will also accept an integer constant, integer variable or integer expression as argument and will then return an integer value.

(g) Functions used for type conversion (REAL, INT)

The function REAL is used to change an integer constant, integer variable or the value of an integer expression into the equivalent real number. For example, REAL(I) will produce a real value equivalent to the value of the integer held in the location I.

The function INT is used to change the value obtained from a real constant, real variable or real expression into an integer, by truncating the real number. Examples are INT(-1.6) = -1, INT(2.9) = 2 The following points should be noted:

(i) The argument of REAL may also be a real constant, real variable or real expression and the argument of INT may also be an integer constant, integer variable or integer expression. However, there does not seem much point in using the functions under these circumstances!

(ii) When an arithmetic assignment of the form X=I is made, in effect the statement X=REAL(I) is obeyed. Similarly, I=X is effectively obeyed as I=INT(X).

(iii) Use of the function REAL is necessary when the effects of integer division are to be avoided. For example, if I=6 and J=4 then I/J = 1; whereas REAL(I)/REAL(J) or REAL(I)/J produces 1.50. However, it should be noted that REAL(I/J) = 1.0 since the integer division takes place before the number is converted to real.

(iv) The use of the function REAL in an arithmetic expression is quite different from the use of REAL in a type statement like REAL L as was used in program EX32.

A summary of the simple intrinsic functions considered in this section is given in the table below.

Name	Definition	Argument	Value
ABS	absolute value x	real integer	real integer
ACOS	principal value (radians) of $\cos^{-1} x$, $-1 \leq x \leq +1$	real	real
ASIN	principal value (radians) of $\sin^{-1} x$, $-1 \leq x \leq +1$	real	real
ATAN	principal value (radians) of $\tan^{-1} x$	real	real
COS	cos x , x in radians	real	real
COSH	cosh x	real	real
EXP	e^x	real	real
INT	convert to integer value	real integer	integer integer
LOG	$\log_e x$, x>0	real	real
LOG10	$\log_{10} x$, x>0	real	real
REAL	convert to real value	integer real	real real
SIN	sin x , x in radians	real	real
SINH	sinh x	real	real
SQRT	$+ \sqrt{x}$, x$\geq$0	real	real
TAN	tan x , x in radians	real	real
TANH	tanh x	real	real

It should be noted that intrinsic functions must   not   be   used   in DATA   or PARAMETER statements.   In particular, this means that if the symbolic name PI is given to the value of π in a PARAMETER statement, the   value must be given explicitly and not generated by means of the function ATAN.

3.5   FURTHER EXAMPLE PROGRAMS

In this section, some problems are discussed together   with   programs which solve them.

3.5.1   Solution of two Simultaneous Equations

The solution (x,y) of the simultaneous equations

$$ax + by = c$$
$$dx + ey = f$$

is given by

$$x = \frac{ce - bf}{ae - bd} \quad, \quad y = \frac{af - cd}{ae - bd}$$

provided $ae - bd \neq 0$.

The   program   described   in   this   section   reads   values   for   the coefficients   of   the   equation   and   calculates   the   solution.   The following points were considered when writing the program:

(i)   There   is   no   reason to suppose that the coefficients in the equations are restricted to integer values.   Hence, real   values   are assumed and read as data.

(ii)   A solution will only exist if $ae - bd \neq 0$.   It   would   be useful   to   check   this   by incorporating a test in the program.   The necessary instructions to do this are considered in the next chapter.

(iii) The   expression $ae - bd$ occurs in the calculation of both x and y.   It is clearly more efficient to calculate its value only once and   store   it.   The   variable DENOM is used for this purpose in the program.

(iv)   It   is sensible to arrange the printed results so that anyone reading them knows exactly to what entity the various numbers   refer. Thus the initial data values as well as the final answer are printed. It is worth spending some effort to make the results look presentable and this has been attempted in these specimen programs.

(v)   It is useful to check, where possible, for   gross   errors   in the   results.   For   example,   an error could be made in the formulae programmed for the calculation of x and y.   A check can   be   made   by calculating the residuals:

$$r_1 = ax + by - c \qquad\qquad r_2 = dx + ey - f$$

for the solutions x and y. Clearly there will be cause for concern if these residuals are large and further investigation will be necessary. Unfortunately, it is not true that small residuals indicate an accurate solution in all cases. A discussion of this point is beyond the scope of this text and may be found in books on Numerical Analysis.

A program to produce the solution of the equations is as follows:

```
      PROGRAM EX33
CCCC  SOLUTION OF A PAIR OF SIMULTANEOUS EQUATIONS
      READ *,A,B,C,D,E,F
CCCC  CALCULATE DENOM, X AND Y
      DENOM=A*E-B*D
      X=(C*E-B*F)/DENOM
      Y=(A*F-C*D)/DENOM
CCCC  CALCULATE THE RESIDUALS
      R1=A*X+B*Y-C
      R2=D*X+E*Y-F
CCCC  PRINT THE RESULTS AND SUITABLE TEXT
      PRINT *,'SOLUTION OF A PAIR OF SIMULTANEOUS EQUATIONS'
      PRINT *
      PRINT *,'THE EQUATIONS ARE:'
      PRINT *,A,' X + ',B,' Y = ',C
      PRINT *,D,' X + ',E,' Y = ',F
      PRINT *
      PRINT *,'SOLUTION IS  X = ',X,' Y = ',Y
      PRINT *,'RESIDUALS ARE  R1 = ',R1,' R2 = ',R2
      END
```

When run using the data record

   1.5 -0.2 2.3 3.1 1.7 2.8

the results from the program were:

```
SOLUTION OF A PAIR OF SIMULTANEOUS EQUATIONS

THE EQUATIONS ARE:
     1.500000      X +    -2.000000E-01 Y =      2.300000
     3.100000      X +     1.700000     Y =      2.800000

SOLUTION IS  X =     1.410095     Y =    -9.242902E-01
RESIDUALS ARE  R1 =     2.910383E-11 R2 =      0.000000
```

The value given in the results for R1 should be regarded with caution, the actual value being almost entirely rounding error.

3.5.2   Evaluation of a Cubic Polynomial

A program to evaluate the polynomial $ax^3 + bx^2 + cx + d$ for given values of a,b,c,d and x is described in this section. The following points were considered when writing the program:

(i)   The coefficients a,b,c,d and the value of x are read as data.

(ii) The obvious way to evaluate the polynomial by using the expression   A*X**3+B*X**2+C*X+D   is rather inefficient since it involves 6 multiplications and 3 additions. Fewer arithmetic operations are required if the polynomial is re-written in the equivalent form ((A*X+B)*X+C)*X+D. This form is called NESTED MULTIPLICATION. In this example only 3 multiplications and 3 additions are required.

(iii) A much more useful program would be to tabulate the polynomial for a whole range of values of x. This can be done quite easily by making the program repeat some of the instructions several times and this type of operation is considered in the next chapter. The program to evaluate the cubic polynomial is given below:

```
      PROGRAM EX34
CCCC  CUBIC POLYNOMIAL BY NESTED MULTIPLICATION
      READ *,A,B,C,D,X
      Y=((A*X+B)*X+C)*X+D
      PRINT *,´CUBIC POLYNOMIAL BY NESTED MULTIPLICATION´
      PRINT *
      PRINT *,´POLYNOMIAL COEFFICIENTS OF DESCENDING POWERS´
      PRINT *,A,B,C,D
      PRINT *,´VALUE OF X = ´,X
      PRINT *,´VALUE OF POLYNOMIAL = ´,Y
      END
```

When run using the data record
    1.23   2.567   6.82   7.98   0.52
the results from the program were:

```
CUBIC POLYNOMIAL BY NESTED MULTIPLICATION

POLYNOMIAL COEFFICIENTS OF DESCENDING POWERS
      1.230000         2.567000         6.820000         7.980000
VALUE OF X =      5.200000E-01
VALUE OF POLYNOMIAL =      12.39346
```

3.5.3 Evaluation of Gould's Function

Gould's function $\phi(r)$ is used in the calculation of the time taken to change the level in a reservoir which is discharging over a weir. It is defined as:

$$\phi(r) = \frac{2}{3} \log_e \frac{\sqrt{r + \sqrt{r} + 1}}{|\sqrt{r} - 1|} - \frac{2}{\sqrt{3}} \left(\tan^{-1} \frac{2\sqrt{r} + 1}{\sqrt{3}} - \theta \right)$$

where r is the ratio of the current water level to the level at which the rate of inflow to the reservoir is equal to the rate of outflow and $\theta = \pi/6$ if r<1 and $\pi/2$ if r>1. The program described in this section calculates $\phi(r)$ for a given value of r. The following points were considered when writing the program:

(i) The value of r is obviously required as data. With the FORTRAN 77 statements considered so far it is not possible to test whether r<1 or r>1 within the program and assign the appropriate value to θ. Hence another input data value (called z) is also read. This is given the value 6.0 if r<1 and the value 2.0 if r>1. Then the value of θ can be calculated as π/z, where π can be generated inside the program by the expression 4.0*ATAN(1.0)

(ii) Since the quantities $\sqrt{r}$ and $\sqrt{3}$ occur several times in the expression, they are calculated separately and stored in locations ROOTR and ROOT3 respectively.

The program to perform this calculation is given below.

```
      PROGRAM EX35
CCCC  CALCULATION OF GOULD'S FUNCTION
      READ *,R,Z
CCCC  CALCULATION OF PI,THETA AND SQUARE ROOTS OF 3 AND R
      PI=4.0*ATAN(1.0)
      THETA=PI/Z
      ROOTR=SQRT(R)
      ROOT3=SQRT(3.0)
CCCC  CALCULATION OF PHI
      A=2.0/3.0*LOG(SQRT(R+ROOTR+1.0)/ABS(ROOTR-1.0))
      B=2.0/ROOT3*(ATAN((2.0*ROOTR+1.0)/ROOT3)-THETA)
      PHI=A-B
CCCC  PRINT RESULTS
      PRINT *,'CALCULATION OF GOULD''S FUNCTION'
      PRINT *
      PRINT *,'R = ',R,'PHI(R) = ',PHI
      END
```

When run using the data record

        1.5   2.0
the results were:

CALCULATION OF GOULD´S FUNCTION

    R =   1.500000   PHI(R) =   1.970855

The following points about the program should be noted:
   (i)   It is usually better to split a complicated expression into
several parts and calculate each part   separately.   In   the   program
φ(r) has been split into two parts. This facilitates checking that
the expression has been correctly programmed.   Such testing would
probably consist of inserting temporary instructions (which can be
removed later) to print out the values of each part so that these can
be checked against a hand calculation.   For   example, the extra
statement   PRINT *,A,B   might be inserted before   PHI=A-B .
   (ii)   It is tempting to program the expression for calculating A as
2/3*LOG...   This would be disastrous   because   the   integer   division
rule would cause A to have the value zero.   Hence the expression must
be as in the program, where 2.0/3.0 is used.
   (iii) ROOT3   cannot   be   calculated by using   SQRT(3)   because SQRT
will not accept an integer argument.
   (iv)   In   the   first   PRINT   statement,   the apostrophe in the name
Gould´s Function has to be doubled to avoid being   mistaken   for   the
end marker of the character string as described in section 2.2.
   (v)   As PHI is not defined if   r = 1,   since   this   would   imply
division   by   zero, a   test   to   check whether this case has occurred
should really be incorporated into the program. Statements to do this
sort of test are described in chapter 4.

3.5.4 Distances Travelled by a Salesman

A salesman is based at his home town H and has to visit towns A, B, C
and then return home.   The positions of the towns are given by a pair
of cartesian map coordinates (X,Y) and the distance between two towns
is assumed to be the straight line distance between the two pairs of
coordinates.   Hence, if the position of town A is (XA,YA) and town B
is (XB,YB), then the distance between them is taken to be

$$\sqrt{(XA-XB)^2 + (YA-YB)^2} \ .$$

   The program described in this section calculates the distances of
all the routes from H to the three towns A,B,C and back to H. The
following points were considered when writing the program:
   (i)   There are only three distinct routes HABCH, HBCAH and HCABH

since the other three possibilities are just the reverse of these three.

(ii) The required data values are the map coordinates of the towns H, A, B and C.

(iii) From these coordinates the distance between any two towns can be calculated. Thus, for example, the distances between towns A and B will be stored in DAB. Then, the distances of the three routes are calculated and stored in DHABCH, DHBCAH and DHCABH.

(iv) The results to be output are the coordinates of the four towns and the distances of the three routes.

The program to calculate the distances is given below.

```
        PROGRAM EX36
  CCCC  ROUTE CALCULATION FOR SALESMAN PROBLEM
        READ *,XH,YH,XA,YA,XB,YB,XC,YC
  CCCC  CALCULATE THE DISTANCES BETWEEN THE TOWNS
        DHA=SQRT((XH-XA)**2+(YH-YA)**2)
        DHB=SQRT((XH-XB)**2+(YH-YB)**2)
        DHC=SQRT((XH-XC)**2+(YH-YC)**2)
        DAB=SQRT((XA-XB)**2+(YA-YB)**2)
        DAC=SQRT((XA-XC)**2+(YA-YC)**2)
        DBC=SQRT((XB-XC)**2+(YB-YC)**2)
  CCCC  CALCULATE THE DISTANCES OF THE THREE ROUTES
        DHABCH=DHA+DAB+DBC+DHC
        DHBCAH=DHB+DBC+DAC+DHA
        DHCABH=DHC+DAC+DAB+DHB
  CCCC  PRINT THE RESULTS
        PRINT *,´SALESMAN PROBLEM´
        PRINT *
        PRINT *,´THE DISTANCES FOR THE VARIOUS ROUTES ARE´
        PRINT *,´ROUTE  HABCH  OR  HCBAH  ´,DHABCH
        PRINT *,´ROUTE  HBCAH  OR  HACBH  ´,DHBCAH
        PRINT *,´ROUTE  HCABH  OR  HBACH  ´,DHCABH
        PRINT *,´WHERE THE TOWNS ARE´
        PRINT *,´H AT ´,XH,YH
        PRINT *,´A AT ´,XA,YA
        PRINT *,´B AT ´,XB,YB
        PRINT *,´C AT ´,XC,YC
        END
```

When run using the data record

    0.0 0.0 1.5 2.7 8.4 5.3 -4.8 -9.1

the results were

SALESMAN PROBLEM

THE DISTANCES FOR THE VARIOUS ROUTES ARE

ROUTE	HABCH	OR	HCBAH	40.28522
ROUTE	HBCAH	OR	HACBH	45.93202
ROUTE	HCABH	OR	HBACH	40.97069

WHERE THE TOWNS ARE

H AT	0.000000	0.000000
A AT	1.500000	2.700000
B AT	8.400000	5.300000
C AT	-4.800000	-9.100000

3.6   EXERCISES

1.   Write FORTRAN 77   arithmetic expressions which correspond to the following algebraic expressions. All variables   are   expressed   by   a single letter such as "x" or "a".

(a) $x + y^3$

(b) $\dfrac{a+b}{c+d}$

(c) $a - \dfrac{b}{cd}$

(d) $\dfrac{1}{xy}$

(e) $x^2 + 2.5x + 3.6$

(f) $\dfrac{a(b+c)}{d}$

(g) $a + \dfrac{b}{c+d}$

(h) $2xe^x$

(i) $\sqrt{a^2 + b^2 - 2ab \sin c}$

(j) $\log_e (x + \sqrt{x^2 + 1})$

2.   Evaluate the   following   arithmetic   expressions   or   statements, assuming   the   standard   type convention.   The values stored are: A = 2.0, B = 5.65, X = 1.4, Y = 0.7, I = 2, J = 3, K = 5.

(a) A+B*X-Y
(b) (A+B)*(X-Y)
(c) A*X/Y*J
(d) I+J/K
(e) X*Y**I
(f) I*K/J*(J+1)
(g) I*K/(J*(J+1))
(h) I*K/J/J+1
(i) M=A+B*I/J
(j) M=X/Y*I/J

3.   Write   a   program   which   reads   in   a   temperature F (in degrees Fahrenheit) and converts it   to   the   equivalent   temperature   C   (in degrees Centigrade) using the formula

$$C = \frac{5}{9} (F - 32)$$

The program should print the values of F and C together with suitable text.

4. Write a program which reads the coefficients of the quadratic equation

$$ax^2 + bx + c = 0, \quad a \neq 0$$

and which calculates the two roots of the equation, which are given by

$$x = \frac{-b + \sqrt{b^2 - 4ac}}{2a} \qquad\qquad x = \frac{-b - \sqrt{b^2 - 4ac}}{2a}$$

The data provided should be such that $b^2 > 4ac$.

5. If a sum of money P is invested at an annual interest rate of I% which is compounded n times per year, then the capital C after k years is given by:

$$C = P \left(1 + \frac{I}{100n}\right)^{nk}$$

Write a program which reads values for P, I, n, k and calculates C.

6. In a particular electrical circuit, the time scale response E(t) is given by the formula

$$E(t) = 1 - (\cos 0.975t + 0.216 \sin 0.975t) \ e^{-1.21t}$$

Write a program which reads in a value for t and calculates E(t).

7. For a girder of cross section as indicated in the diagram, the second moment of area about the Neutral Axis (I_{NA}) is given by:

$$I_{NA} = \frac{1}{12}(b_1 d_1^3 + b_2 d_2^3 + b_3 d_3^3) + A_1(h-c-\frac{1}{2}d_1)^2 + A_2(d_3 + \frac{1}{2}d_2 - c)^2 + A_3(c - \frac{1}{2}d_3)^2$$

where $A_1 = b_1 d_1$ $A_2 = b_2 d_2$ $A_3 = b_3 d_3$ $h = d_1 + d_2 + d_3$

and

$$c = \frac{A_1(h - \frac{1}{2}d_1) + A_2(d_3 + \frac{1}{2}d_2) + \frac{1}{2}A_3 d_3}{A_1 + A_2 + A_3}$$

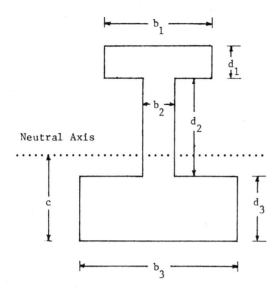

Write a program which reads values for

$$b_1, b_2, b_3, d_1, d_2, d_3,$$

and prints out these values together with values for c and I_{NA}.

Specimen data: b_1 = 60.0, b_2 = 15.0, b_3 = 90.0,

$$d_1 = 20.0, \ d_2 = 70.0, \ d_3 = 30.0,$$

where all measurements are in millimetres.

CHAPTER 4
CONTROL STATEMENTS

All the programs considered so far have consisted of a sequence of statements that are obeyed in the order in which they appear in the program. If this were always the case, every sequence of statements requiring repetition would have to be written several times. This is obviously not desirable. Also statements should only be obeyed when they are meaningful. For example, in program EX33 it is meaningless to divide by the value of A*E-B*D unless that value is non-zero.

The ability to repeat a group of statements influences the way in which one thinks about performing tasks. For example, suppose that it is required to output the sum of three values given as data. Using only the information given in chapters 2 and 3, the statements

```
        READ *,A,B,C
        SUM=A+B+C
        PRINT *,´ THE SUM IS´,SUM
```

could be used. If there were 100 values to add together, this approach would require 100 names for the input values. However, it is also possible to use a running total and to add the values one at a time as they are read, as in the following program.

```
        PROGRAM EX41
        SUM=0.0
        READ *,X
        SUM=SUM+X
        READ *,X
        SUM=SUM+X
        READ *,X
        SUM=SUM+X
        PRINT *,´ THE SUM IS ´,SUM
        END
```

This is a longer program, but it should be noted that the statements

```
        READ *,X
        SUM=SUM+X
```

are repeated three times, and only one name is used for the input data. If there were 100 values to sum, these statements would be repeated 100 times! The desire to be able to do this without writing the statements 100 times becomes overwhelming. The control statement that most conveniently does this is called the DO statement.

The purpose of CONTROL STATEMENTS is to control the order in which the program statements are obeyed. They make it possible to repeat a sequence of statements many times or miss statements out altogether. The control statements considered in this chapter are CONDITIONAL STATEMENTS, which are used to make decisions; DO STATEMENTS, which are used to repeat sequences of statements; STOP STATEMENTS, which cause the program to be terminated at a point other than the physical end of the program; and GOTO STATEMENTS, which cause a "jump" to another statement in the program.

4.1 CONDITIONAL STATEMENTS

Conditional statements make it possible for a program to take logical decisions. For example, in program EX36 (see section 3.5.4), which determined the distance travelled by a salesman when visiting three towns, the distances for all possible routes were printed. With the aid of conditional statements, the program can be written to make the computer print only the shortest journey.

There are a number of conditional statements, of which the BLOCK IF statement is probably the most powerful and simple. It enables, subject to some well-defined criterion, one of two alternative sequences of statements to be obeyed.

4.1.1 The BLOCK IF Statement

As a simple example, consider the problem of reading in two values and printing the larger of the two. The statements to do this are:

```
        PROGRAM EX42
        READ *,A,B
        IF (A.GT.B) THEN
            BIG=A
        ELSE
            BIG=B
        ENDIF
        PRINT *,BIG
        END
```

In this example, when A is greater than B, the LOGICAL EXPRESSION A.GT.B is "true"; while when A is not greater than B, the expression is "false". When the logical expression A.GT.B is "true", the statement BIG=A is obeyed, followed by the PRINT statement. When the logical expression is "false", the statement BIG=B is obeyed, followed by the PRINT statement. Thus, by the time the PRINT statement is obeyed, the value of BIG will be the larger of A and B.

Note that in this example the statements BIG=A and BIG=B have been indented. Although the extra spaces are ignored by the compiler, they make the program structure clearer and hence easier to correct if errors are made.

4.1.2 Logical Expressions

Before proceeding to look at the full definition of the BLOCK IF statement, it is necessary to define what is meant by a logical expression. This is an expression which is either "true" or "false". In its simplest form a logical expression is one of

  A.GT.B   (A is greater than B)
  A.LT.B   (A is less than B)
  A.NE.B   (A is not equal to B)
  A.GE.B   (A is greater than or equal to B)
  A.LE.B   (A is less than or equal to B)
  A.EQ.B   (A is equal to B)

In these examples, A and B represent any well-defined values that are mutually compatible. For example, if X and Y are real variables,

  X+Y.GT.3.4
  INT(X/Y).EQ.5
  SIN(X).GT.COS(X+Y)

are all valid logical expressions.

If it is necessary to check to see if two conditions are both "true", they can be made into a single logical expression using the .AND. operator. For example, if it is required to check that a point (x,y) is in the first quadrant (that is, both x and y coordinates are positive), all that is needed is to test the logical expression

  X.GT.0.0 .AND. Y.GT.0.0

When this is "true" (that is, both x>0 and y>0), the point is in the first quadrant. Similarly, a course of action may depend on whether or not a value lies outside a given range. For example, a value "x" lies outside the range "a" to "b" if either x<a or x>b. This can be tested by using the logical expression

  X.LT.A .OR. X.GT.B

This expression is "true" if either of the two conditions x<a or x>b is true, otherwise it is "false".

It is normally a meaningless exercise to test two real   values   for equality,   because   of   rounding   errors.   Hence   the   .EQ. and .NE. operators should not usually be used when comparing real   quantities. The   appropriate   logical   expression   for testing whether or not two real quantities are almost equal (that   is,   the   difference   between them is insignificant) is

          ABS(A-B).LE.EPS

where EPS is the tolerance in the difference that can be accepted.

   Should the items being compared be of different types, a conversion is made. Assuming the normal type conventions, the logical expression

          A.GT.N

is interpreted as

          (A-N).GT.0.0

4.1.3 The General Form of the BLOCK IF Statement

The BLOCK IF statement has the general form

          IF (logical expression) THEN
              statements A
          ELSE
              statements B
          ENDIF

where the separate parts of the statement   must   occur   on   different program lines, as indicated.

   The statements which are to be obeyed as a result of this statement are   blocked   off   into   two   disjoint   groups,   "statements   A" and "statements B".   The group "statements A" form the IF BLOCK   and   the group   "statements   B"   form   the   ELSE   BLOCK   of   the   conditional statement.   The entire   statement   is   referred   to   as   a   BLOCK   IF statement.   When the logical expression is "true", "statements A" are obeyed and "statements B" are ignored. When the logical expression is "false", "statements A" are ignored and "statements B" are obeyed.

   The end of the   first   group   of   statements   ("statements   A")   is indicated   by   the   ELSE statement and the end of the second group of statements ("statements B") is   indicated   by   the   ENDIF   statement. Under   normal circumstances the statement obeyed after "statements A" have been obeyed is that immediately following the   ENDIF   statement. This   is   also   the   case   when "statements B" are obeyed rather than "statements A".

   The   ELSE   block   may   be omitted, in which case the ENDIF statement terminates the IF block.   In this   case,   the   IF   statement   has   no effect   should   the   logical expression be "false", and the statement following the ENDIF statement is obeyed. To illustrate this,   program EX42 (see section 4.1.1) is rewritten as follows

```
PROGRAM EX43
READ *,A,B
BIG=B
IF (A.GT.B) THEN
    BIG=A
ENDIF
PRINT *,BIG
END
```

In this example, "statements A" consists of the single statement
BIG=A. Usually there will be more than one statement in this group.
The effect of program EX43 is that BIG is set equal to B and then a
test is made to see if A is greater than B. If it is, BIG is re-set
to the value of A and the value of BIG is printed. Should A be less
than or equal to B, the IF statement has no effect and the value of
BIG, which in this case remains equal to B, is printed.

4.1.4 Nested IF Statements

IF statements can be inserted inside an IF BLOCK (or ELSE BLOCK),
provided they lie completely within the IF BLOCK (or ELSE BLOCK).
For example, consider the problem of evaluating the mathematical
function f(x), where

$$f(x) = x^2 \qquad\qquad x < -1$$
$$= x \qquad\qquad -1 \le x < 0$$
$$= x(1-x) \qquad\qquad 0 \le x < 1$$
$$= (x-1)^2 \qquad\qquad x \ge 1$$

To evaluate y=f(x) for a known value of x, the following conditional
statement could be used

```
IF (X.LT.-1.0) THEN
    Y=X*X
ELSE
    IF (X.LT.0.0) THEN
        Y=X
    ELSE
        IF (X.LT.1.0) THEN
            Y=X*(1.0-X)
        ELSE
            Y=(X-1.0)**2
        ENDIF
    ENDIF
ENDIF
```

As a result of this statement, the value of f(x) is stored in Y. In

this example there are three IF statements. Two of them appear inside
the first BLOCK IF statement, and one appears inside both of the
other BLOCK IF statements. The IF blocks are said to be NESTED one
inside the other.

When using the BLOCK IF statement in its general form, the
following points should be noted:

(i)   When a BLOCK IF statement is used inside another BLOCK IF
statement, the rule for matching the ENDIFs with the corresponding
IFs is the same as for closing and opening brackets in arithmetic
expressions, as described in section 3.2.2. This can be illustrated
as follows

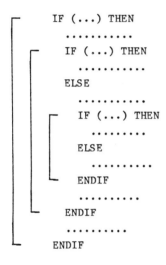

```
      IF (...) THEN
         ..........
         IF (...) THEN
            ..........
         ELSE
            ..........
            IF (...) THEN
               .........
            ELSE
               ..........
            ENDIF
            ..........
         ENDIF
         ..........
      ENDIF
```

(ii) Control cannot be passed to ENDIF, ELSE or ELSEIF (see next
section) statements in the program by means of a GOTO statement,
which is described in section 4.4.

(iii) An IF block can only be entered through the IF statement and
an ELSE block can only be entered through the ELSE statement. This
means that they cannot be jumped into from the outside by means of a
GOTO statement.

4.1.5 The ELSEIF Statement

In the example given in the last section there were three successive
ENDIF statements. To simplify this, the ELSEIF statement is
available to combine the ELSE with the IF. It does not require an
ENDIF statement of its own, and is considered to be part of the
previous IF clause. Using the ELSEIF statement, the example can be
written

```
IF (X.LT.-1.0) THEN
   Y=X*X
ELSEIF (X.LT.0.0) THEN
   Y=X
ELSEIF (X.LT.1.0) THEN
   Y=X*(1.0-X)
ELSE
   Y=(X-1.0)**2
ENDIF
```

The ELSEIF statement is said not to increase the level of the IF statement, which is the number of IFs passed without passing the corresponding ENDIF statement in a BLOCK IF statement. Additional IF statements can appear inside IF blocks. Note that with this construction, when a group of statements following a THEN have been obeyed, the next statement to be obeyed is the one following the next ENDIF statement.

4.1.6 The Logical IF Statement

Program EX43 in section 4.1.3, which prints the larger of two values, can be written more compactly using a logical IF statement as follows

```
PROGRAM EX44
READ *,A,B
BIG=B
IF (A.GT.B) BIG=A
PRINT *,BIG
END
```

In this case, the statement BIG=A which follows the logical expression is obeyed when the expression is "true", otherwise the statement is ignored. In both cases, the next instruction to be obeyed is the one in the natural sequence of the program. The following diagram gives a clear picture of the effect of the logical IF statement.

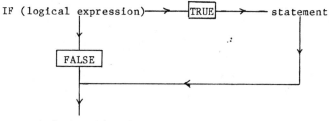

Notice that the word THEN is <u>not</u> used in a logical IF statement. The
statement following the logical expression must be a <u>single</u>
unconditional statement.   If a sequence of statements is controlled
by the logical expression, a BLOCK IF statement should be used.

4.2   THE DO STATEMENT

The DO statement enables a group of statements to be repeated for a
specified number of times. As an example, consider the problem of
summing 100 input values discussed at the beginning of this chapter.
This can be done by the following program:

```
      PROGRAM EX45
CCCC  PROGRAM TO READ AND SUM 100 VALUES
      SUM=0.0
      DO 10 I=1,100
         READ *,X
         SUM=SUM+X
   10 CONTINUE
      PRINT *,'THE SUM IS' ,SUM
      END
```

In this program, SUM acts as an accumulator. It is set to zero
initially and is incremented by each value as it is read.   I is
called the DO variable. It is given an initial value of 1, then the
statements down to and including the statement labelled 10 are
obeyed. These statements are called the DO LOOP. After statement 10
has been obeyed, control is returned to the DO statement, the next
value of I is selected and the statements down to 10 are repeated.
This process is continued until all values for I (100 in this case)
have been used. The values used for I are defined in the first line
of the DO statement, in this case

          DO 10 I=1,100

by I=1,100. The 1 indicates the first value to be used, 100 indicates
the final value to be used and the value of I is assumed to increase
by 1 each time the statement is obeyed. The CONTINUE statement is a
dummy statement indicating the end of the DO loop. Any executable
statement except a control statement can be labelled as the terminal
statement of the DO loop. If a CONTINUE statement is used as the
terminal statement, the program is easier to read.

   When all of the values for I have been used, the statement
following the statement labelled 10 is obeyed. There is nothing
sacred about the label 10. Any integer in the range 1 to 99999 could
be used (see section 2.1) provided the statement label is unique and

the statement with the given label appears after the DO statement.

4.2.1 Nested DO Statements

It is possible to have conditional statements within the DO loop
provided they are contained completely within the DO loop. In the
previous example, suppose that the range, the largest and the
smallest of the set of 100 input values had been required, as well as
the sum. The program might be written:

```
      PROGRAM EX46
CCCC  PROGRAM TO FIND THE SUM, LARGEST, SMALLEST AND RANGE
      READ *,X
      SUM=X
      BIG=X
      SMALL=X
      DO 10 I=2,100
         READ *,X
         IF (X.GT.BIG) THEN
            BIG=X
         ELSEIF (X.LT.SMALL) THEN
            SMALL=X
         ENDIF
         SUM=SUM+X
   10 CONTINUE
      RANGE=BIG-SMALL
      PRINT *,´THE SUM IS ´,SUM,´ THE LARGEST IS ´,BIG,
     1   ´THE SMALLEST IS ´,SMALL,´ AND THE RANGE IS ´,RANGE
      END
```

The logic on which this program is based is:

(i)   Read the first value and assign it to SUM, SMALL and BIG.
SUM is used to hold the sum of the values read so far, SMALL the
smallest value read so far, and BIG the largest.

(ii) Read the next value and store it in X. Check to see if it is
bigger than the largest value read so far. If it is, store it in
BIG. Otherwise check to see if it is smaller than the smallest value
read so far. If it is, store it in SMALL.

(iii) Add the new value to SUM and repeat from (ii) until all of
the data has been used. When no values are left, print the results.

There is no reason why the statements inside a DO loop should not
include other DO statements. However, two DO loops must not straddle
one another. The following diagram illustrates the correct (and
incorrect) nesting of DO loops.

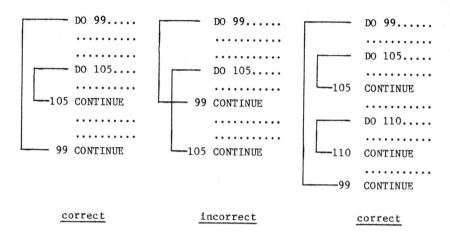

| correct | incorrect | correct |

The second (inner) DO statement in the first example could have another DO statement as part of its DO loop. In the third example, the first DO loop can have 110 as the label for the terminal statement in place of 99, provided that this DO loop does not contain an instruction to jump to the statement labelled 99. The one CONTINUE would then terminate the first and the last DO loops.

4.2.2 The General Form of the DO Statement

Having discussed the simple DO statement, it is now possible to specify the general form, which is

```
        DO label variable=E1,E2,E3
            ...................
    label ...................
```

where E1, E2 and E3 represent integer or real expressions.

The labelled statement which terminates the DO loop must appear after the DO statement. To make it clear where the DO loop ends, it is recommended that the labelled statement is always of the form

```
    label CONTINUE
```

The variable is called the DO VARIABLE and is either a real or integer variable. The statements within the DO loop are obeyed first with the DO variable taking the value E1, then the value E1+E3, and so on, and finally the value E1+(n−1)E3. The integer "n" is the number of times the loop is to be obeyed and is given by

$$n = \text{integer part of } ((E2-E1)/E3 + 1)$$

The only occasions when the DO loop is not obeyed "n" times are when "n" is negative or zero, in which case the statements in the DO loop are not obeyed at all, or when an exit is made as the result of a jump instruction. E3 may be omitted, in which case it is assumed to have the value 1.

The following points should be noted

(i)   The DO variable can be used within the DO loop but its value must not be altered.

(ii) E1, E2 and E3 are evaluated on entry to the DO loop and are held constant throughout the DO loop, even if they refer to variables that are altered within the DO loop. For example, the statements

```
        N=10
    DO 99 I=1,N
        N=N+1
    99 CONTINUE
```

will cause the DO loop to be executed 10 times with I=1, 2, 3, 4, 5, 6, 7, 8, 9 and 10. However, on exit from the DO loop, N will have the value 20.

(iii) It is not permitted to jump into a DO loop from outside that loop.

(iv) On exit from a DO loop, the DO variable retains the last value assigned to it. This means that if exit is caused through using up all the values in the DO variable list, that is E1, E1+E3, E1+2*E3,...E1+(n-1)*E3 then the value on exit will be E1+n*E3.   The reason for this is that the DO variable is assigned its new value before a check is made to determine whether or not all of the values defined in the DO variable list have been used. Thus in the example given in note (ii) the value of I will be 11 when the DO statement has been completed.

(v)   DO loops can be nested within IF blocks, ELSE blocks or ELSEIF blocks but must not straddle two blocks.

4.2.3 Summing a Finite Series

The following example illustrates the use of DO statements.   The value of the finite series

$$1 - x + \frac{x^2}{2!} - \frac{x^3}{3!} + \frac{x^4}{4!} - \frac{x^5}{5!} + \frac{x^6}{6!} - \frac{x^7}{7!} + \frac{x^8}{8!} - \frac{x^9}{9!}$$

is required for various values of x, where

```
    2!=       2*1
    3!=     3*2*1
    4!=   4*3*2*1
```

and so on.

Before writing the FORTRAN 77 statements to evaluate the sum, it should be noted that a person doing this calculation by hand would not compute each term in the series from scratch, but would use the information obtained from computing earlier terms, since a simple formula connects each term with the preceding term.   For example,

$$\frac{x^7}{7!} = \frac{x}{7} \cdot \frac{x^6}{6!}$$

since

$7! = 7*6*5*4*3*2*1 = 7*(6*5*4*3*2*1) = 7*6!$

and the term in x^6 would be computed before the term in x^7.

Thus, as with many computing problems, the question of how to advance the calculation one step has to be considered. Once this has been resolved, the complete solution can be obtained by taking the appropriate number of steps. Having decided how the calculation can be extended one step at a time, all that remains is to decide how to take the first step; that is, how to initialise the variables.

In the given example, the terms in the series are denoted by T_0, T_1, T_2,.... Then $T_0 = 1$, $T_1 = -x$ and the general term is given by

$$T_n = (-1)^n \frac{x^n}{n!} = -\frac{x}{n}(-1)^{n-1}\frac{x^{n-1}}{(n-1)!} = -\frac{x}{n}T_{n-1}$$

Thus T_2 can be calculated from T_1 by using the above formula with n=2. Next T_3 can be calculated from T_2 by giving "n" the value 3 and the remaining terms are calculated in a similar way. Each time a new term is calculated it is added to the sum. The value of the sum can be set initially to $T_0 + T_1 = 1-x$ and the current term to $T_1 = -x$. The sum can then be built up step by step. Using T to denote the current term, N to indicate which term this is and SUM to be the sum of the series, the instructions to sum the series for a given value of X are:

```
        T=-X
        SUM=1.0-X
        DO 15 N=2,9
            T=-X*T/N
            SUM=SUM+T
    15 CONTINUE
```

Note how the solution is obtained by assuming that the result is known to a point and then advancing one step. Repetition of this step gives the final answer. The initial values for the variables are chosen to be consistent with the statements that follow in the main loop. The DO variable is used in the DO loop in a natural way to modify the value of T.

Having written the sequence of statements needed to compute the value of the series for one value of "x", it is a simple matter to compute the sum for several different values of "x" . This is done by including this section of program inside a loop that controls the values assigned to "x". Thus the complete program could be written

```
        PROGRAM EX47
CCCC    PROGRAM TO TABULATE A FINITE SERIES
        DO 10 X=0.1,1.05,0.1
           T=-X
           SUM=1.0-X
           DO 15 N=2,9
              T=-X*T/N
              SUM=SUM+T
15         CONTINUE
           PRINT *,´SUM = ´,SUM,´ WHEN X = ´,X
10 CONTINUE
        END
```

The following points about this program should be noted

(i)   The program contains a DO loop nested within another DO loop. This arises quite naturally from the way the solution to the problem is approached.

(ii)   In the outer DO loop, the value for E2 has been set as 1.05 to ensure that the last value used for X is 1.0. This is because real numbers cannot always be stored without small errors occurring. For example, when using a hand calculator with 6 digit capacity, the nearest value to 2/3 that can be stored is 0.666667. Adding this value three times gives a value of 2.00001. Similar errors, but on a smaller scale, occur in all computers. The best way of ensuring that the complete range of values is used is to make the last value equal to a number half way between the last value required and the first value not required. However, when using integers no such problem exists and the actual limits can be used.

(iii) The analysis used in the construction of this program should be considered carefully. First the kernel of the problem (that is, how to proceed from one stage to the next) was examined. The instructions for the solution to the kernel were written and inserted in a loop. Then the initialisation statements were inserted in front of this loop and all enclosed in an outer loop which modified the value of x. The instructions were not written by starting at line 1.

(iv)   An alternative method of solving this problem is considered in exercise 5 at the end of this chapter.

4.3 THE STOP STATEMENT

Programs should stop being executed when they come to a logical end. This may or may not be at the physical end of the program. Clearly, a simple mechanism for stopping execution of the program at an intermediate point is desirable. In FORTRAN 77 this is done by using the STOP statement which is simply written

       STOP

This statement can appear anywhere a normal statement is permitted.

  As an example, consider a program that reads in a data item, processes the data and then repeats the sequence. One way of indicating that there is no more data to be processed is to include a fictitious item at the end of the data and to test for this item being read. For example, if the input data represents the frequencies with which an event occurred in certain time intervals, a correct value cannot be negative. Using I to denote the frequency in the program, a negative value can be detected and the program terminated by the statements:

       READ *,I

       IF (I.LT.0) STOP

Another use of the STOP statement is when something is obviously wrong, such as division by zero or by a very small quantity. If there is no "cure", the program must stop with an indication of the error, as in the following example:

       IF (ABS(B).LT.1.0E-8) THEN

           PRINT *, *** B IS TOO SMALL***   B= ,B

           STOP

       ENDIF

       C=A/B

4.4 THE GOTO STATEMENT

Sometimes the number of repetitions of a loop is not known at the outset. For example, if a function is defined as an infinite series, the sequence for computing successive terms must be broken according to some prescribed criterion. One way to do this in FORTRAN 77 is to use an IF statement combined with a GOTO statement.

  The simplest form of the GOTO statement is

       GOTO label

This statement will cause the statement with the appropriate label to be executed next, instead of the statement in the natural sequence. There are however a few restrictions on the position of the statement with the given label. These are

  (i) It is not permitted to jump to a statement within a DO loop unless the GOTO is also within that DO loop.

  (ii) It is not permitted to jump into an IF or ELSE block from outside that block.

  (iii) ELSE, ELSEIF and ENDIF statements cannot be labelled.

  There are other forms of the GOTO statement, which are discussed in chapter 10. Care is needed when using GOTO statements, since

injudicious use can lead the unwary to produce programs which work
"correctly" sometimes and not at other times.

4.4.1 Summing an Infinite Series

Suppose that it is necessary to compute the approximate value of the
sum of the convergent infinite series

$$1 - x + \frac{x^2}{2!} - \frac{x^3}{3!} + \frac{x^4}{4!} - \frac{x^5}{5!} + \frac{x^6}{6!} - \frac{x^7}{7!} + \frac{x^8}{8!} - \ldots$$

ignoring terms that are less than 10^{-5} in magnitude.

The approach is that used in program EX47.   Each term in the series
is computed from its predecessor. Assuming that T is the (n-1)-th
term, the next term (the n-th term) is given by

$$- \frac{x}{n} T$$

This term is now the current term and is stored in T. If its value is
significant, it is added to the sum and it becomes the last computed
term. The value of "n" is increased by 1 and, since the same relation
holds between T and its successor as before, the loop can be
repeated.

The sequence of the computation can be expressed as follows
(i)   Initialise all variables.
(ii)   Add the term to the sum.
(iii) Compute the next term and, if this is significant repeat from
step (ii). Otherwise, print the value of the sum.

The relevant piece of program then becomes

```
        N=1
        SUM=1.0
        T=-X
    15 SUM=SUM+T
        N=N+1
        T=-X*T/N
        IF (ABS(T).GT.1.0E-5) GOTO 15
        PRINT *,´THE SUM IS ´,SUM,´ WHEN X IS ´,X
```

To obtain the sum of the series for several values of "x", this piece
of program is included in a DO loop that controls the values assigned
to "x".   It should be noted that this technique is only applicable to
certain types of infinite series.

4.5 EXAMPLE PROGRAMS

In this section, a number of other programs which use control
statements are described.

4.5.1 Shortest Route Between Three Towns

A salesman living at town H has to visit three towns A, B and C and
then return home. The program reads in the co-ordinates for H, A, B
and C and prints the shortest route for the salesman to take. The
distance between two towns at (x_1,y_1) and (x_2,y_2) is taken to be

$$\sqrt{(x_1-x_2)^2 + (y_1-y_2)^2}$$

This is an extension of the problem solved earlier in section 3.5.4.

```
      PROGRAM EX48
      READ *,XH,YH,XA,YA,XB,YB,XC,YC
CCCC  WE HAVE READ IN THE CO-ORDINATES OF THE TOWNS.
CCCC  IN THE FOLLOWING, IDENTIFIERS STARTING WITH A D REPRESENT
CCCC  DISTANCES AND THE REMAINING CHARACTERS INDICATE THE ROUTE
      DHA=SQRT((XH-XA)**2+(YH-YA)**2)
      DHB=SQRT((XH-XB)**2+(YH-YB)**2)
      DHC=SQRT((XH-XC)**2+(YH-YC)**2)
      DAB=SQRT((XA-XB)**2+(YA-YB)**2)
      DAC=SQRT((XA-XC)**2+(YA-YC)**2)
      DBC=SQRT((XB-XC)**2+(YB-YC)**2)
      DHABCH=DHA+DAB+DBC+DHC
      DHBCAH=DHB+DBC+DAC+DHA
      DHCABH=DHC+DAC+DAB+DHB
CCCC  PRINT THE HEADING FIRST AS THIS IS ALWAYS REQUIRED
      PRINT *,'THE SHORTEST ROUTE VIA ALL THE TOWNS IS ',
      IF (DHABCH.LT.DHCABH) THEN
         IF (DHBCAH.GT.DHABCH) THEN
            PRINT *,' H, A, B, C, H       WHERE:'
         ELSE
            PRINT *,' H, B, C, A, H       WHERE:'
         ENDIF
      ELSEIF (DHBCAH.GT.DHCABH) THEN
         PRINT *,' H, C, A, B, H      WHERE:'
      ELSE
         PRINT *,' H, B, C, A, H      WHERE:'
      ENDIF
CCCC  NOTICE THAT THE IF BLOCK IS ITSELF A BLOCK IF STATEMENT
      PRINT *,' H IS AT    ',XH,YH
      PRINT *,' A IS AT    ',XA,YA
      PRINT *,' B IS AT    ',XB,YB
      PRINT *,' C IS AT    ',XC,YC
      END
```

Once again, the distances between the various towns must be computed
and used to determine the path lengths HABCH, HACBH and HBACH. The
other possible routes are simply these in the reverse order.   Having
computed the distances, the smallest value can be selected by the
computer (using a conditional statement in the program) and the
required result printed.

   When run with the data record
   2.0 1.0 3.5 8.0 7.0 4.32 812.0 81.0
the results were

    THE SHORTEST ROUTE VIA ALL TOWNS IS
    H, B, C, A, H   WHERE:
    H IS AT   2.000000   1.000000
    A IS AT   3.500000   8.000000
    B IS AT   7.000000   4.320000
    C IS AT   812.0000   81.00000

4.5.2 The Cube Root of a Number

The program described in this section uses the Newton-Raphson
iterative scheme to determine the cube root of a value given as data.
If "a" is the number whose cube root is to be found, the method is to
set up a sequence of values defined by the relation

$$x_{n+1} = x_n - (x_n^3 - a)/(3x_n^2), \quad n=0,1,2,\ldots$$

Provided $x_n \neq 0$, the members of the sequence will get closer and closer
to the cube root. Hence the calculation of the sequence can stop when

$$|x_{n+1} - x_n| < tol$$

where "tol" is a measure of the accuracy required for the cube root.
The technique used is called iteration.

   Since each term in the sequence can be calculated from the previous
term, it is only necessary to retain two successive approximations at
any stage.   These will be stored in locations X0 and X1. The
iterative process is as follows:

(i)   Set X0 to an initial guess at the cube root.

(ii)   Compute the next term X1 from the value of X0.

(iii) If X0 and X1 are not sufficiently close, that is, $|X1-X0| > tol$
then re-set X0 to the current value of X1 and repeat step (ii);
otherwise continue to the next step of the program with the desired
solution in X1.

   For the given example

$$X1 = X0 - (X0^3 - A)/(3X0^2) = X0 + (A - X0^3)/(3X0^2) = X0 + DX0$$

   where

$$DX0 = (A-X0^3)/(3X0^2)$$

The program has been designed to read in a value A, for which the cube root is required, and A/3.0 is taken as the initial approximation to the cube root. Successive approximations are calculated and printed out. When two successive approximations are such that their difference DX0 is less than 0.00001 the loop is terminated. The current value of X1 is taken as the cube root and a check residual X1**3 - A is calculated to give some indication of the accuracy obtained when the program terminates. The program is

```
      PROGRAM EX49
CCCC  PROGRAM TO CALCULATE CUBE ROOTS
      READ *,A
      IF (ABS(A).LT.1.0E-5) THEN
          PRINT *,A,´ IS TOO SMALL´
      ELSE
          PRINT *,´THE SEQUENCE OF APPROXIMATIONS TO ´,
     1       ´THE CUBE ROOT IS´
          X1= A/3.0
   20     X0=X1
          DX0=(A-X0**3)/(3.0*X0**2)
          X1=X0+DX0
          PRINT *,X1
          IF (ABS(DX0).GE.1.0E-5) GOTO 20
CCCC  NO CHECK ON THE NUMBER OF ITERATIONS HAS BEEN INCLUDED
CCCC  BECAUSE THE SEQUENCE IS KNOWN TO BE RAPIDLY CONVERGENT
          PRINT *,´THE FINAL RESULT IS A = ´,A,
     1       ´THE CUBE ROOT = ´,X1
          PRINT *, ´CHECK RESIDUAL IS ´,X1**3-A
      ENDIF
      END
```

When this program was run with 3.5 being read as the value of the variable A, the results were

```
THE SEQUENCE OF APPROXIMATIONS TO THE CUBE ROOT IS
     1.634921
     1.526416
     1.518338
     1.518294
     1.518294
THE FINAL RESULT IS A=    3.500000    THE CUBE ROOT =    1.518294
CHECK RESIDUAL IS      2.910383E-11
```

Since the Newton-Raphson scheme cannot be guaranteed to converge to
the correct result for all problems, it is good practice to restrict
the program to a limited number of iterations by inserting a counter
in the loop and terminating the loop if this counter exceeds some
prearranged value.

4.5.3 Roots of a Quadratic Equation

The program described on the next page reads the coefficients of a
set of quadratic equations and determines their roots. The program
terminates when all the coefficients read are zero.
   In this problem there are a number of situations that could arise.
The roots could be real, the roots could be complex, the data given
could represent a linear equation (the coefficient of x^2 being zero),
or the data could even be invalid. A decision concerning the action
to be taken under each of these circumstances must be made at the
outset. The solution that follows allows the possibility of the
coefficient of x^2 being zero, in which case the equation is treated
as linear.
   The equation being solved is assumed to be $ax^2+bx+c=0$, and the
solution is computed from the well-known formula

$$x = \frac{-b \pm \sqrt{(b^2-4ac)}}{2a}$$

unless the value of "a" is zero. In this case, the root is assumed to
be x = -c/b, provided the value of "b" is non-zero.
   The program first tests to ensure that "a", "b" and "c" are not all
zero.   Next a test is made to see whether or not "a" is zero. If "a"
is non-zero, the equation is a genuine quadratic and can be solved
using the formula.   However, it is not permitted to take the square
root of a negative value. Thus when "a" is non-zero there are two
possible cases.   These are $b^2 \geq 4ac$ which means that the roots are
real; and $b^2 < 4ac$,   which means that the roots are complex.   The
program must allow for both cases.
   If "a" is zero, the equation reduces to the linear form
        bx + c = 0,
in which case a further test is needed to test whether or not "b" is
zero.   If "b" is zero, the equation is INVALID, otherwise the result
is -c/b. There is no need for a test on "c" because the program
would have stopped had "a", "b" and "c" all been zero.
   Since obscure errors frequently turn up long after a program was
written, it is important to document programs adequately and comments
should be used to help explain the logic used in the design of the
program.

```
        PROGRAM EX410
CCCC    CALCULATION OF ROOTS OF A QUADRATIC
        PRINT *,'THE FOLLOWING TABLE GIVES THE ROOTS',
       1    ' OF A*X**2+B*X+C=0'
     10 PRINT *
        READ *,A,B,C
        IF ((ABS(A)+ABS(B)+ABS(C)).EQ.0.0) STOP
CCCC    THIS IS THE EXCEPTIONAL CASE WHERE A TEST FOR
CCCC    THE EQUALITY OF REALS IS REASONABLE
CCCC    STOP IF ALL THREE OF A, B AND C ARE ZERO ON INPUT
        PRINT *,'A=',A,'B=',B,'C=',C
        IF (A.NE.0.0) THEN
CCCC       ONLY ENTER THIS BLOCK IF THE EQUATION IS A
CCCC       GENUINE QUADRATIC
           DISCR=B**2-4.0*A*C
           R=-0.5*B/A
           IF (DISCR.GE.0.0) THEN
              D=SQRT(DISCR)*0.5/A
              PRINT *,'THE REAL ROOTS ARE:  ',R+D,
       1            '  AND  ',R-D
           ELSE
              COMP=0.5*SQRT(-DISCR)/A
              PRINT *,'THE COMPLEX ROOTS ARE: ',R,'  +',
       1          COMP,'I'
              PRINT *,'                       AND   ',R,'  -',
       1          COMP,'I'
           ENDIF
        ELSE
CCCC       THIS BLOCK IS ONLY ENTERED WHEN A IS ZERO AND
CCCC       HENCE THE EQUATION TO BE SOLVED IS LINEAR
           IF (B.EQ.0.0) THEN
              PRINT *,'                 INVALID EQUATION'
           ELSE
              PRINT *,'EQUATION IS LINEAR AND HAS A ROOT',
       1          -C/B
           ENDIF
        ENDIF
        GOTO 10
        END
```

The test data for this program should be chosen to ensure that all possible routes through the program are tested and all possible cases are considered. A little time spent selecting suitable test data is well worth the effort.

When program EX410 was tested using the data
   1.0 2.0 1.0
   1.0 -2.0 1.0
   1.0 2.0 -1.0
   1.0 2.0 3.0
   1.0 3.0 0.0
   1.0 0.0 3.0
   0.0 3.0 1.0
   0.0 0.0 7.0
   0.0 0.0 0.0
the following results were obtained

```
THE FOLLOWING TABLE GIVES THE ROOTS OF A*X**2+B*X+C=0


A=    1.000000    B=    2.000000    C=    1.000000
THE REAL ROOTS ARE:       -1.000000       AND      -1.000000


A=    1.000000    B=   -2.000000    C=  · 1.000000
THE REAL ROOTS ARE:        1.000000       AND       1.000000


A=    1.000000    B=    2.000000    C=   -1.000000
THE REAL ROOTS ARE:        4.142136E-01  AND      -2.414214


A=    1.000000    B=    2.000000    C=    3.000000
THE COMPLEX ROOTS ARE:    -1.000000        +     1.414214    I
                   AND    -1.000000        -     1.414214    I


A=    1.000000    B=    3.000000    C=    0.000000
THE REAL ROOTS ARE:        0.000000       AND      -3.000000


A=    1.000000    B=    0.000000    C=    3.000000
THE COMPLEX ROOTS ARE:     0.000000        +     1.732051    I
                   AND     0.000000        -     1.732051    I


A=    0.000000    B=    3.000000    C=    1.000000
EQUATION IS LINEAR AND HAS A ROOT                 -3.333333E-01


A=    0.000000    B=    0.000000    C=    7.700000
                   INVALID EQUATION
```

Due to the limitations of the input and output routines considered so far, these results are not laid out as neatly as they could be. However, they should be scrutinised to ensure that they are correct! In the foregoing results it appears that all cases have been tested. Data that was inconsistent was used, repeated roots, real roots and complex roots were obtained and all of the results were satisfactory. This program could be run for a long time using different data and yield satisfactory results. However, there are circumstances in which the program results are inadequate. For example, if A=1.0, B=1.0E12 and C=1.0E12, the roots produced by the program are 0 and -1.0E12. Unfortunately the root with smaller magnitude should be -1.0, not zero. The reason for this is that, because B is very large compared to A, the value of B**2-4.0*A*C is indistinguishable from that of B**2 because of the limited accuracy of the computer. The value of -B+SQRT(DISCR) is zero, large errors having been introduced due to cancellation. This type of calculation should be avoided in numerical work whenever possible.

The difficulty can be avoided in this example since the root with smaller magnitude can be calculated in a different manner. It is well-known that the roots x_1 and x_2 of a quadratic are related by the equation:

$$x_1 x_2 = \frac{c}{a} \; .$$

The smaller root can be calculated from this expression and in the case considered this yields the value -1.0 which was quoted earlier. This should serve as a warning that carefully thought out tests are needed before a program can be genuinely called correct.

When a solution is obtained as the difference of two "almost equal" quantities, it has to be treated with extreme caution. Inevitably an answer of reduced accuracy is produced. This type of error is often called a subtractive cancellation error. Whenever possible, calculations should be reformulated to avoid this situation. Inexperienced programmers often draw unjustified conclusions from results which are a combination of arithmetic errors. A careful examination is always needed to ensure that results are meaningful.

4.6 EXERCISES

1. Write a program which reads a value and prints whichever of the messages
    THE GIVEN VALUE IS POSITIVE
    THE GIVEN VALUE IS NEGATIVE
    THE GIVEN VALUE IS ZERO
is appropriate.

2. Write a program which reads three numbers and prints them in a column with the largest at the top and the smallest at the bottom of the column.

3. A man wishes to compare the repayments on a loan of 1,000 pounds taken out over a five year period for various rates of interest based on two different schemes. For scheme A the monthly repayments are

$$\frac{100+5x}{6} \text{ pounds}$$

while for scheme B the monthly repayments are

$$\frac{5x(1+x/100)^5}{6(1+x/100)^5-6} \text{ pounds,}$$

the rate of interest being x%. Write a program which prints a table of values in three columns with headings

X	REPAYMENTS	REPAYMENTS
	SCHEME A	SCHEME B

in which "x" takes the values 1,2,3,4,5,6,7,8,9,10,11,12,13,14,15.

4. A simple beam of length L and uniform cross-section has a single concentrated load P applied at a distance A from the left-hand end. The deflection Y of the beam at a point a distance X from the left-hand end is given by the formula:

$$Y = -\frac{PBX}{6EIL}[\ 2L(L-X) - B^2 - (L-X)^2]\qquad 0 \le X \le A$$

$$= -\frac{PA(L-X)}{6EIL}[\ 2LB - B^2 - (L-X)^2]\qquad A \le X \le L$$

where E is Young's Modulus, I is the second moment of area and B=L−A.

Write a program which reads in values for P, L, A, E, I and which tabulates Y for X = 0, 0.1L, 0.2L, 0.3L,...,0.9L, L.

Typical data for this problem might be:

$$P = 227 \text{ kg.}, \quad A = 1650 \text{ mm.}, \quad L = 3910 \text{ mm.},$$
$$E = 21000 \text{ kg/mm}^2., \quad I = 1.04*10^6 \text{ mm}^4.$$

5. Re-write program EX47 to evaluate the given series using nested multiplication. To do this, the series is written as

$$1-x(1-\frac{x}{2}(1-\frac{x}{3}(1-\frac{x}{4}(1-\frac{x}{5}(1-\frac{x}{6}(1-\frac{x}{7}(1-\frac{x}{8}(1-\frac{x}{9})))))))).$$

6. When water is discharged at a rate of Q cubic metres/second from a pipe of diameter D metres, the friction coefficient f can be calculated indirectly from the empirical formula

$$F = -2 \log_{10}(\frac{A}{D} + \frac{BD}{Q}F)\ ,$$

where $f = F^{-2}$ and $A = 1.35135*10^{-4}$, $B = 2.247338*10^{-6}$

F can be found from the given formula by the following method

(i)   An initial approximation F_0 is given to F

(ii) $F_1 = -2 \log_{10}(\frac{A}{D} + \frac{BD}{Q} F_0)$ is calculated.

(iii) If $|F_1 - F_0| \leq 10^{-10}$ then the value F_1 is accepted as the solution of the equation and f is calculated from it.   Otherwise, replace F_0 by F_1 and calculate a new value for F_1 by repeating step (ii).

Write a program which will read in values for D, Q and an initial approximation F_0. The program should use the method outlined above to calculate f. It should also incorporate a counter to record the number of times that the value of F_1 is calculated.   If this counter exceeds 20, the program should be terminated with the message "SOLUTION NOT FOUND".

Typical data for this problem might be:

$D = 0.5$ metres, $Q = 0.5$ m^3/sec, $F_0 = 10.0$.

7. A man always records numbers by writing them from right to left instead of from left to right. Thus, when he means 1234, he writes 4321.   Write a program which reads a five digit integer supplied by this man, converts it to the correct value and prints the given value and the true value.   Modify the program so that a sequence of five digit integers is read and the digits of each number in the sequence are reversed.   The end of the sequence is indicated by a zero.

8. Write a program to read in an integer and determine whether or not it is a prime number. The program should print an answer of the form ... IS A PRIME or ... IS NOT A PRIME.   To determine whether or not a number, "m", is a prime simply check to see if it is exactly divisible by one of $2, 3, 5, 7, 9, 11, \ldots, \sqrt{m}$.

9. Write a program to determine the roots of a quadratic equation using the modified scheme suggested at the end of section 4.5.3.

CHAPTER 5
ARRAYS

An ARRAY is the means by which a program can reference many different storage locations using a single name. To access a particular element or component some additional information has to be provided. This is called the SUBSCRIPT. In this chapter the manipulation of arrays is described, first in their simplest form and then more generally.

5.1 A SIMPLE APPLICATION OF AN ARRAY

It is often necessary to store a large set of data whose individual elements all have something in common, such as a set of marks obtained by different students in an examination. Rather than allocate a different name to each storage location used for each item of data, a single name is given to the whole sequence of storage locations, a particular item being identified by its position in the sequence.

As an example, suppose that a set of 100 examination marks is to be stored. The whole sequence of storage locations used could be identified by the collective name MARK. The first storage location can be referred to as MARK(1), the second as MARK(2), and so on, the last being referred to as MARK(100). This construction is consistent with the mathematical notation of using a subscript and representing the 100 marks by

$$m_1, m_2, m_3, \cdots\cdots\cdots\cdots m_{100}.$$

Any particular element is specified by giving the name, MARK followed by a SUBSCRIPT, which consists, in this case, of a single SUBSCRIPT EXPRESSION in brackets. For example, MARK(I) is the name of an element of the array MARK and the subscript expression is an integer variable I, whose value is used to identify the particular element. It is possible for subscripts to contain more than one subscript expression, as described in section 5.7. When only one subscript expression is present, the array is said to be ONE-DIMENSIONAL. The subscript expression, which is examined in detail in section 5.4, may be an integer constant, integer variable or integer expression.

The name which the programmer chooses for the array must obey the normal rules for names (see section 2.2). It is necessary to state explicitly in the program that a particular name refers to an array rather than a simple variable and to specify the bounds of the subscript expressions so that the storage space required can be allocated for the array. This is usually accomplished by means of a DIMENSION statement, which is described in section 5.3.

5.2 EXAMPLE PROGRAMS

Suppose the average mark obtained by a set of "n" candidates in an examination is required. It could be obtained by the following program which does not use arrays.

```
        PROGRAM EX51
  CCCC  AVERAGE OF A SET OF N MARKS
        SUM=0.0
        READ *,N
        DO 11 I=1,N
            READ *,MTEMP
            PRINT *,MTEMP
  CCCC        READS AND PRINTS ONE MARK PER RECORD
            SUM=SUM+MTEMP
     11 CONTINUE
        AVRGE=SUM/N
        PRINT *,´AVERAGE MARK IS ´,AVRGE
        END
```

The following points should be noted:

(i) The marks are integers, one being on each data record. This would be wasteful if N were large.

(ii) No record of the marks is retained in the store, since each new mark is read and assigned to the integer variable MTEMP, overwriting the previous value.

Suppose the problem is extended, and the number of candidates with more than the average mark is required. In this case, the average is not known until all the data has been read. It is essential, therefore, to store the data in such a way that a comparison with the average can be made when this is known. One way to store the data is to use an ARRAY and the program may then be written:

```
      PROGRAM EX52
CCCC  AVERAGE OF A SET OF MARKS AND THE NUMBER OF
CCCC  CANDIDATES OBTAINING MORE THAN THE AVERAGE MARK
      DIMENSION MARK(100)
      READ *,N
      SUM=0.0
      DO 11 I=1,N
          READ *,MARK(I)
          PRINT *,MARK(I)
          SUM=SUM+MARK(I)
   11 CONTINUE
      AVRGE=SUM/N
      PRINT *,´AVERAGE MARK IS ´,AVRGE
CCCC  SEARCHES FOR MARKS ABOVE THE AVERAGE
      M=0
      DO 12 I=1,N
          IF (AVRGE.LT.MARK(I)) M=M+1
   12 CONTINUE
      PRINT *,´NUMBER OF CANDIDATES WITH MORE ´,
     1   ´THAN THE AVERAGE MARK IS ´,M
      END
```

The following points about this program should be noted:
(i)   The statement DIMENSION MARK(100) allocates the hundred storage locations

        MARK(1), MARK(2), MARK(3), ..., MARK(100)

for the array elements. As the program assumes that N is at most 100, it would be better to test whether N lies between 1 and 100. This can be done by the block IF statement

```
      IF (N.LT.1 .OR. N.GT.100) THEN
          PRINT *,´N OUT OF RANGE, N IS ´,N
          STOP
      ENDIF
```

(ii) The input and output statements

```
      READ *,MARK(I)
      PRINT *,MARK(I)
```

read and print one value at a time. There are other forms of read and write statements which would allow the set of marks to be treated as one data record. These are discussed later in section 5.5.

(iii) The ARRAY ELEMENT MARK(I) can be used in arithmetic expressions and conditional statements wherever a simple integer variable may be used. Examples of this are

```
      SUM=SUM+MARK(I)
      IF (AVRGE.LT.MARK(I)) M=M+1
```

(iv)   The   last PRINT statement in the program is continued over to
another line. This is signified by a 1 in position 6.

(v)   MARK(I)   refers   to   each   element   of the array in turn as I
changes value under the control of the DO loop.

It   will be appreciated that it takes longer to locate a particular
array element in the store than it does to locate a simple   variable.
This   is   because   the   position of the required array element in the
sequence of storage locations used for the   whole   array   has   to   be
determined.   Thus,   if   the   same array element is to be used several
times, it is good programming practice to locate the element once and
store   its value in a simple variable. For example, the left-hand set
of statements below are more efficient than the right-hand set.

```
10 READ *,K                      10 READ *,MARK(I)
20 IF (K.EQ.-1) GOTO 30          20 IF (MARK(I).EQ.-1) GOTO 30
   I=I+1                            SUM=SUM+MARK(I)
   SUM=SUM+K                        I=I+1
   MARK(I)=K                        GOTO 10
   GOTO 10                       30 I=I-1
30 .......
```

5.3 THE DIMENSION STATEMENT

Storage   must   be   allocated   for each element of an array before any
information can be assigned to it.   The   allocation   of   storage   is
usually   specified by a non-executable DIMENSION STATEMENT which must
be included at the beginning of the   program   before   any   executable
statement   in the program.   In main programs each array bound must be
a constant integer expression. This is not necessary in   subprograms,
which are described in chapter 7.

The general form of the DIMENSION statement is

        DIMENSION list

where the "list" is a list of array names, with   the   bounds   of   the
subscript   expressions associated   with   each   array specified   in
brackets.

If   only   one   bound   is   given   for a subscript, the result of the
constant integer expression must   define   a   positive   integer   which
specifies   the   greatest   value   that   can   be taken by the subscript
expression. The least value is then assumed to be   1.   When   a   lower
bound other than 1 is required, the lower bound is specified followed
by a colon and the upper bound. The subscript expression can take all
integer   values   from   the   lower bound up to and including the upper
bound. Obviously the upper bound must be greater than or equal to the
lower bound! For example,

        DIMENSION A(3)

allocates the three real storage locations A(1), A(2) and A(3), and

        DIMENSION M(-1:1)

allocates the three integer storage locations M(-1), M(0) and M(1).

  More than one array may be specified by the same DIMENSION statement, for example,

        DIMENSION A(3),B(0:2),M(-1:1)

allocates the storage locations for A(1), A(2), A(3), B(0), B(1), B(2), M(-1), M(0) and M(1). Here A and B are arrays of real variables and M is an array of integer variables, all with three elements.

  More than one DIMENSION statement may be used in the same program. For example, if the two DIMENSION statements

        DIMENSION A(3)

        DIMENSION M(-1:1)

appear in a program, the first allocates three real elements to the array A and the second allocates three integer elements to the array M.

  If it is desirable to give a name to an array which is contrary to the implied type, a TYPE STATEMENT as described in section 2.5 must be used. The bounds for the subscript expressions may be specified in this statement, in which case the array must not be redefined in a DIMENSION statement. The statement

        INTEGER HSTGRM(0:2)

allocates storage for the three elements of the integer array HSTGRM, namely HSTGRM(0), HSTGRM(1) and HSTGRM(2). Alternatively, the following two statements would achieve the same result

        INTEGER HSTGRM

        DIMENSION HSTGRM(0:2)

  If a number of arrays with the same bounds for their subscript expressions are used and these bounds require changing for different runs of the program it is better to use a PARAMETER statement (see section 2.7), so that only one statement will need to be changed between runs. Any constant integer expression can be used in a DIMENSION statement, for example

        INTEGER DIM

        PARAMETER (DIM=4)

        DIMENSION X(DIM),Y(DIM),Z(2*DIM-1)

5.4 SUBSCRIPT EXPRESSIONS

Subscript expressions may take any integer value, which may be positive, zero or negative within the range of integer values specified in the DIMENSION statement or its equivalent. They may be integer constants, integer variables, or integer expressions which

are evaluated to locate the required element of the array at the time
the statement involving the array element is carried out. If the
array A has its first element in A(1), A(3) is the third element of
the array A and if "i" represents the current value of the integer
variable I, A(I) is the i-th element of the array A. The element
represented by A(I*(M-1)+J) depends on the current values of I, M
and J. When M=4, I=2 and J=3, the array element is A(9).

5.5 INPUT AND OUTPUT OF ONE-DIMENSIONAL ARRAYS

Values can be read and assigned to individual elements of an array by
including the array elements in the list of a READ statement. In a
similar way, individual elements of an array can be part of the list
of a PRINT statement. Examples of this, are given in program EX52 in
section 5.2. One value is read from each data record into the
appropriate element of the array MARK, then a copy of the value is
printed out.

The following are examples of READ statements which involve array
elements. The statement

        READ *,N,X,A(2),I(1)

reads the first four numbers from the next available data record and
assigns their values to the integer variable N, the real variable X,
the real array element A(2) and the integer array element I(1)
respectively. The statement

        READ *,A(1),A(2),A(3),A(4)

reads four real numbers from the input data and stores them in the
elements A(1), A(2), A(3) and A(4) of the array A. The statement

        READ *,(A(I),I=1,4)

is a more compact form of the last example. The construction
(A(I),I=1,4) is called an IMPLIED DO LOOP. It is essential for large
amounts of input data when the bounds of the implied DO loop (1 and 4
in the example) are integer variables or expressions. This READ
statement can be easily altered to read "n" values, where "n" is the
value of the integer variable N at the time the READ statement is
executed, as in the following example

        DIMENSION A(50)
        READ *,N
        READ *,(A(I),I=1,N)

Here the DIMENSION statement allocates 50 storage locations to the
array A. The second statement reads an integer value from the next
available data record and assigns it to the integer variable N. Then
N real values, which start on the next record, are read in sequence
and assigned to the N array elements A(1), A(2), A(3), ..., A(N).
This form of statement will go to subsequent data records to find

sufficient data, but if there is any additional data remaining on the last physical record after the list is completed, this remaining data is lost (see section 2.3.2).

It should be noted that the DIMENSION statement which allocates the storage for the array A has to state a fixed array size. An error will occur if N is greater than the specified size of the array (in this case 50). When N is less than 50, there will be elements of the array A which are undefined and should not be used, until they are assigned a value.

The general form of an implied DO loop for a one-dimensional array A is

          (A(I),I=int1,int2,int3)

where I represents any integer variable; "int1", "int2" and "int3" being integer constants, integer variables or integer expressions. The statement refers initially to the array element A(int1), then to A(int1 + int3), then to A(int1 + 2*int3), and so on until the value of the subscript expression exceeds "int2", when the process is terminated. If "int3" is omitted, a default value of 1 is assumed.

Implied DO loops can appear at any point in the list of an input or an output statement. Examples of input statements which use an implied DO loop are

          READ *,(A(I),I=1,5,2)

which reads information into A(1), A(3) and A(5) respectively; and

          READ *,(A(I),I=4,0,-2)

which reads consecutive numbers and stores the first in A(4), the second in A(2), and the third in A(0).

It is possible to use the array name only (without a subscript) in the READ statement. For example,

          READ *,A

reads information into every element of the array A. There must be at least enough data items available for all the array elements specified by the DIMENSION statement for the array A.

There is a list-directed output statement corresponding to each of the above list-directed input statements. PRINT replaces READ and the information is copied from the elements of the array and printed out. Each PRINT statement starts printing out at the beginning of a new line and therefore all the information to be printed out on a single line must be specified by the same PRINT statement. Examples of list-directed PRINT statements are

          PRINT *,N,X,A(2),I(1)
          PRINT *,A(1),A(2),A(3),A(4)
          PRINT *,(A(I),I=1,4)
          PRINT *,(A(I),I=1,N)
          PRINT *,A

It should be noted that an implied DO loop is treated as a single item in the list. Hence a statement such as

        PRINT *,X,Y,(A(I),I=1,N),Z,(B(I),I=10,1,-1)

is valid. When there is insufficient room on a line of output for the next value, a new line of output is automatically started.

   Arrays may be initialised by using a DATA statement. For example, the statement

        DATA (A(I),I=1,3) / 3*0.0 /

sets the values of the array elements A(1), A(2) and A(3) to zero. Similarly, the pair of statements

        DIMENSION X(100)
        DATA X / 100*1.0 /

will set all the elements of the array X to the value 1.0.

5.6 PROGRAMS WHICH USE ONE-DIMENSIONAL ARRAYS

The following examples illustrate the way in which arrays may be used and manipulated.

5.6.1 Average of a Set of Examination Marks

Program EX52 described in section 5.2 is rewritten to use an implied DO loop in the READ and PRINT statements. This program calculates the average mark obtained by "n" candidates in an examination and determines the number of candidates with more than the average mark.

   The program assumes that the number of candidates is available on the first data record and the marks, which are integer values, are on the remaining data record(s). The number of candidates and their marks are printed in a list followed by the average. The marks are totalled in the DO loop terminating at label 11 and the average is stored in AVRGE. The average mark is then used in the second pass through the data (the DO loop terminating at label 12) to find the number of candidates who scored more than the average. This quantity is stored in M and is printed when the DO loop ends. The program on the next page produced the results

THE   5 CANDIDATES HAD THE FOLLOWING MARKS
        20   30   40   50   60
AVERAGE MARK IS   40.00000
NUMBER OF CANDIDATES WITH MORE THAN THE AVERAGE MARK IS   2

when run with the data records

```
      5
      20 30 40 50 60
```

It should be noted that the program checks the value of N which is read. If it is less than 1 or greater than 100, the program stops. The real variable SUM is used to accumulate the sum of the marks, which are held in the integer array, MARK. Had an integer variable (INTSUM, say) been used for this, it would have been necessary to use the intrinsic function REAL in the statement which calculates the average, that is

        AVRGE=REAL(INTSUM)/N

in order to avoid the difficulty of integer division.

```
      PROGRAM EX53
CCCC  AVERAGE OF A SET OF MARKS AND THE NUMBER OF CANDIDATES
CCCC  OBTAINING MORE THAN THE AVERAGE MARK
      DIMENSION MARK(100)
CCCC  IT IS ASSUMED THAT THERE ARE NO MORE THAN 100 CANDIDATES
CCCC  THE PROGRAM TERMINATES IF N IS LESS THAN 1
CCCC  OR N GREATER THAN 100
      READ *,N
      IF (N.LT.1 .OR. N.GT.100) THEN
          PRINT *,'N OUT OF RANGE, N IS ',N
          STOP
      ENDIF
      PRINT *,'THE ',N,' CANDIDATES HAD THE FOLLOWING MARKS'
      READ *,(MARK(I),I=1,N)
      PRINT *,(MARK(I),I=1,N)
CCCC  CALCULATE THE SUM AND AVERAGE
      SUM=0.0
      DO 11 I=1,N
          SUM=SUM+MARK(I)
   11 CONTINUE
      AVRGE=SUM/N
      PRINT *,'AVERAGE MARK IS ',AVRGE
CCCC  SCAN THE CANDIDATES FOR THOSE WITH MARKS ABOVE THE AVERAGE
      M=0
      DO 12 I=1,N
          IF (AVRGE.LT.MARK(I)) M=M+1
   12 CONTINUE
      PRINT *,'NUMBER OF CANDIDATES WITH MORE ',
     1    'THAN THE AVERAGE MARK IS ',M
      END
```

5.6.2 Linear Exchange Sort

The program considered in this section reads an integer N and a list
of N real numbers, sorts them into descending order, and prints out
the ordered list.

The method of sorting used by the program is called the linear
exchange sort, which is relatively simple but not very efficient for
large values of N. There are much more sophisticated and efficient
methods which are described in the specialist literature on sorting.

In this method, a search is made for the largest value in the list
and this value is exchanged with the first value in the list. A
search is then made from the second position and the next largest
value found is exchanged with the second value in the list and so on.
This process may be implemented by having a variable AMAX to which is
assigned a copy of the largest value encountered so far in the search
and an integer IMAX which records its position in the list.

Initially the unsorted values are contained in the array elements
A(1),A(2),A(3),...,A(N). When the largest value is in its correct
position, the elements to be sorted are A(2),A(3),...,A(N). This is
a similar problem, the only difference being the position of the
start of the list! The first of the unsorted elements is denoted by
A(I) and I is given the value 1 initially, then 2, and so on.

This allows the algorithm to be written as follows:

(i)   Set I=1.

(ii)   Set IMAX=I and AMAX=A(IMAX); that is, start by assuming that
the first element is the largest.

(iii) Examine the elements A(I+1), A(I+2), ..., A(N) and compare
them with AMAX. Whenever an element is found which exceeds AMAX a
copy of the value is placed in AMAX and IMAX is set equal to the
value of the subscript expression. When the end of the list is
reached, AMAX will hold a copy of the largest value and IMAX will
hold its position in the list. The value in A(I) is placed in the
position indicated by IMAX and then the value held by AMAX is
assigned to A(I).

(iv) Increase I by 1, since there is one less unsorted value in
the list at each stage. Repeat from (ii) until all the elements are
in order; that is, repeat steps (ii) and (iii) with I=1,2, ...,N-1.
The algorithm may be accomplished by the following statements:

```
      DO 11 I=1,N-1
         IMAX=I
         AMAX=A(IMAX)
         DO 12 J=I+1,N
            IF (A(J).GT.AMAX) THEN
               AMAX=A(J)
               IMAX=J
            ENDIF
12       CONTINUE
         A(IMAX)=A(I)
         A(I)=AMAX
11 CONTINUE
```

The program is completed by incorporating appropriate statements for input and output, and then becomes:

```
      PROGRAM EX54
CCCC  SORTING A LIST OF NUMBERS INTO DESCENDING ORDER
      DIMENSION A(100)
      READ *,N
      IF (N.LT.1 .OR. N.GT.100) THEN
         PRINT *,´N OUT OF RANGE, N IS ´,N
         STOP
      ENDIF
CCCC  READ VALUES AND PRINT IN ORIGINAL ORDER
      READ *,(A(I),I=1,N)
      PRINT *,´LIST IN INPUT ORDER´
      PRINT *,(A(I),I=1,N)
CCCC  THE SORTING PROCESS
      DO 11 I=1,N-1
         IMAX=I
         AMAX=A(IMAX)
         DO 12 J=I+1,N
            IF (A(J).GT.AMAX) THEN
               AMAX=A(J)
               IMAX=J
            ENDIF
12       CONTINUE
         A(IMAX)=A(I)
         A(I)=AMAX
11 CONTINUE
CCCC  SORTING COMPLETED, PRINT IN SORTED ORDER
      PRINT *,´LIST IN DESCENDING ORDER´
      PRINT *,(A(I),I=1,N)
      END
```

When the program was run with the data records

```
4
7.0 4.0 8.0 9.0
```

the results were:

LIST IN INPUT ORDER
       7.000000   4.000000   8.000000   9.000000
LIST IN DESCENDING ORDER
       9.000000   8.000000   7.000000   4.000000

5.6.3 Evaluation of an N-th Degree Polynomial

The following program reads an integer "n" and the "n+1" coefficients
of the n-th degree polynomial

$$f(x) = a_n x^n + a_{n-1} x^{n-1} + \ldots\ldots\ldots\ldots + a_1 x + a_0.$$

It prints a table of values of $f(x)$ and $f'(x)$ for x=-3.0(1.0)3.0,
where $f'(x)$ denotes the derivative of $f(x)$. The notation
x=-3.0(1.0)3.0 means that "x" takes the values -3.0, -2.0, -1.0, 0.0,
1.0, 2.0 and 3.0.
   In section 3.5.2, program EX34 evaluated the cubic polynomial

$$ax^3 + bx^2 + cx + d$$

for a given value of x. Using nested multiplication, the cubic could
be rewritten as

$$a_3 x^3 + a_2 x^2 + a_1 x + a_0 = ((a_3 x + a_2)x + a_1)x + a_0.$$

This can be evaluated by the process

```
f=a
   3
f=f.x+a
       2
f=f.x+a
       1
f=f.x+a
       0
```

which can be written in the more compact form

```
f=a
   3
Repeat for i=2,1,0
f=f.x+a
       i
```

This can be easily extended to evaluate a polynomial of degree "n" as
follows

$$f=a_n$$

Repeat for $i=n-1,n-2,\ldots,1,0$

$$f=f.x+a_i$$

The expression for $f'(x)$ is

$$f'(x)=na_n x^{n-1}+(n-1)a_{n-1}x^{n-2}+\ldots\ldots+2a_2 x+a_1$$

which is similar to the expression for $f(x)$, but with each coefficient a_i replaced by ia_i and the corresponding power of x reduced by one.

This can be evaluated by modifying the process given above as follows:

$$f'=n.a_n$$

Repeat for $i=n-1,n-2,\ldots,2,1$

$$f'=f'.x+i.a_i$$

A program to carry out these calculations is as follows:

```
      PROGRAM EX55
CCCC  TABULATION OF A POLYNOMIAL AND ITS DERIVATIVE
      DIMENSION A(0:10)
      READ *,N
      READ *,(A(I),I=N,0,-1)
      PRINT *,'    X               F(X)             F''(X)'
CCCC  NOTE TWO QUOTES ARE REQUIRED IN A CHARACTER STRING
CCCC  TO DISTINGUISH IT FROM A TERMINATOR
      DO 11 X=-3.0,3.5,1.0
         FX=A(N)
         FDASH=N*A(N)
         DO 12 I=N-1,1,-1
            FX=FX*X+A(I)
            FDASH=FDASH*X+I*A(I)
   12    CONTINUE
         FX=FX*X+A(0)
         PRINT *,X,FX,FDASH
   11 CONTINUE
      END
```

This program was used to tabulate

$$f(x)=x^4+4x^3+6x^2+4x+1=(1+x)^4,$$

by providing the data records

```
4
1.0 4.0 6.0 4.0 1.0
```

The results were

X	F(X)	F´(X)
−3.000000	16.00000	−32.00000
−2.000000	1.000000	−4.000000
−1.000000	0.000000	0.000000
0.000000	1.000000	4.000000
1.000000	16.00000	32.00000
2.000000	81.00000	108.0000
3.000000	256.0000	256.0000

5.6.4 A Common Error

Two students were asked to write a piece of FORTRAN 77 to find the sum of all the __distinct__ values in an ordered array, M. The statements from the first student were

```
      S=M(1)
10 DO 20 I=2,N
         IF (M(I).EQ.M(I-1)) GOTO 10
         S=S+M(I)
20 CONTINUE
      PRINT *,S
```

while those from the second student were

```
      S=M(1)
      DO 15 I=2,N
         IF(M(I).EQ.M(I-1)) GOTO 15
         S=S+M(I)
15 CONTINUE
      PRINT *,S
```

If __all__ the values contained in the array are distinct, both sets of statements give the correct result. However, when the array contains two identical values, the first set of statements go into an infinite loop. As an example, suppose that the array M contains the values 5, 8, 10, 11, 11, 12, ... When I has the value 5, both M(I) and M(I−1) will have the value 11. In the first case, control is returned to the initial line of the DO statement as a result of the IF statement and the DO variable (I) is re-initialised. This means that the DO loop will be repeated __from the beginning__ with I taking values 2, 3, 4 and 5 as before. When I is 5 again, the statement GOTO 10 is obeyed and the control variable is re-initialised. The program is now in an infinite loop that will be broken only when overflow occurs or the program runs out of time. The second set of statements give the correct result, since when I has the value 5, control passes to the CONTINUE statement and I is incremented.

5.7 TWO-DIMENSIONAL ARRAYS

Two-dimensional arrays are similar to one-dimensional arrays, except that two subscript expressions are required to specify a particular element. They can be used to record information about problems in two dimensions. For example, the two subscript expressions could correspond to grid lines on a map and the value of the array element itself could give some characteristic of the point, such as its height or its temperature. Usually the distances corresponding to these subscript expressions would be constant for each direction, although this is not essential.

The conventional mathematical way of writing down a two-dimensional array is

$$
\begin{array}{cccccccc}
a_{11} & a_{12} & a_{13} & \cdot\cdot & \cdot\cdot & \cdot\cdot & \cdot\cdot & a_{1n} \\
a_{21} & a_{22} & a_{23} & \cdot\cdot & \cdot\cdot & \cdot\cdot & \cdot\cdot & a_{2n} \\
a_{31} & a_{32} & a_{33} & \cdot\cdot & \cdot\cdot & \cdot\cdot & \cdot\cdot & a_{3n} \\
\cdot\cdot & \cdot\cdot & \cdot\cdot & \cdot\cdot & \cdot\cdot & \cdot\cdot & \cdot\cdot & \cdot\cdot \\
\cdot\cdot & \cdot\cdot & \cdot\cdot & \cdot\cdot & \cdot\cdot & \cdot\cdot & \cdot\cdot & \cdot\cdot \\
a_{m1} & a_{m2} & a_{m3} & \cdot\cdot & \cdot\cdot & \cdot\cdot & \cdot\cdot & a_{mn}
\end{array}
$$

The above array is known in mathematics as an (mxn) matrix; that is, a rectangular arrangement having "m" rows and "n" columns. The elements are written row by row, one row per line if possible. The ARRAY ELEMENT A(I,J) contains the value of the matrix element a_{ij}. That is, a particular element a_{ij} of a two-dimensional array is selected by its two subscript expressions. The first subscript expression I indicates the row and the second subscript expression J the column in which the entity lies.

When the compiler allocates storage locations for a two-dimensional array, a linear sequence of storage of size equal to the total number of elements, mxn, is allocated. Elements

$$a_{11}, \ a_{21}, \ \ldots\ldots, \ a_{m1}$$

are stored in positions 1 to m of the linear sequence; elements

$$a_{12}, \ a_{22}, \ \ldots\ldots, \ a_{m2}$$

are stored in positions m+1 to 2m of the sequence, and so on. This is known as column major ordering and hence matrices are stored column

by column.   The programmer does not have to worry about this detail
in most uses of two-dimensional arrays, but the implications are
discussed in chapter 7 when arrays are used as the parameters of
subprograms.

An array can have up to 7 subscript expressions. An array that
requires "k" subscript expressions is called a k-dimensional   array.
The corresponding entry in the DIMENSION statement described in
section 5.3 must specify the bounds for each of the "k" subscript
expressions, for example, the statement
        DIMENSION A(3,2)
allocates storage for the two-dimensional array A whose elements are
stored in the order A(1,1), A(2,1), A(3,1), A(1,2), A(2,2), A(3,2).

It should be noted that the lower bound of each subscript has the
default value 1, since no lower bound was given explicitly.   The
statement
        DIMENSION A(2:3,0:1)
allocates storage for the two-dimensional array A whose elements are
stored in the order A(2,0), A(3,0), A(2,1), A(3,1).

Although it is possible to have up to seven-dimensional arrays in
FORTRAN 77, in this book only one and two-dimensional arrays are
used.   A detailed account of the way in which array elements are
accessed is given in appendix 2.

A matrix can be read by statements of the form:
        DIMENSION A(20,20)
        READ *,M,N
        DO 11 I=1,M
          READ *,(A(I,J),J=1,N)
     11 CONTINUE
The matrix is read in row by row, with each new row starting on a new
data record. It is assumed that A will have no more than 20 rows or
20 columns, and in any particular case only M rows and N columns are
occupied, the values of M and N being supplied as data.   The output
of an array can be achieved in a similar way.

It is possible to read an (mxn) matrix with the quantities in the
same order as in the previous example by the statement
        READ *,M,N,((A(I,J),J=1,N),I=1,M)
In this case, each new row need not necessarily start on a new data
record.

This double subscript expression form of the IMPLIED DO LOOP can
also be used in a DATA statement to set initial values in a matrix.
For example, the statement
        DATA ((CBD(I,J),J=1,8),I=1,8) / 64*0.0 /
initially sets the elements CBD(1,1) to CBD(8,8) of the array CBD to
zero.

It should be noted that, if a read statement contains just the array name without an implied do loop, the values for the whole array are read in the order in which the elements are stored, that is in column order. Similarly, if a DATA statement just contains the array name without an implied do loop, all the elements of the array are given the listed values.

5.8 PROGRAMS USING TWO-DIMENSIONAL ARRAYS

This section contains a number of example programs which use two-dimensional arrays.

5.8.1 Transpose of a matrix

This program reads two integers into locations named M and N, then the elements of an (mxn) matrix into an array. It then prints the matrix whose rows are the columns of the original matrix. In mathematical terms, this is the transpose of the original matrix.

The maximum value of N is taken to be 8 to make sure that each row of the matrix is printed on one line of line printer output without overflowing onto the next. The program checks that the values of N and M lie within the range defined by the dimension statement. If they do not, it stops. The values of M and N are available on the first data record and each new row of the matrix starts on a new data record.

This program does not require any manipulation of the matrix elements, since all that is necessary is to pick out the elements in column order for printing.

```
      PROGRAM EX56
CCCC  PROGRAM TO READ A MATRIX AND PRINT ITS TRANSPOSE
      DIMENSION A(8,8)
      READ *,M,N
      IF (M.LT.1.OR.M.GT.8.OR.N.LT.1.OR.N.GT.8) STOP
      DO 11 I=1,M
         READ *,(A(I,J),J=1,N)
   11 CONTINUE
      PRINT *,´THE ´,N,´ BY ´,M,´ MATRIX IS´
      DO 12 J=1,N
         PRINT *,(A(I,J),I=1,M)
   12 CONTINUE
      END
```

The program with input data

```
3 2
1.0 4.0
2.0 5.0
3.0 6.0
```

produced the following output

```
THE            2 BY            3 MATRIX IS
    1.000000        2.000000        3.000000
    4.000000        5.000000        6.000000
```

5.8.2 Verification of a Knight's Tour

A knight's tour is defined as a sequence of 63 knight's moves on a chessboard, in which the knight visits every square once. The program checks if a sequence of 63 moves forms a knight's tour. Each square on the chessboard is identified by a pair of integer coordinates (r,c) which specify the row and column in which the square lies. The data consists of a list of the squares that are to be visited by the knight. As each square is visited, its coordinates are printed. If an invalid move is encountered, an appropriate message is printed and the program terminated. If the coordinates of 64 squares have been printed, all the moves were valid and the message "IS A KNIGHT'S TOUR" is printed on a new line.

A valid knight's move is from the present square to one which is either one horizontal square and two vertical squares or two horizontal squares and one vertical square away.

	1	2	3	4	5	6	7	8
1								
2			X		X			
3		X				X		
4				K				
5		X				X		
6			X		X			
7								
8								

This is illustrated in the diagram, where each square marked X is a valid knight's move from the square marked K. Mathematically this can be expressed by the statement that a move from the present square (r_p, c_p) to a new square (r_n, c_n) is a valid knight's move if

$$(r_n - r_p)^2 + (c_n - c_p)^2 = 5.$$

In the program, the chessboard is represented by a two-dimensional array CBD where, for example, CBD(1,1) represents the square in the top left hand corner. Initially all elements of CBD are set to zero and whenever a square is visited for the first time the value of the appropriate element of CBD is reset to 1. As the coordinates of each new square to be visited are read, a check is made to see whether the square exists on the chessboard (that is, both coordinates lie in the range 1 to 8); whether the move is a valid knight's move and whether the square has been visited previously.

The algorithm can be summarised as follows:

(i)   Read in the coordinates (r_p, c_p) of the initial position and check that it is on the chessboard.

(ii)   Read in the coordinates (r_n, c_n) of the next square to which the knight moves. Check if it is on the chessboard; if it is not, print an appropriate message.

(iii) Check that it is a valid knight's move, that is,

$$(r_n - r_p)^2 + (c_n - c_p)^2 = 5$$

If not then flag an invalid move.

(iv) Check whether the knight has previously visited the square; that is, whether the value stored in the array representing square (r_n, c_n) is equal to one. If it does, print a message that the square has been previously visited and terminate the program; otherwise set the array element equal to 1.

(v)   If 63 valid moves have been completed, print the message "IS A KNIGHT'S TOUR"; otherwise, set $r_p = r_n$ and $c_p = c_n$, and repeat from step (ii).

With a test set of moves, the program on the next page based on the above algorithm printed out

1	3
3	4
2	6
4	7
5	5
7	5

INVALID KNIGHT'S MOVE FROM   5,   5 TO   7,   5

```
        PROGRAM EX57
CCCC    KNIGHT'S TOUR
        INTEGER CBD,RP,CP,RN,CN
        DIMENSION CBD(8,8)
        DATA CBD/64*0/
CCCC    READ THE COORDINATES OF THE PRESENT SQUARE
        READ *,RP,CP
        PRINT *,RP,CP
CCCC    CHECK THAT THE SQUARE LIES ON THE CHESSBOARD
        IF (RP.LT.1 .OR. RP.GT.8) GOTO 10
        IF (CP.LT.1 .OR. CP.GT.8) GOTO 10
CCCC    LOOP TO READ THE COORDINATES OF THE NEXT SQUARE
        DO 11 K=1,63
            CBD(RP,CP)=1
CCCC        KNIGHT MARKED ON THE CHESSBOARD
            READ *,RN,CN
            PRINT *,RN,CN
CCCC        CHECK THAT THE SQUARE LIES ON THE CHESSBOARD
            IF (RN.LT.1 .OR. RN.GT.8) GOTO 10
            IF (CN.LT.1 .OR. CN.GT.8) GOTO 10
CCCC        CHECK IF IT IS A VALID KNIGHT'S MOVE
            IF ((RN-RP)**2+(CN-CP)**2.NE.5) THEN
                PRINT *,'INVALID KNIGHT''S MOVE FROM',RP,',',CP,
     1          ' TO',RN,',',CN
                STOP
            ELSEIF (CBD(RN,CN).EQ.1) THEN
                PRINT *,'NOT A KNIGHT''S TOUR, SQUARE ',RN,',',
     1          CN,' REVISITED'
                STOP
            ELSE
                RP=RN
                CP=CN
            ENDIF
   11   CONTINUE
        PRINT *,'IS A KNIGHT''S TOUR'
        STOP
   10   PRINT *,'LAST MOVE NOT ON THE CHESSBOARD'
        END
```

5.8.3 Distance Travelled by a Salesman

This section describes a modification of the program discussed in section 4.5.1. The program reads an integer "n" and a list of the values of the longitudinal and latitudinal co-ordinates in kilometres of "n" towns numbered 1, 2, 3, ..., n. It then forms a two-dimensional array containing the distances between town "i" and town "j". The program next calculates the total distance along a route from a home town through a number of other towns, returning to the home town. The program is capable of processing a set of routes, a typical route being specified by an integer "k" (the number of towns on the route) and a list of the "k" towns in the order in which they are visited. The program terminates when a route of 0 towns is read. The program carries out the following steps

(i)   The longitudinal and latitudinal co-ordinates of the "n" towns (x_i, y_i) are given in kilometres and are provided in the following order

```
n
x₁   y₁
x₂   y₂
..   ..

..   ..
xₙ   yₙ
```

$$
\begin{array}{cc}
n & \\
x_1 & y_1 \\
x_2 & y_2 \\
.. & .. \\
.. & .. \\
x_n & y_n
\end{array}
$$

These are stored in one-dimensional arrays X and Y respectively.

(ii)   A matrix DIST is formed of the distances between all the towns. For example DIST(I,J) is set equal to

$$(x_i - x_j)^2 + (y_i - y_j)^2$$

It should be noted that DIST(I,J) = DIST(J,I) and DIST(I,I) = 0.0.

(iii) The number, "k", of towns on a route is read. If k=0, the program terminates, otherwise the towns on the route are read and stored in an integer array named ROUTE. The number of the starting town is also assigned to ROUTE(K+1) to simplify the calculations of the distance travelled. The route is then printed.

(iv) The number representing a town should be in the range 1 to "n" and, if any are not, the message IS NOT VALID is printed and the program considers the next route.

(v)   The length of the route is the sum of

DIST(ROUTE(I),ROUTE(I+1))   for I=1,2,...,K

That is, the subscript expressions of DIST are ROUTE(I), ROUTE(I+1) which are integer array elements. These in turn are selected by the subscript expressions I, I+1 of the integer array ROUTE.

The length of the route is evaluated and printed in the following form:

TOTAL DISTANCE TRAVELLED IS ... KILOMETRES

A possible way of programming this algorithm is as follows:

```
        PROGRAM EX58
CCCC    DISTANCES TRAVELLED BY A SALESMAN
        INTEGER ROUTE,DIM
        PARAMETER (DIM=17)
        DIMENSION X(DIM),Y(DIM),DIST(DIM,DIM),ROUTE(DIM+1)
CCCC    READ THE COORDINATES OF THE TOWNS
        READ *,N
        DO 11 I=1,N
           READ *,X(I),Y(I)
     11 CONTINUE
CCCC    CALCULATE ENTRIES IN THE DISTANCE MATRIX
        DO 12 I=1,N
           DIST(I,I)=0.0
           DO 13 J=I+1,N
              DIST(I,J)=SQRT((X(I)-X(J))**2+(Y(I)-Y(J))**2)
              DIST(J,I)=DIST(I,J)
     13    CONTINUE
     12 CONTINUE
CCCC    READ THE ROUTE TO BE FOLLOWED
     15 READ *,K
        IF (K.EQ.0) STOP
        READ *,(ROUTE(I),I=1,K)
        K1=K+1
        ROUTE(K1)=ROUTE(1)
        PRINT *,'ROUTE',(ROUTE(I),I=1,K1)
CCCC    CHECK FOR INVALID ROUTE
        DO 14 I=1,K
           IF (ROUTE(I).LT.1 .OR. ROUTE(I).GT.N) THEN
              PRINT *,'IS NOT VALID'
              GOTO 15
           ENDIF
     14 CONTINUE
CCCC    CALCULATE THE LENGTH OF THE ROUTE
        TDIST=0.0
        DO 16 I=1,K
           TDIST=TDIST+DIST(ROUTE(I),ROUTE(I+1))
     16 CONTINUE
        PRINT *,'TOTAL DISTANCE TRAVELLED IS ',TDIST,' KILOMETRES.'
        GOTO 15
        END
```

With the input data

```
4
0.0 0.0
4.0 6.0
-3.0 9.0
-2.0 -1.0
3
1 4 3
2
2 5
0
```

the program gave the following results

```
ROUTE           1         4         3         1
TOTAL DISTANCE TRAVELLED IS      21.77278     KILOMETRES.
ROUTE           2         5         2
IS NOT VALID
```

It should be noted that the particular distance array formed by the above data could be set up using a DATA statement. The program would then start with the statements:

```
        INTEGER ROUTE,DIM
        PARAMETER (DIM=4)
        DIMENSION X(DIM),Y(DIM),DIST(DIM,DIM),ROUTE(DIM+1)
        DATA ((DIST(I,J),I=1,4),J=1,4) /
     1    0.0, 7.211103, 9.486833, 2.236068,
     2    7.211103, 0.0, 7.615773, 9.219544,
     3    9.486833, 7.615773, 0.0, 10.04988,
     4    2.236068, 9.219544, 10.04988, 0.0 /
```

The statements from

```
        READ *,N
        DO 11 I=1,N
```

to

```
     12 CONTINUE
```

inclusive would be omitted; and N replaced by DIM in the statement

```
        IF (ROUTE(I).LT.1 .OR. ROUTE(I).GT.N) THEN
```


5.9 EXERCISES

1. Write a program which reads in a set of examination marks, which are integers in the range 0 to 100, and finds their mean and standard deviation. The set is terminated by -1. The program should check if

the marks are all valid and list any that are not, together with
their positions in the list of marks.   In this case, the program
should terminate with an appropriate comment.

If all the marks m_i, i=1,2,...,n are valid, the program should find
their mean M and standard deviation S from the formulae

$$M = \frac{1}{n} \sum_{i=1}^{n} m_i$$

$$S^2 = \frac{1}{n} \sum_{i=1}^{n} m_i^2 - M^2$$

Specimen data, one mark per data record

17 75 61 34 56 54 117 84 11 60 0 42 59 36 54 41 67 -1

2. Write a program which takes the same set of marks used for
exercise 1 and finds the median mark.   The median is the middle mark
in the ordered list of marks. If the number of candidates is even,
the average of the middle two marks may be taken to be the median.

3. Write a program which takes the same set of marks used for
exercise 1 and gives under the following heading

        A   B   C   D   E

the number of candidates obtaining marks in the ranges 100 to 80, 79
to 60, 59 to 40, 39 to 20 and 19 to 0 respectively.

4. Write a program which reads the coefficients and right-hand sides
of the equations

$$u_{11}x_1 + u_{12}x_2 + \ldots\ldots\ldots\ldots + u_{1n}x_n = b_1$$
$$u_{22}x_2 + \ldots\ldots\ldots\ldots + u_{2n}x_n = b_2$$
$$\ldots\ldots\ldots\ldots\ldots\ldots\ldots\ldots\ldots$$
$$u_{nn}x_n = b_n$$

and solves them by back-substitution.   The technique is to obtain
x_n from the last equation, then x_{n-1} from the next to the last
equation and so on.   Test your program with the data appropriate for

solving the equations

$$4x_1 + 2x_2 + x_3 = -7$$
$$3x_2 - x_3 = 5$$
$$2x_3 = 2 .$$

5. A list of the roll numbers of students who obtained grade A in Latin and a list of the roll numbers of students who obtain grade A in Mathematics is to be compared to determine how many students obtained grade A in both subjects. Write two programs to compare these lists where, for the first program each list is ordered so that the roll numbers are increasing, and for the second program there is no order to the lists.

6. A two-dimensional array A is set up to represent flights from a given airport for the next twenty-four hour period. The information is stored in the array A with each flight represented by one row with

A(I,1) = flight number,

A(I,2) = number of seats currently available,

A(I,3) = the row index of the entry for the next flight
        to the same destination.

In the case of no other flights to a given destination A(I,3)=0. The array A is arranged such that the flight numbers are in ascending order. Write a program which uses a binary search technique to locate a given flight number in the table, and which reserves the seats on the required flight. If insufficient seats are available on the flight, the next available flight number is printed. The reservation must be made on a single flight or not at all. Appropriate comments such as

"... seats reserved on flight number ... "

"Insufficient number of seats on flight number ...,
    next flight is number ... "

"No available flights "

should be printed.

The binary search technique to find the position in an ordered list of elements A(I), I=1,2, ...,N of a value X, which lies between A(1) and A(N) is as follows:

(i)   Check that X lies between A(1) and A(N).

(ii)   Set TOP=1, BOTTOM=N.

(iii) Evaluate MID=(TOP+BOTTOM)/2.

(iv)   If A(MID)=X, the position is the value of MID, then stop.
       If A(MID)>X, set BOTTOM=MID; otherwise set TOP=MID.
       Return to step (iii) if TOP≠BOTTOM.
       If TOP=BOTTOM, the value X is not in the list.

7. A table of the ratio A*/A against the Mach number M for air flowing in a duct is given below.

A*/A	1.0000	0.9553	0.8502	0.7212	0.5926	0.4770	0.3793	0.2996	0.2362
M	1.00	1.25	1.50	1.75	2.00	2.25	2.50	2.75	3.00

A* is the flow area for Mach number 1 and A is the flow area for Mach number M.

Use a modified form of the binary search technique described in exercise 6 to locate the interval in which a given value of the ratio A*/A lies and obtain the corresponding Mach number.

If R is the value of the ratio A*/A and R lies in the interval (R_1, R_2), the required value M of the Mach number is given by the linear interpolation formula

$$M = M_1 + \frac{(R - R_1)}{(R_1 - R_2)} (M_1 - M_2),$$

where M_1 and M_2 are the corresponding Mach numbers to the area ratios R_1 and R_2 respectively.

Specimen data: (a) 0.7, (b) 0.4770

8. Write a program which lists the prime numbers between 2 and N, using N = 1000 as test data.

Hint: Starting with 2 as the first prime number, obtain the other prime numbers by checking that they are not exactly divisible by a smaller prime number. Note that it is not necessary to determine if a number is divisible by any number greater than $\sqrt{N}$.

CHAPTER 6
FORMATTED INPUT AND OUTPUT

In this chapter, a description is given of the method of defining the
arrangement of numbers and character strings by the programmer.
Formatted output enables the programmer, rather than the compiler, to
specify the layout of the numbers and character strings which form
the results. Formatted input means that the data read by the program
must be presented in a pre-determined format. This can be
advantageous when large volumes of data are to be processed.

6.1 SHORTCOMINGS OF LIST-DIRECTED OUTPUT

The output produced using a list-directed PRINT statement, as
described in chapter 2, is not always satisfactory for a number of
reasons. Most of these may have been noticed already. For example,
since the number of positions of a line of output which a number
occupies is predetermined by the compiler, large unsightly gaps can
be left in the output. Thus, when the program

```
      PROGRAM EX61
      READ *,I,J
      PRINT *,´DERBY COUNTY ´,I,´, MANCHESTER UNITED ´,J
      END
```

was run using the data
   3 1
the results were

    DERBY COUNTY   3, MANCHESTER UNITED   1

The layout would be improved if the gaps between the Y and the 3 and
between the D and the 1 were reduced. Unfortunately, this cannot be
done when using list-directed output.

Another shortcoming is the form in which real numbers are printed. This will also vary according to the compiler. It means that the number of decimal digits output cannot be altered. For example, seven digits may be printed when only one or two are significant. It also means that, if the compiler is set to print the exponential form of numbers which are numerically less than one, the programmer cannot have such numbers printed in decimal form. In addition, the predetermined layout of the output implies that the maximum amount of data that can be printed on any one line is also predetermined. For example, suppose that a compiler allows 16 character positions for the output of a real number and that the maximum number of characters to a line of line printer output is 132. An attempt to print 20 real numbers on one line using list-directed output as implemented by this compiler would cause a rather untidy overflow of the output onto the next line.

Finally, one of the main reasons for laying down a standard for FORTRAN is so that a program which works on one computer will give the same results, subject to rounding errors, when run on a different machine. When list-directed output is used, this will not necessarily happen. For example, when the program

```
        PROGRAM EX62
        PRINT *,´                 X        X-SQUARED´,
     1       ´          X-CUBED´
        DO 11 X=1.0,1.5,0.2
           XSQ=X*X
           PRINT *,X,XSQ,X*XSQ
    11  CONTINUE
        END
```

was run at Salford, the results were

X	X-SQUARED	X-CUBED
1.000000	1.000000	1.000000
1.200000	1.440000	1.728000
1.400000	1.960000	2.744000

If the program were run using a compiler which allocated only twelve line printer positions to each real number, the results would be

X	X-SQUARED	X-CUBED
1.000000	1.000000	1.000000
1.200000	1.440000	1.728000
1.400000	1.960000	2.744000

In spite of these shortcomings, it should be remembered that list-directed output is much simpler to use than formatted output and that there are fewer things that can go wrong with it.

Within FORTRAN 77, there are a number of ways of formatting output. The more commonly used methods are described in this chapter, brief details of the others being given in chapter 10.

6.2 EXAMPLE PROGRAMS

To illustrate the use of formatted output, two of the example programs considered earlier in the book are rewritten to improve the layout of their results.

The first to be rewritten is program EX62 from section 6.1. The rewritten version of this program is

```
        PROGRAM EX63
        PRINT 100
        DO 11 X=1.0,1.5,0.2
            XSQ=X*X
            PRINT 101,X,XSQ,X*XSQ
     11 CONTINUE
    100 FORMAT (´  X    X-SQUARED  X-CUBED´)
    101 FORMAT (1X,F3.1,5X,F4.2,5X,F5.3)
        END
```

The results of running this program are

X	X-SQUARED	X-CUBED
1.0	1.00	1.000
1.2	1.44	1.728
1.4	1.96	2.744

The layout of the results from this program does not depend on the compiler being used, unlike the layout of the results from program EX62.

The PRINT statements in this program reference FORMAT statements which define the arrangement of the output. The arrangement of individual items in the output list is governed by the FORMAT EDIT DESCRIPTORS, or simply EDIT DESCRIPTORS, in the FORMAT statement. Thus for example, the value of X is arranged in a manner defined by the format edit descriptor F3.1 in the FORMAT statement labelled 101. The construction of the formatted PRINT statement and the FORMAT statement are described in detail in sections 6.3 and 6.4 respectively. In this section only their effect is described.

The first PRINT statement in the example program,

        PRINT 100

together with the associated FORMAT statement labelled 100 cause the
output of the character string

    ^X^^^X-SQUARED^^X-CUBED

where ^ represents a space character. It should be noted that in
FORMAT statements, any space characters in a character string are
part of the character string. They are normally present in the
output. The exception is when the space character is a line printer
CARRIAGE CONTROL CHARACTER. These are described in detail in section
6.4.8, but it should be noted here that when the first character in a
line of output from a formatted PRINT statement is a space character,
it is not printed but causes the line printer to advance one line.

    The second PRINT statement in the program,

        PRINT 101,X,XSQ,X*XSQ

together with the associated FORMAT statement labelled 101 causes the
output of a line of numbers. The format edit descriptor 1X in the
FORMAT statement specifies a space character which is not printed but
acts as a carriage control character as described above.   The first
three positions on the line of output are allocated for the value of
X, the arrangement of this number being specified by the format edit
descriptor F3.1 in the FORMAT statement. The first of these three
positions is reserved for the digit before the decimal point, the
second for the decimal point, and the third for the one place of
decimals specified by the .1 part of the format edit descriptor.
Five space characters, specified by the first occurrence of the
format edit descriptor 5X in the FORMAT statement, separate this
number from the value of XSQ, which is allocated four positions on
the line of output. This is achieved by the format edit descriptor
F4.2, which allocates two character positions for digits after the
decimal point as specified by the .2 part of the format edit
descriptor and one position for the decimal point itself. This
leaves one character position for a digit before the decimal point.
Five space characters, specified by the second occurrence of the
format edit descriptor 5X in the FORMAT statement, separate this
number from the value of X*XSQ, which occupies five character
positions. This is specified by the format edit descriptor F5.3 in
the FORMAT statement, which allocates one position before the decimal
point, one for the decimal point and three places of decimals.

    As a second illustration of formatted output, consider the
following rewritten version of program EX56 from section 5.8.1.   It
should be noted that in this version of the program, it is possible
to print up to 20 numbers on a line of output, so the maximum size of
the subscript specified in the DIMENSION statement has been changed

accordingly.

```
          PROGRAM EX64
          DIMENSION A(20,20)
          READ *,M,N
          IF (M.LT.1 .OR. M.GT.20 .OR. N.LT.1 .OR. N.GT.20) STOP
          DO 11 I=1,M
             READ *,(A(I,J),J=1,N)
       11 CONTINUE
          PRINT 100,N,M
          DO 12 J=1,N
             PRINT 101,(A(I,J),I=1,M)
       12 CONTINUE
      100 FORMAT (´ THE ´,I2,´ BY ´,I2,´ MATRIX IS´)
      101 FORMAT (20(1X,F5.2))
          END
```

The results of running this program with the data used for program EX56 were

```
   THE  2 BY  3 MATRIX IS
    1.00  2.00  3.00
    4.00  5.00  6.00
```

As with program EX63, the PRINT statements in the program now reference FORMAT statements which define the arrangement of the output. The statement
          PRINT 100,N,M
together with the associated FORMAT statement labelled 100 cause the output of the character string THE^, where ^ indicates a space character. This is followed by the current value of the integer variable N in the next two positions of the line, then the character string ^BY^, the current value of the integer variable M in the next two positions of the line, and finally the character string ^MATRIX^IS.

The second PRINT statement in the program,
          PRINT 101,(A(I,J),I=1,M)
together with the associated FORMAT statement labelled 101 cause the output of the j-th column of the array named A on a line of line printer output. Five positions are allocated for each number: two positions before the decimal point, the decimal point in the third position, then two places of decimals. A space character is to be inserted before each number except the first, where the format edit descriptor 1X is treated as a carriage control character.

6.3 THE FORMATTED PRINT STATEMENT

The general form of this statement is

        PRINT label,list

where "list" is a list of constants, variables and expressions, each one separated from the next by a comma.   The label is that of a FORMAT statement which must appear somewhere in the program.   With the exception that the arrangement of the output on the line printer is imposed by the FORMAT statement rather than by the compiler, the effect of the statement is the same as that of the list-directed PRINT statement described in chapter 2.   It should be noted that any number of PRINT statements can reference the same FORMAT statement. This statement reduces to

        PRINT label

if no variables are to be printed.

6.4 THE FORMAT STATEMENT

The general form of this statement is

     label FORMAT (edit descriptor list)

where the label (which must be present) is referenced by at least one input/output statement in the program.   The edit descriptor list will be described later in this section.   FORMAT statements are non-executable, and may be inserted at any point in the program.   It is normal practice to group them immediately before the END statement, as this causes the least interference when reading the logical flow of the program, but the language does not require this to be done. Usually, high numbers (100, 101, 102, ...) are used as labels of FORMAT statements, but this is also merely a convention.

    The edit descriptor list mentioned in the general form of the FORMAT statement consists of a number of format edit descriptors which are normally separated by commas.   The format edit descriptors can specify the number of positions on a line of output which a number is to occupy (called the FIELD WIDTH), or a character string or its equivalent, or the position where the next number or character string is to be printed.   The format edit descriptors used in program EX63 are the character string in the FORMAT statement labelled 100 and 1X, F3.1, 5X, F4.2, 5X and F5.3 in the FORMAT statement labelled 101.   Likewise, the format edit descriptors used in program EX64 are I2, 1X, F5.2 and the character strings.   Note that different types of format edit descriptor may be used in the same FORMAT statement.

    It may be that a number is too big to fit into the number of positions on the line of output allocated by the edit descriptor.   If

this happens, a string of asterisks of appropriate length is printed
instead.   As an example of this, suppose that the data supplied to
program EX64 in section 6.2 had been

    3 2

    1.0 4.0

    124.2 -84.7

    12.427 -8.472

The results of running the program with this data are

    THE   2 BY 3 MATRIX IS

    1.00 ***** 12.43

    4.00 ***** -8.47

Neither 124.2 nor -84.7 can be printed using the format edit
descriptor F5.2, since both numbers require three character positions
before the decimal point and this edit descriptor only allocates two.
It should be noted that the minus sign occupies a character position.

    If   there is a possibility that the value produced may be
incompatible with the format edit descriptor specified for output,
the program should incorporate a check which results in the use of an
alternative edit descriptor if necessary.

    There follow detailed specifications of the more commonly used edit
descriptors. Further edit descriptors are described in chapter 10.

6.4.1 The X-format Edit Descriptor

Space characters can be output using a character string containing
space characters, such as ´   ´. Alternatively, X-format can be
used. The general form of this edit descriptor is

    wX

which specifies that space characters are to be output in the next
"w" positions of the line. This edit descriptor is similar to the
character string in a FORMAT statement in that it does not cause
numbers from the store of the computer to be output. It is usually
used to improve the layout of results or to provide a space character
for carriage control.

6.4.2 The I-format Edit Descriptor

Integer numbers are output using I-format. The general form of this
edit descriptor is

    Iw

where "w", an unsigned integer number, represents the field width.
This is the number of character positions reserved for the number on

the line of output. The output is right justified, with a leading minus sign if the number being output is negative. In this case, a character position is required for the minus sign. If the number is positive, a character position for the sign may not be required, since whether or not the plus sign is printed depends on the compiler being used. Usually the plus sign is not printed, in which case the edit descriptor I4 can be used to output any integer from −999 to 9999 inclusive.

Examples of output using the edit descriptor I4 are

VALUE TO BE OUTPUT	ACTUAL OUTPUT
7812	7812
12	^^12
−32	^−32
0	^^^0
−7812	****

Note that asterisks are printed in the last case because −7812 requires five character positions and the edit descriptor I4 only allocates four.

As an example of a formatted PRINT statement, consider

        PRINT 100,IOTA,JELLY,KNAVE
    100 FORMAT (1X,I4,I3,I6)

If the values of IOTA, JELLY and KNAVE at the time that this statement is obeyed are 34, 567 and −8 respectively, the output is

    ^^34567^^^^−8

The space character generated as a result of the 1X format edit descriptor is not printed, as it is the carriage control character. The first four characters in the output are caused by outputting the value of IOTA using the I4 format edit descriptor; the next three characters are caused by outputting the value of JELLY using the I3 format edit descriptor, and the next six characters are caused by outputting the value of KNAVE using the I6 format edit descriptor.

If it is necessary to have the field completely filled with space characters when the number being output is zero, a modified form of I-format is used, namely

    Iw.0

Thus, four space characters will be "printed" if the edit descriptor I4.0 is used to output zero.

It should be noted that the value of the field width "w" must not be zero and also that only integer quantities can be output using I-format. Other types must be output using the format appropriate to them.

When the same I-format edit descriptor is used several consecutive times in a format specification, an abbreviation of the form

    rIw   or   rIw.0

may be used, where "r" represents an integer called a REPEAT SPECIFICATION. This indicates the number of times that the edit descriptor is to be repeated. Thus, if the values of integer variables IOTA, JELLY and KNAVE are 34, 567 and -8 respectively, the output which results from the statements

        PRINT 100,IOTA,JELLY,KNAVE
    100 FORMAT (1X,3I4)

is

   ^^34^567^^-8

This is the same as the output which results from the statements

        PRINT 100,IOTA,JELLY,KNAVE
    100 FORMAT (1X,I4,I4,I4)

6.4.3 The F-format Edit Descriptor

Real numbers can be output using F-format. The general form of this edit descriptor is

    rFw.d

where "r" is a repeat specification, "w" specifies the field width and "d" specifies the number of decimal places to be output. If "r" is omitted, a value of 1 is assumed for it. The first "w-d-1" positions of the field contain the whole number part of the real number, arranged in the same way as described in section 6.4.2; position "w-d" contains the decimal point; and positions "w-d+1" to "w" inclusive contain the fractional part of the real number. Thus the edit descriptor F6.2 will allocate a field width of six characters for the output of a real number. The first three positions of the field contain the whole number part of the number, position four the decimal point, and positions five and six the fractional part.

   Examples of output using the edit descriptor F6.2 are

VALUE TO BE OUTPUT	ACTUAL OUTPUT
483.76	483.76
12.9	^12.90
-0.076	^-0.08
0.00448	^^0.00
-126.3	******

It should be noted that the value to be output is rounded when necessary according to the normal rules of arithmetic, and that asterisks are printed in the last case because -126 requires four character positions and F6.2 only specifies three character positions to the left of the decimal point.

   As an example of a formatted PRINT statement which uses F-format edit descriptors, consider

```
      PRINT 100,ALPHA,BETA,GAMMA
  100 FORMAT (1X,F6.3,2F8.4)
```
If the values of ALPHA, BETA and GAMMA at the time that the PRINT
statement is obeyed are 3.14159, 12.8 and −641.36 respectively, the
output will be
```
  ^3.142^12.8000********
```
Note that the asterisks are printed because −641.3600 occupies more
than eight character positions.

   Clearly, care must be taken when choosing the values for "w" and
"d".   The requirement of a character position for the decimal point,
and the desirability of at least one digit to the left of the decimal
point and of a character position for the sign means that "w" should
normally be at least three greater than "d".

6.4.4 The E-format Edit Descriptor

Real numbers can also be output using E-format. If there is doubt as
to the magnitude of the number being output, then use of F-format can
result in a complete or partial failure of output. A number which is
too large in magnitude for the field width results in the output of
asterisks, while a number which is too small in magnitude will be
rounded on output to zero. In cases like this, E-format is a useful
alternative. The general form of this edit descriptor is
```
     rEw.d
```
where "r" is a repeat specification which, if omitted, is taken to be
1; "w" specifies the field width and "d" specifies the number of
significant digits that are to be output.

   The form of the output is leading spaces (if any); followed by a
sign, which may be replaced by a space character if the number is
positive, depending on the compiler; then a zero; a decimal point;
"d" digits; and a four character field indicating the exponent. This
last consists of an E followed by a sign and two digits. Thus the
edit descriptor E14.6 will allocate a field width of 14 characters
for the output of a real number, the form of the output being
```
  ^p0.ddddddEsdd
```
where ^ represents a space character; "p" a plus or a minus sign or a
space character; "d" a decimal digit, and "s" a plus or a minus sign.
   Examples of output using the edit descriptor E14.6 are

VALUE TO BE OUTPUT	ACTUAL OUTPUT
783.4	^^0.783400E+03
0.0007834	^^0.783400E−03
−7834086.78	^−0.783409E+07

It should be noted that the form of the output requires room in the
field width for the characters represented by p0. and for the

characters represented by Esdd. In this case, if "w" is chosen to be
at least seven greater than "d", the real number will be printed no
matter what compiler is used.

As an example of a formatted PRINT statement which uses the E-
format edit descriptor, consider

```
      PRINT 100,TRUE,GRIT
   100 FORMAT (1X,E16.9,2X,E10.3)
```

If the values of TRUE and GRIT are 0.000001786 and -1583216.28
respectively, the output will be

   ^0.178600000E-05^^-0.158E+07

As with I-format and F-format, asterisks will be printed if the
field width is insufficient to hold the number of characters being
printed. Thus E12.8 results in twelve asterisks being printed, no
matter what number is being output.

6.4.5 The A-format Edit Descriptor

In the introduction to this section on the FORMAT statement, it was
stated that character strings can be used in FORMAT statements as
edit descriptors. For example, program EX61 could be written using a
FORMAT statement as

```
      PROGRAM EX65
      READ *,I,J
      PRINT 100,I,J
   100 FORMAT (´ DERBY COUNTY ´,I1,
     1    ´, MANCHESTER UNITED ´,I1)
      END
```

When this program was run using the data

   3 1

the result was

   DERBY COUNTY 3, MANCHESTER UNITED 1

The D of DERBY is the first character on the line of output because
the space character in front of the D in the FORMAT statement is a
carriage control character, which is not printed. Unlike previous
examples, this carriage control character arose from a character
string rather than by using the 1X format edit descriptor. In fact,
the carriage control character in the earlier examples could always
have been written as ´ ´ rather than as 1X.

An alternative way of writing this program is to include the
character strings in the list following the PRINT statement. The

program then becomes

```
      PROGRAM EX66
      READ *,I,J
      PRINT 100,´DERBY COUNTY ´,I,´, MANCHESTER UNITED ´,J
  100 FORMAT (1X,A,I1,A,I1)
      END
```

The output from this program is the same as that from program EX65, provided the same data is used. Note that, in this program, the edit descriptor list could have been written

   1X,2(A,I1)

where the value "2" is a repeat specification.

   An A in a FORMAT edit descriptor list indicates that a character string is to be printed at that point in the output. The general form of this edit descriptor is

   rA   or   rAw

where "w" specifies the field width and "r" is a repeat specification which, if omitted, is taken to be 1. In the first case, the number of character positions on the line of output is specified by the length of the character string being output, while in the second case the number of character positions is specified by "w".

   Normally, A-format is only used when dealing with character variables, as will be described in chapter 8. When character constants are being output, it is usual to include the appropriate character strings in the FORMAT statement.

6.4.6 The Slash Edit Descriptor

The slash (/) edit descriptor in an output list indicates that the current line of output is to be terminated. This is especially useful when printing headings for output. As an example, consider

```
      PRINT 100
  100 FORMAT (10X,´FORTRAN 77´,/,10X,´**********´)
```

These statements result in the two lines

```
      FORTRAN 77
      **********
```

being printed. If the programmer wishes, the commas before and after the slash can be omitted, so that the FORMAT statement above is written

```
  100 FORMAT (10X,´FORTRAN 77´/10X,´**********´)
```

This is the normal practice.

   It should be noted that the new line of output started as a result of the slash edit descriptor still needs a carriage control character

to start it.   Thus each line of output from the example   starts   with
nine blank characters, because the first blank character on each line
is taken to be the carriage control character.

Two   successive   slash   edit   descriptors   cause   a blank line to be
output.   The statements

          PRINT 100
     100 FORMAT (10X,´FORTRAN 77´//10X,´**********´)
result in the three lines

          FORTRAN 77

          ****
being   printed.   Following the usual practice, the commas before and
after the slashes have been omitted in this example.

6.4.7 The Colon Edit Descriptor

The colon (:) edit descriptor terminates output of a   line   if   there
are   no more items in the output list.   It has no effect if there are
more items in the list.   As   with   the   slash   edit   descriptor,   the
commas   before   and   after   the colon can be omitted.   As an example,
consider the statements

          PRINT 100,(L(I),I=1,N)
     100 FORMAT (´ NO 1 = ´,I1,:,´ NO 2 = ´,I1,:,
        1   ´ NO 3 = ´,I1,:,´ NO 4 = ´,I1)
If the values of   N,   L(1),   L(2) and   L(3)   are   3,   5,   7   and   1
respectively, these statements will result in the characters

     NO 1 = 5 NO 2 = 7 NO 3 = 1
being   printed.   If   the   colons   are   omitted,   so   that the FORMAT
statement reads

     100 FORMAT (´ NO 1 = ´,I1,´ NO 2 = ´,I1,
        1   ´ NO 3 = ´,I1,´NO 4 = ´,I1)
the statements would result in the characters

     NO 1 = 5 NO 2 = 7 NO 3 = 1 NO 4 =
being printed.

6.4.8 Carriage Control Characters

As   mentioned   earlier,   the   first character of each line printed is
used to control the vertical   movement   of   the   paper   in   the   line
printer.   This is true whether it is a number or part of a character
string.   The first character on every line of line printer output   is
called   the   CARRIAGE   CONTROL   CHARACTER.   This is normally a space
character, which instructs the machine to advance   the   line   printer
paper by one line and can be set by putting 1X or ´^´ at the start of

the format specification, where ^ indicates a space character.   Note
that, for example, 26X at the start of the format specification means
an output of 25 space characters on the next line, since the first
space character is the carriage control character.   Similarly,
^^FRED^ at the start of the format specification causes the output of
the <u>four</u> characters FRED.   For further guidance, the reader is
referred to programs EX63, EX64, EX65 and EX66.

There are four valid carriage control characters in FORTRAN 77.   In
addition to the space character, these are +, 0 (zero) and 1.   Their
effects are as follows.

+   Do not advance the line printer paper.

^   Advance the line printer paper by one line.

0   Advance the line printer paper by two lines.

1   Advance the line printer paper to the top of the next page.

It should be noted that the + carriage control character   effectively
overwrites the previous line of output. Inexperienced programmers
should be very careful when using the 1 carriage control character
since, if it were inadvertently used within a loop, a considerable
wastage of paper would result.

As an example of the output given using this feature of FORTRAN 77,
consider the statements

```
        PRINT 100,´THIS´
        PRINT 101
        PRINT 102
    100 FORMAT (´1´,A)
    101 FORMAT (´ IS AN´/´+      EXAMPLE´)
    102 FORMAT (´0OF CARRIAGE CONTROL´)
```

The output as a result of these statements is

    THIS
    IS AN EXAMPLE

    OF CARRIAGE CONTROL

The output starts at the top of   a   new   page   because   the   carriage
control character for the first line of output is the 1 in the FORMAT
statement associated with the first PRINT statement.   The second line
of   output is caused by the second PRINT statement, which outputs the
two records IS^AN and ^^^^^^EXAMPLE on the same line. This is because
the + carriage control character causes the second record to
overwrite the first.   The blank line is caused because the 0 carriage
control   character   in the FORMAT statement associated with the third
PRINT statement causes the line printer paper to be advanced   by   two
lines.   Note   that   carriage control characters other than the space
character are normally produced by character strings.

It   is   advisable   to   specify   the   carriage   control   character

explicitly in every case. For example,
```
      PRINT 100,N
  100 FORMAT (1X,I2)
```
and
```
      PRINT 100,N
  100 FORMAT (I3)
```
where N holds 6 would both cause ^6 to be printed, the first
character being taken as the carriage control character in both
cases. If, however, N holds 106, the first PRINT statement causes
two asterisks to be printed in the first two positions of the line.
This is because the field is not wide enough for the number being
output.   If N holds 106, the second PRINT statement causes 06 to be
printed at the top of a new page of output. This is because the 1 is
taken as the carriage control character.   Thus, for example, an
attempt to output 206 using the second PRINT statement could cause a
failure, because 2 is not a valid carriage control character.

It has already been mentioned that a carriage control character is
required at the start of a line of output formed as a result of a
slash character. This was seen in section 6.4.6, when
```
  100 FORMAT (10X,´FORTRAN 77´/10X,´**********´)
```
was shown to result in nine space characters followed by FORTRAN 77
being printed on the first line of output and nine space characters
followed by ********** being printed on the second.

Finally, it should be noted that carriage control characters are
only used in formatted output.   List-directed output can only be
printed after advancing the line printer paper precisely one line,
which is done automatically.

6.4.9 Repeat Specifications

Repeat specifications used with single I-format, F-format, E-format
and A-format edit descriptors have been described previously. If a
sequence of edit descriptors is to be repeated, it must be enclosed
in brackets and a repeat specification placed before the opening
bracket. For example, program EX64 in section 6.2 required the
specification of twenty fields for the output of real numbers. This
could be done by the FORMAT statement
```
  101 FORMAT (1X,F5.2,1X,F5.2,1X,F5.2,1X,F5.2,1X,F5.2,
     1    1X,F5.2,1X,F5.2,1X,F5.2,1X,F5.2,1X,F5.2,1X,
     2    F5.2,1X,F5.2,1X,F5.2,1X,F5.2,1X,F5.2,1X,F5.2,
     3    1X,F5.2,1X,F5.2,1X,F5.2,1X,F5.2)
```
Clearly, this is a very long and cumbersome statement. It is
shortened considerably when it is written as
```
  101 FORMAT (20(1X,F5.2))
```

The two FORMAT statements have the same effect, but the use of the repeat specification 20 makes the second form more acceptable.

The X-format, slash and colon format edit descriptors must be enclosed in brackets when a repeat specification is used, as must character constants such as ´**********´. Thus the statement

     100 FORMAT (10X,´FORTRAN 77´/10X,´**********´)

given in section 6.4.6 could be written as

     100 FORMAT (10X,´FORTRAN 77´/10X,10(´*´))

where 10(´*´) has the same effect as ´**********´.

Finally, consider the example given in section 6.4.7. The PRINT statement and associated FORMAT statement in this example could be written

       PRINT 100,(I,L(I),I=1,N)
     100 FORMAT (´ NO ´,I1,´ = ´,I1:´ NO ´,I1,´ = ´,I1:
     1   ´ NO ´,I1,´ = ´,I1:´ NO ´,I1,´ = ´,I1)

The output is the same as that given in section 6.4.7. Using a repeat specification in the FORMAT statement, these statements could be written

       PRINT 100,(I,L(I),I=1,N)
     100 FORMAT (4(´ NO ´,I1,´ = ´,I1:))

6.5 INTERACTION BETWEEN OUTPUT LIST AND FORMAT

As was seen in the last section, control of the layout of output depends on the items in the output list of the PRINT statement and on the edit descriptors in the FORMAT statement. Frequently the number of items in the output list differs from the number of edit descriptors in the format specification.

If there are fewer items in the output list than edit descriptors in the FORMAT statement, printing is terminated when all the items have been printed. Program EX64 (see section 6.2) illustrates this.

When there are fewer edit descriptors than output list items, a new line of output is started and the edit descriptors are repeated when they have all been used once. If there are no inner brackets within the edit descriptor list, repetition starts with the first edit descriptor in the list. For example, the statements

       PRINT 100,A,B,C,D
     100 FORMAT (1X,2F5.2)

cause the values of A and B to be printed on one line and the values of C and D on the next. After the first line has been printed, repetition starts from the 1X edit descriptor. Hence the output is as if the statements had been

       PRINT 100,A,B,C,D
     100 FORMAT (1X,2F5.2/1X,2F5.2)

When there are inner brackets in the edit descriptor list, the situation is rather more complicated. Repetition starts from the left-hand bracket which corresponds to the last inner right-hand bracket. As an example, consider the statements

        PRINT 100,A,B,C,D
    100 FORMAT (1X,2(F5.2,2X))

The last inner right-hand bracket occurs after the format edit descriptor 2X, so that the repetition starts from the left-hand bracket before the format edit descriptor F5.2. Thus the given statements are equivalent to

        PRINT 100,A,B,C,D
    100 FORMAT (1X,2(F5.2,2X)/2(F5.2,2X))

since the space character used as a carriage control character for the first line is not repeated. This could cause a runtime error as described in section 6.4.8. It can be put right by inserting an extra pair of inner brackets, so that the statements become

        PRINT 100,A,B,C,D
    100 FORMAT ((1X,2(F5.2,2X)))

In this case, the left-hand bracket which corresponds to the last inner right-hand bracket is the one before the format edit descriptor 1X, so the whole edit descriptor list is repeated. Thus these statements give the same output as the statements

        PRINT 100,A,B,C,D
    100 FORMAT (1X,2(F5.2,2X)/1X,2(F5.2,2X))

Great care must be taken when using inner brackets. For example, the repeated edit descriptor 10(´*´) is normally equivalent to ´**********´. If repetition occurs when using the FORMAT statement

    100 FORMAT (1X,I6,´**********´,F5.2)

it will start with the 1X edit descriptor. However, if repetition occurs in the FORMAT statement

    101 FORMAT (1X,I6,10(´*´),F5.2)

it will start with the 10(´*´) edit descriptor. This could cause a runtime error as described in section 6.4.8, since the first character on the second line of output is an asterisk, which is not one of the allowed carriage control characters. The statement equivalent to the first FORMAT statement is

    100 FORMAT ((1X,I6,10(´*´),F5.2))

6.6 EXAMPLE PROGRAMS

In this section, the layout of the results from two of the example programs given in earlier chapters is improved. The section also includes a program which has a table of mortgage repayments as output.

6.6.1 Roots of a Quadratic Equation

In section 4.5.3, a program for finding the roots of a quadratic equation was discussed. Unfortunately, the layout of the results of this program was rather untidy. In the revised version which follows, formatted output is used to improve the layout.

```
       PROGRAM EX67
CCCC   ROOTS OF QUADRATIC EQUATIONS, USING FORMATTED OUTPUT
CCCC   NOT A VALID METHOD IF B**2 IS MUCH GREATER THAN 4*A*C
       PRINT 100
    10 READ *,A,B,C
       IF (ABS(A)+ABS(B)+ABS(C).EQ.0.0) STOP
       IF (A.NE.0.0) THEN
          DISCR=B**2-4.0*A*C
          R=-0.5*B/A
          IF (DISCR.GE.0.0) THEN
             D=0.5*SQRT(DISCR)/A
             PRINT 101,A,B,C,R+D,R-D
          ELSE
             COMP=0.5*SQRT(-DISCR)/A
             PRINT 102,A,B,C,R,COMP,R,COMP
          ENDIF
       ELSE
          IF (B.EQ.0.0) THEN
             PRINT 103,A,B,C
          ELSE
             PRINT 104,A,B,C,-C/B
          ENDIF
       ENDIF
       GOTO 10
   100 FORMAT (6X,'THE FOLLOWING TABLE GIVES THE ROOTS OF',
      1    ' THE EQUATION'/25X,'A*X**2+B*X+C=0'//6X,'A',6X,'B',
      2    6X,'C',21X,'ROOTS')
   101 FORMAT (2X,3(1X,F6.3),13X,F6.3,' AND ',F6.3)
   102 FORMAT (2X,3(1X,F6.3),4X,F6.3,'+',F6.3,'*I AND ',F6.3,
      1    '-',F6.3,'*I')
   103 FORMAT (2X,3(1X,F6.3),18X,'INVALID')
   104 FORMAT (2X,3(1X,F6.3),18X,F6.3)
       END
```

As the program logic was described in section 4.5.3, only the formatted PRINT statements are discussed here. The statement

```
      PRINT 100
```
in conjunction with the associated FORMAT statement causes the output of the headings.   Note the use of the slash edit descriptor to   start a   new   line   of   output,   a pair of them being used to print a blank line.   The FORMAT statements labelled 101, 102, 103 and 104   describe the output of the coefficients and roots of the equation in the cases where the   roots   are   real,   complex   conjugates,   non-existent   and coincident   respectively.   Note   how   the   repeat   edit   descriptor 3(2X,F6.3) provides fields for the coefficients in these statements.

   The program assumes that all numbers to be printed are in the range from -9.999 to 99.999 inclusive.   This is because the edit descriptor F6.3   has been used to output all the numbers: an attempt to output a number outside this range would cause six asterisks to be printed   in the field.   It follows that the program would require modification if it were necessary to print numbers outside this range.

   The   results,   using   the   same data as was used for program EX410, were

```
        THE FOLLOWING TABLE GIVES THE ROOTS OF THE EQUATION
                         A*X**2+B*X+C=0


     A      B      C                       ROOTS
   1.000  2.000  1.000              -1.000 AND -1.000
   1.000 -2.000  1.000               1.000 AND  1.000
   1.000  2.000 -1.000               0.414 AND -2.414
   1.000  2.000  3.000      -1.000+ 1.414*I AND -1.000- 1.414*I
   1.000  3.000  0.000               0.000 AND -3.000
   1.000  0.000  3.000       0.000+ 1.732*I AND  0.000- 1.732*I
   0.000  3.000  1.000                   -0.333
   0.000  0.000  7.700                   INVALID
```

6.6.2 Distance Travelled by a Salesman

The program on the next page is a revised   version   of   program   EX58 from   section   5.8.3.   It   finds   the   total distance travelled by a salesman when using   a   number   of   specified   routes.   The   results obtained   when   this program was run using the same input data as was used for program EX58 were

```
   ROUTE IS FROM   1 TO   4 TO   3 TO   1
   TOTAL DISTANCE TRAVELLED IS     21.7728 KILOMETRES.
   ROUTE IS FROM   2 TO   5 TO   2
   THIS ROUTE IS NOT VALID.
```

The revised program is as follows

```
      PROGRAM EX68
CCCC  DISTANCES TRAVELLED BY A SALESMAN, USING FORMATTED OUTPUT
      INTEGER ROUTE,DIM
      PARAMETER (DIM=17)
      DIMENSION X(DIM),Y(DIM),DIST(DIM,DIM),ROUTE(DIM+1)
      READ *,N
      DO 11 I=1,N
         READ *,X(I),Y(I)
   11 CONTINUE
      DO 12 I=1,N
         DIST(I,I)=0.0
         DO 13 J=I+1,N
            DIST(I,J)=SQRT((X(I)-X(J))**2+(Y(I)-Y(J))**2)
            DIST(J,I)=DIST(I,J)
   13    CONTINUE
   12 CONTINUE
   15 READ *,K
      IF (K.EQ.0) STOP
      READ *,(ROUTE(I),I=1,K)
      K1=K+1
      ROUTE(K1)=ROUTE(1)
      PRINT 100,(ROUTE(I),I=1,K1)
      DO 14 I=1,K
         IF (ROUTE(I).LT.1 .OR. ROUTE(I).GT.N) THEN
            PRINT 101
            GOTO 15
         ENDIF
   14 CONTINUE
      TDIST=0.0
      DO 16 I=1,K
         TDIST=TDIST+DIST(ROUTE(I),ROUTE(I+1))
   16 CONTINUE
      PRINT 102,TDIST
      GOTO 15
  100 FORMAT (' ROUTE IS FROM ',I2,17(' TO ',I2:))
  101 FORMAT (' THIS ROUTE IS NOT VALID.')
  102 FORMAT (' TOTAL DISTANCE TRAVELLED IS ',F10.4,
     1 ' KILOMETRES.')
      END
```

Note the use of the colon edit descriptor in the FORMAT statement
labelled 100. Since some routes are shorter than others, it is

necessary to suppress superfluous TO´s in the output which this statement generates, which is why the colon is used.

6.6.3 Table of Mortgage Repayments

In many scientific, business and engineering applications, it is desirable to present numeric data in the form of a table. Examples are actuarial tables, tide tables, diving pressure tables, tables of atomic weights and the distance table used in the example program in section 6.6.2. As an example of this, program EX69 on the next page gives monthly mortgage repayments at various rates of interest on a principal which is read in as data. The repayments are made over periods of 5, 10, 15, 20 and 25 years.

The formula for calculating the monthly mortgage repayments is

$$x = \frac{\dfrac{Pr}{1200}\left[1 + \dfrac{r}{1200}\right]^{12t}}{\left[1 + \dfrac{r}{1200}\right]^{12t} - 1}$$

where "x" is the monthly repayment, "P" is the principal, "r" is the rate of interest as a percentage, and "t" is the time in years over which repayments are to be made.

The basis of the program is the calculation of the monthly repayments. The table is output a row at a time, so it is necessary to calculate all the repayments in that row. The most convenient way of storing the repayments is to use an array and the output of a row of the table may then be achieved by the statement

```
      PRINT 100,RATE,(X(I),I=1,5)
```

where 100 is the label of the FORMAT statement which defines how the output is to be arranged, RATE holds the interest rate, and the elements of the array X hold the repayments.

The calculation of the repayments is carried out in the DO loop labelled 13. Note that this could have been done by the statements

```
      DO 13 I=1,5
         TIME=5*I
         X(I)=MONEY*RATE/1200.0*(1.0+RATE/1200.0)**(12*TIME)/
   1        ((1.0+RATE/1200.0)**(12*TIME)-1.0)
      13 CONTINUE
```

where TIME is an integer variable which holds the period over which the principal is to be repaid and MONEY is a real variable which holds the principal. This loop, when followed by the PRINT statement, would cause the output of a row of the table. It will be

noted   that RATE does not change along a row of the table, so that it
increases efficiency if the calculations of RATE/1200.0 and
1.0+RATE/1200.0   are   done   outside   the   loop.   Likewise,
(1.0+RATE/1200.0)**(12*TIME) appears twice, so this should be
calculated by a separate statement within the loop.

The program can thus be written as follows

```
            PROGRAM EX69
      CCCC  MORTGAGE REPAYMENTS ON AN AMOUNT READ IN AS DATA
      CCCC  FOR VARIOUS RATES OF INTEREST AND OVER VARIOUS
      CCCC  PERIODS OF REPAYMENT
            INTEGER YEAR
            REAL MONEY
            DIMENSION YEAR(5),MONTH(5),X(5)
            READ *,MONEY
            DO 11 I=1,5
               YEAR(I)=5*I
               MONTH(I)=12*YEAR(I)
         11 CONTINUE
            PRINT 100,MONEY,(YEAR(I),I=1,5)
            DO 12 RATE=5.0,16.0,2.0
               R=RATE/1200.0
               R1=1.0+R
               DO 13 I=1,5
                  R2=R1**MONTH(I)
                  X(I)=MONEY*R*R2/(R2-1.0)
         13      CONTINUE
               PRINT 101,RATE,(X(I),I=1,5)
         12 CONTINUE
            PRINT 102
        100 FORMAT (7X,´MONTHLY REPAYMENTS FOR BORROWING ´,
          1    F9.2,´ POUNDS´/7X,49(´*´)//7X,´OVER VARIOUS´,
          2    ´ PERIODS AT VARIOUS RATES OF INTEREST´/7X,
          3    49(´*´)//1X,62(´.´)/´ :´,15X,´:´,12X,
          4    ´PERIODS OF REPAYMENT´,12X,´:´/´ :´,15X,´:´,
          5    44(´.´),´:´/´ : INTEREST RATE :´,5(1X,I2,´ YRS :´)/
          6    ´ :´,15(´.´),´:´,5(8(´.´),´:´))
        101 FORMAT (´ : ´,F4.1,´ PER CENT :´,5(1X,F6.2,´ :´))
        102 FORMAT (´ :´,15(´.´),´:´,5(8(´.´),´:´))
            END
```

The calculation and printing of a row of repayments is done by the
DO loop labelled 12, by which the interest rate is incremented and
succeeding rows of the table are printed. Note that, before entering

the loop, the repayment periods used are stored in the array MONTH, which avoids doing the same calculation for each row of the table.

The statement

        PRINT 100,MONEY,(YEAR(I),I=1,5)

together with the FORMAT statement labelled 100, causes the output of the headings of the table. In the FORMAT statement, two slash edit descriptors together (//) are used to print a blank line. Apart from this, the first character on each line of output is a space character, which acts as the carriage control character. Note the use of the repeat edit descriptor 49(´*´) to print 49 asterisks. The framework of the table is provided by a suitable arrangement of dots and semicolons. The use of repeat edit descriptors to do this should be noted. The repeat edit descriptor 5(1X,I2,´ YRS :´) is used to print the line

    : INTEREST RATE : 5 YRS : 10 YRS : 15 YRS : 20 YRS : 25 YRS :

This prints five occurrences of a space, a two-character integer field (used to print the appropriate value from the array YEAR), and the characters ´YRS´:.

Each line of the table is output by the second PRINT statement which has associated with it the FORMAT statement labelled 101. Note the use of the repeat edit descriptor 5(1X,F6.2,´´:´) in this statement. The third PRINT statement, with its associated FORMAT statement, causes the output of the line of dots and semicolons which terminates the table.

The results of running the program using 25000.0 as input data were

```
         MONTHLY REPAYMENTS FOR BORROWING  25000.00 POUNDS
         **************************************************


         OVER VARIOUS PERIODS AT VARIOUS RATES OF INTEREST
         **************************************************


     ................................................................
     :              :           PERIODS OF REPAYMENT            :
     :              :..............................................:
     : INTEREST RATE :  5 YRS : 10 YRS : 15 YRS : 20 YRS : 25 YRS :
     :..............:.......:.......:.......:.......:........:
     :  5.0 PER CENT : 471.78 : 265.16 : 197.70 : 164.99 : 146.15 :
     :  7.0 PER CENT : 495.03 : 290.27 : 224.71 : 193.82 : 176.69 :
     :  9.0 PER CENT : 518.96 : 316.69 : 253.57 : 224.93 : 209.80 :
     : 11.0 PER CENT : 543.56 : 344.38 : 284.15 : 258.05 : 245.03 :
     : 13.0 PER CENT : 568.83 : 373.28 : 316.31 : 292.89 : 281.96 :
     : 15.0 PER CENT : 594.75 : 403.34 : 349.90 : 329.20 : 320.21 :
     :..............:.......:.......:.......:.......:........:
```

6.7 FORMATTED INPUT

When a programmer supplies the data for a program, it is natural to use list-directed input. It may be that data is supplied from another source, in which case it is probable that all of the data on a record will not be used by the program. In such circumstances, formatted input is used.

As an example, consider the following rewritten version of program EX64, which was described in section 6.2.

```
      PROGRAM EX610
      DIMENSION A(20,20)
      READ 100,M,N
      IF (M.LT.1 .OR. M.GT.20 .OR. N.LT.1 .OR. N.GT.20) STOP
      DO 11 I=1,M
         READ 101,(A(I,J),J=1,N)
   11 CONTINUE
      PRINT 102,N,M
      DO 12 J=1,N
         PRINT 103,(A(I,J),I=1,M)
   12 CONTINUE
  100 FORMAT (2I2)
  101 FORMAT (8F10.0)
  102 FORMAT (´ THE ´,I2,´ BY ´,I2,´ MATRIX IS´)
  103 FORMAT (20(1X,F5.2))
      END
```

When supplied with the data
```
   ^3^2
  1.0^^^^^^^4.0
  2.0^^^^^^^5.0
  3.0^^^^^^^6.0
```
the results were the same as those of running program EX64.

In this program, the FORMATTED READ STATEMENTS
```
      READ 100,M,N
```
and
```
      READ 101,(A(I,J),J=1,N)
```
read data records on which data is arranged as specified by FORMAT statements labelled 100 and 101 respectively. The general form of the formatted READ statement is
```
      READ label,list
```
so that it is similar to the PRINT statement. The label is that of the FORMAT statement which specifies how data is arranged on the data

record.   The construction of this statement is as described in
section 6.4.   The effect of the edit descriptors is slightly
different.

   The edit descriptors which are normally used in conjunction with a
formatted READ statement are I-format, F-format, X-format BN-format,
BZ-format and A-format.   The latter is described in chapter 8.   The
others are described in the following sections.

6.7.1 The I-format Edit Descriptor

As when used for output, the general form of this is
   rIw
where "w" specifies the number of positions on the data record which
are to contain the number being read.   The repeat specification "r"
may be omitted, in which case the value 1 is assumed.   Any blank
characters are ignored unless the entire field is blank, in which
case zero is read.   It is possible to override this so that blanks
are understood to mean zero, as is described in section 6.7.4.
Repetition of edit descriptors is as described in section 6.4.9.
   As an example, consider
        READ 100,I,J,K,(L(M),M=1,4)
     100 FORMAT (I2,2I3,2(I1,I2))
If the data record contains
   ^12^^3^45^6^7^
the statement results in

VARIABLE	VALUE	POSITIONS ACCESSED
I	1	1 and 2
J	2	3, 4 and 5
K	34	6, 7 and 8
L(1)	5	9
L(2)	6	10 and 11
L(3)	0	12
L(4)	7	13 and 14

As with the other edit descriptors described in this section, the
same FORMAT statement can be used for input as for output.   For
example,
        READ 100,I,J,K,(L(M),M=1,4)
        PRINT 100,I,J,K,(L(M),M=1,4)
     100 FORMAT (1X,I2,2I3,2(I1,I2))
when the data record is
   0^12^^3^45^6^7^
results in the output
   ^1^^2^345^60^7
The 0 in the input data record is ignored, since the edit descriptor

1X causes one character to be ignored. The positions accessed and
the input and output values can be seen from the following table

FORMAT	POSITIONS	INPUT	VARIABLE	VALUE	OUTPUT
I2	2 and 3	^1	I	1	^1
I3	4 5 and 6	2^^	J	2	^^2
I3	7 8 and 9	3^4	K	34	^34
I1	10	5	L(1)	5	5
I2	11 and 12	^6	L(2)	6	^6
I1	13	^	L(3)	0	0
I2	14 and 15	7^	L(4)	7	^7

Note that blank characters are ignored on input, so that 3^4 is read
as 34, except that if the entire field is blank, zero is assumed.

6.7.2 The F-format Edit Descriptor

The general form of this is as stated in section 6.4.3, namely
    rFw.d
where "w" specifies the field width and "r" is a repeat specification
which can be omitted. If the number in the appropriate field on the
data record contains a decimal point, "d" is ignored. This is
frequently the case, when the edit descriptor is often written as
    Fw.0
If the number in the appropriate field on the data record does not
contain a decimal point, this format specifies that the last "d"
digits form the fractional part of the number being read.   Blank
characters, although counted as part of the field, are ignored unless
this has been overridden, as is described in section 6.7.4.
    As an example, consider
            READ 100,A,B,C,D
        100 FORMAT (F10.0,F10.4,F10.2,F10.6)
where the data record contains
    1.0^^^^^^^^^3.4^^7^^12345^^^^^67^^^^^^^^^
The result is that the values of A, B, C and D are 1.0, 3.47, 123.45
and 0.000067 respectively.   Using the edit descriptor F10.0, the
contents of positions 1-10 of the data record (1.0^^^^^^^^) are read
into A.   Using the edit descriptor F10.4, the contents of positions
11-20 (^^3.4^^7^^) are read into B as 3.47, since blank characters
within the field are ignored.   The 0 and the 4 in these edit
descriptors are ignored, since there is a decimal point in each
field.   Using the edit descriptor F10.2, the contents of positions
21-30 (12345^^^^^) are read into C as 123.45. This is because, since
there is no decimal point in the field, the 2 in the edit descriptor
specifies that the last two non-blank characters in the field (namely
45) are taken as the fractional part of the number and the other

non-blank characters (namely 123) as the whole number part. Finally,
using the edit descriptor F10.6, the contents of positions 31-40
(67^^^^^^^^) are read into D as 0.000067. As there is no decimal
point in this field, the 6 in the edit descriptor specifies that the
last six non-blank characters in the field are to be taken as the
fractional part of the number. Because there are only two non-blank
characters in the field, these are taken as the right-most digits in
the fractional part; the remaining digits being assumed to be zeros.

6.7.3 The X-format Edit Descriptor

As was described in section 6.4.1, the general form of this is
    wX
When used in a FORMAT statement for input, the appropriate field in
the data record is ignored. As an example, consider
        READ 100,A,I
    100 FORMAT (2X,F3.1,3X,I2)
where the data record contains
    1234567890
This results in A and I being given values 34.5 and 90 respectively.
This is because the contents of positions 1 and 2 of the data record
are ignored; the contents of positions 3, 4 and 5 are read into A, a
decimal point being assumed between the second and third digits in
the field; the contents of positions 6, 7 and 8 are ignored; and the
contents of positions 9 and 10 are read into I.

6.7.4 The BN-format and BZ-format Edit Descriptors

These edit descriptors can be used to specify the interpretation of
blank characters in an input numeric field. On output, they are
ignored.

   It was stated in sections 6.7.1 and 6.7.2 that blank characters in
an input field are ignored. This convention can be replaced by one
which assumes that blank characters represent zeros if a BZ-format
edit descriptor appears in the edit descriptor list before the
appropriate numeric edit descriptor. As an example, consider the
statements
        READ 100,I,J
    100 FORMAT (I4,BZ,I4)
If the data record being read contains
    ^12^^12^
the result is that I is given the value 12 and J the value 120, since
the blank character in position eight of the data record is
interpreted as zero.

The normal convention can be reasserted by including a BN-format edit descriptor in the edit descriptor list. As an example, consider the statements

```
        READ 100,I,J,K
    100 FORMAT (I4,BZ,I4,BN,I4)
```

If the data record being read contains

```
    ^12^^12^^12^
```

the result is that I is given the value 12, J the value 120 and K the value 12.

As some implementations of FORTRAN 77 have taken the default setting to be that blanks imply zeros rather than blanks are ignored, it is strongly recommended that all FORMAT statements which contain numeric edit descriptors and which are used in conjunction with READ statements should commence with a BN-format edit descriptor. In most cases, this confirms the default setting, but it will ensure that programs are portable. It is of interest to note that the default setting in FORTRAN 66 was that blanks imply zeros.

6.8 EXERCISES

1. Modify program EX53 from section 5.6.1 to improve the appearance of the output so that, if the data given in the text is used, the output will be

```
    THE    5 CANDIDATES HAD THE FOLLOWING MARKS
      20,  30,  40,  50,  60
    AVERAGE MARK IS   40.00
    NUMBER OF CANDIDATES WITH MORE THAN THE AVERAGE MARK IS   2
```

2. Modify program EX55 from section 5.6.3 so that the layout of the results is improved. The values of "x" should be printed correct to one decimal place and the values of f(x) and f´(x) in exponential form showing five significant figures so that, for the data given, the output becomes

X	F(X)	F´(X)
-3.0	0.16000E+02	-0.32000E+02
-2.0	0.10000E+01	-0.40000E+01
-1.0	0.00000E+00	0.00000E+00
0.0	0.10000E+01	0.40000E+01
1.0	0.16000E+02	0.32000E+02
2.0	0.81000E+02	0.10800E+03
3.0	0.25600E+03	0.25600E+03

3. Modify the solution to exercise 4 of chapter 5 so that, for the data given, the output is

```
THERE ARE 3 EQUATIONS TO BE SOLVED, WHICH ARE
 -7.000 =    1.000 X3 +    2.000 X2 +   4.000 X1
  5.000 =  -1.000 X3 +    3.000 X2
  2.000 =    2.000 X3


THEIR SOLUTION IS
  X1 =  -3.000, X2 =    2.000, X3 =   1.000
```
Your program should be valid for from two to eight equations.

4. An underground gas storage field consists of two injection wells and one production well which are sunk vertically into a large porous rock structure. The injection wells are each of strength "m", and they are situated at points equidistant from the production well, which is of strength "2m". All three wells are in a straight line. Assuming ideal, two-dimensional, horizontal flow conditions, it is possible to show that, when all three wells are operating simultaneously, the stream function for the combined flow is

$$S(x,y) = \frac{m}{2\pi} \tan^{-1}\left[\frac{2a^2xy}{a^2(x^2-y^2)-(x^2+y^2)^2}\right]$$

Write a program which reads values for "m" and "a" and which prints a table showing values of the stream function calculated according to the above formula for x=0.1a(0.1a)2a and y=0.1a(0.1a)a. The output should be of the following form

```
VALUES OF THE STREAM FUNCTION FOR THE GAS STORAGE FIELD PROBLEM
**************************************************************

                      M = 2.0       A = 1.0

           Y = 0.1   Y = 0.2   Y = 0.3      ...      Y = 1.0
  X = 0.1    ...       ...       ...        ...        ...
  X = 0.2    ...       ...       ...        ...        ...
  X = 0.3    ...       ...       ...        ...        ...
   ...
  X = 2.0    ...       ...       ...        ...        ...
```
As data for your program, read in values of 0.5 and 2.0 for "m" and "a" respectively.

5. Rewrite program EX57 from section 5.8.2 so that the output is a diagram showing the knight's tour. The chessboard should be delineated by rows and columns of asterisks, with numbers in the squares indicating the order in which the squares were visited. Hence the form of the output should be

```
*****************************************
*      *      *      *      *      *      *      *      *
*  1  * 22  * 13  *  6  * 63  * 60  * 15  * 18  *
*      *      *      *      *      *      *      *      *
*****************************************
*      *      *      *      *      *      *      *      *
* 12  *  5  * 64  * 21  * 14  * 17  * 62  * 59  *
*      *      *      *      *      *      *      *      *
*****************************************
*      *      *      *      *      *      *      *      *
* 23  *  2  *  7  * 10  * 61  * 58  * 19  * 16  *
*      *      *      *      *      *      *      *      *
*****************************************
*      *      *      *      *      *      *      *      *
*  8  * 11  *  4  * 25  * 20  * 41  * 56  * 35  *
*      *      *      *      *      *      *      *      *
*****************************************
*      *      *      *      *      *      *      *      *
*  3  * 24  *  9  * 52  * 57  * 36  * 43  * 40  *
*      *      *      *      *      *      *      *      *
*****************************************
*      *      *      *      *      *      *      *      *
* 48  * 51  * 26  * 29  * 42  * 39  * 34  * 55  *
*      *      *      *      *      *      *      *      *
*****************************************
*      *      *      *      *      *      *      *      *
* 27  * 30  * 49  * 46  * 53  * 32  * 37  * 44  *
*      *      *      *      *      *      *      *      *
*****************************************
*      *      *      *      *      *      *      *      *
* 50  * 47  * 28  * 31  * 38  * 45  * 54  * 33  *
*      *      *      *      *      *      *      *      *
*****************************************
```

A zero in a square would indicate that the square had not been visited. The output should be the complete tour as above if the moves are all valid, or the tour up to the invalid move if there is an invalid move in the data. As input data for your program, use that suggested by the diagram.

6. Write a program which has as output the outstanding balances each month on a mortgage. Input data for the program is the amount borrowed, the interest rate and the amount repaid each month. The outstanding balance each month is calculated according to the formula

$$B = A \left(1 + \frac{r}{1200} \right) - X$$

where "A" is the outstanding balance from the previous month, "r" is the interest rate and "X" is the amount repaid each month. Output from the program should be of the following form

```
TABLE SHOWING THE MONTHLY BALANCES ON A LOAN OF ... POUNDS
***********************************************************
AT ... PER CENT INTEREST REPAID AT ... POUNDS PER MONTH
*******************************************************
```

		MONTH 1	MONTH 2	MONTH 3	...	MONTH 12
YEAR	1	...	...	...	...	...
YEAR	2	...	...	...	...	...
...						

followed by either

THE MORTGAGE HAS BEEN COMPLETELY REPAID

or

AFTER 50 YEARS, THERE IS A BALANCE OF ... POUNDS

In the first case, the final balance shown in the table should be 0.00, since the final payment will generally be less than "X" pounds. Naturally, there should be only one occurrence of this in the table.

CHAPTER 7
SUBPROGRAMS AND COMMON BLOCKS

This chapter describes how separately compiled sections of FORTRAN 77
can be incorporated into a complete program.

7.1 PROGRAM UNITS

A FORTRAN 77 program may consist of several PROGRAM UNITS. It always
contains a MAIN PROGRAM and it may also contain one or more
SUBPROGRAMS. Each program unit consists of a number of statements
and is terminated by an END statement.

As its name suggests, the main program is the principal program
unit and processing always starts at the first executable statement
in the main program. It is usual to position the main program first
since some compilers insist on this, and to follow it with any
subprograms. The order of the subprograms does not matter. All
programs considered so far have only contained a main program, which
has started with a PROGRAM statement.

A subprogram is a separate program unit which can be CALLED into
use from the main program or from another subprogram. Often a
sequence of instructions which performs a particular computation is
required at several different points in a program unit. It is
laborious and inefficient to write this sequence of instructions at
each point, so a special mechanism is provided whereby the sequence
can be stored separately as a subprogram and be obeyed when desired.
At that stage, a jump is made to the subprogram, the instructions in
the subprogram are obeyed and a jump back is made. This idea is not
new since it was introduced in section 3.4 where intrinsic functions,
such as SQRT, were considered. In a statement like:

        X = -B+SQRT(B**2-4.0*A*C)

the argument of SQRT is evaluated, a jump is made to the intrinsic
function (subprogram) SQRT with this value and the set of
instructions for calculating the square root obeyed. The value of

the square root is then returned to the arithmetic expression and evaluation of the expression continues.

The program unit in which a subprogram is called is termed the CALLING PROGRAM UNIT. It will often be the main program but it can be any other program unit. However, a subprogram may not be called from itself either directly or indirectly via another program unit, that is, RECURSION is specifically forbidden in FORTRAN 77. Subprograms provided as program units are known as EXTERNAL SUBPROGRAMS in contrast to INTRINSIC SUBPROGRAMS such as EXP and SQRT which are provided as part of the language.

There are two main types of subprogram, the FUNCTION SUBPROGRAM and the SUBROUTINE SUBPROGRAM. Conceptually, a function subprogram is like an intrinsic function which is provided by the programmer and not by the system. It calculates a single value and control is returned to the main program with this value. A subroutine subprogram is rather more sophisticated and may be used to perform a number of tasks like sorting a set of values held in an array or producing a particular form of input or output. It is more akin to the READ or PRINT statements considered in chapter 2. A subroutine can be used to return a single value, but its use in these circumstances is usually more clumsy than that of a function.

The concept of a subprogram is very powerful because it allows the possibility of assembling complete libraries of subprograms (written by experts in their own particular field) and of incorporating individual subprograms into particular programs as required. This avoids the programmer having to spend considerable time and effort producing his own subprograms to perform standard mathematical calculations which are available "off the shelf".

There is also a third type of subprogram called a BLOCK DATA SUBPROGRAM which is used for the initialisation of data in a special area of storage called a COMMON BLOCK.

7.2 FUNCTION SUBPROGRAMS

In this section, function subprograms are considered in detail. In most cases the CALL, or use, of the function is in the main program, although a function may be called from any other program unit.

7.2.1 Example of a Function Subprogram

The time taken to change the level of water in a reservoir from h_1 to h_2 is given by:

$$t = \frac{A}{Kb\sqrt{H}} (\phi(r_2) - \phi(r_1))$$

where

A = the average surface area of the reservoir between the two levels

H = the height of the reservoir at which the rate of inflow equals the rate of outflow

b = the length of the weir

K = a constant associated with the design profile of the weir

$$r_1 = h_1/H \qquad r_2 = h_2/H$$

ϕ = Gould's Function, defined in section 3.5.3

A program which reads data values for A, H, b, h_1, h_2 and calculates t is given on the next page. The equation for calculating Gould's Function is so complicated that it would be inappropriate to include it twice. This may be avoided by defining $\phi(r)$ as a function subprogram, the instructions for which are based on lines 7-12 of program EX35 in section 3.5.3 . When used with the data values:

A = 75902 m^2 H = 0.785 m   B = 15.2 m   K = 1.711 units

H1 = 0.3 m   H2 = 0.6 m

the following results were produced:

RESERVOIR PROBLEM

TIME TAKEN TO CHANGE LEVEL OF WATER IN A RESERVOIR

AREA =   75902. H = 0.785 B =   15.2 K = 1.711

TIME TAKEN TO CHANGE LEVEL FROM   0.30 TO   0.60 IS 2375.4 SECONDS

The following points about the program should be noted:

(i) The main program extends from the statement PROGRAM EX71 down to the first END statement. The subprogram defining the function PHI follows the main program and is terminated by the second END statement.

(ii) In the main program, PHI is used in exactly the same way that an intrinsic function would be used - the use of SQRT and PHI in the expression for T should be compared.

(iii) The subprogram starts with the FUNCTION STATEMENT

FUNCTION PHI(R)

which identifies the subprogram as a function subprogram defining a function with the name PHI. It also specifies the number of arguments the function requires, in this case just the value of R. There then follow the instructions for calculating Gould's Function, finishing with an instruction which assigns the calculated value to the name of the function PHI. The RETURN statement then causes control to revert back to the main program at the point in the arithmetic expression at which it left.

```
          PROGRAM EX71
CCCC   TIME TAKEN TO CHANGE THE LEVEL OF WATER IN A RESERVOIR
          REAL K
          READ *,A,H,B,K,H1,H2
CCCC   USE OF THE FUNCTION PHI
          T=A/(K*B*SQRT(H))*(PHI(H2/H)-PHI(H1/H))
          PRINT *,'RESERVOIR PROBLEM'
          PRINT *
          PRINT *,'TIME TAKEN TO CHANGE LEVEL OF WATER IN A RESERVOIR'
          PRINT 100,A,H,B,K
          PRINT 101,H1,H2,T
100   FORMAT(' AREA = ',F10.0,'  H = ',F6.3,'  B = ',F6.1,
     1        '  K = ',F6.3)
101   FORMAT(' TIME TAKEN TO CHANGE LEVEL FROM ',F6.2,' TO ',F6.2,
     1        ' IS ',F6.1,' SECONDS')
          END
CCCC   SUBPROGRAM TO CALCULATE GOULD'S FUNCTION
          FUNCTION PHI(R)
          PARAMETER (ROOT3=1.732050808,PI=3.14159265359,PIBY2=PI/2.0,
     1        PIBY6=PI/6.0)
CCCC   CHECK FOR A NEGATIVE VALUE OF R
          IF (R.LT.0.0) R=ABS(R)
          ROOTR=SQRT(R)
CCCC   CHECK FOR R VERY CLOSE TO 1.0
          IF (ABS(ROOTR-1.0).LT.1.0E-10) THEN
              PHI=1.0E20
              RETURN
          ENDIF
CCCC   SET THE APPROPRIATE VALUE FOR THETA
          IF (R.LT.1.0) THEN
              THETA=PIBY6
          ELSE
              THETA=PIBY2
          ENDIF
CCCC   CALCULATE PHI
          A=2.0/3.0*LOG(SQRT(R+ROOTR+1.0)/ABS(ROOTR-1.0))
          B=2.0/ROOT3*(ATAN((2.0*ROOTR+1.0)/ROOT3)-THETA)
          PHI=A-B
          RETURN
          END
```

(iv) The values of $\sqrt{3}$, $\pi/2$ and $\pi/6$ are set by the PARAMETER statement so that they need not be recalculated every time the function PHI is called.

(v)   A test is made to see whether a negative value for "r" has
been provided and if so, the absolute value is used.   Similarly,
since $\phi(r)$ is not defined if r=1, a test is made to see whether "r"
is within 10^{-10} of 1.0.   If it is, a large value (10^{20}) is assigned
to ϕ.

7.2.2 The FUNCTION Statement

The definition of a function subprogram always starts with a FUNCTION
STATEMENT.   This contains the word FUNCTION, possibly with an
associated type qualifier such as REAL or INTEGER, the name given to
the function and a list of arguments contained in brackets.   These
indicate the information needed to perform the calculation.

The FUNCTION NAME must obey the normal rules for variable names as
described in section 2.2.   It is helpful if the name used is
descriptive of the purpose of the function and clearly the names of
existing intrinsic functions should be avoided.   If the name chosen
for the function is identical to that of an intrinsic function, the
intrinsic function will be used unless the name is declared in an
EXTERNAL statement in the calling program unit, as described in
section 7.5.2.   Also, since the value returned to the calling program
unit is associated with the name of the function, the name is used to
indicate whether the value is of type real or integer according to
the standard type convention or a specific type specification.   If
the type inferred by the type convention is inappropriate, a type
name such as REAL or INTEGER may be placed in front of the word
FUNCTION to indicate the type required.   In this case the function
name must also be declared in a similar type statement in the calling
program unit.   There are other possible function types which are
described in later chapters.

The arguments in the list carry the information from the calling
program unit that is to be used in the calculation of the function
value.   The type and number of arguments will vary depending upon the
nature of the function.   For example, only the real value R was
required in program EX71.   In this section only simple real and
integer variables will be used as arguments, discussion of array
arguments and function arguments being given later in the chapter.
The arguments are separated by commas and the whole list is enclosed
within a pair of brackets.   The pair of brackets must still be
present even if there are no arguments.

The following are examples of FUNCTION statements.
        FUNCTION F(X)
defines a function named F which returns a real value.   It has one
real argument which is represented by X in the function definition.

When the function is called, any real argument may be used in place of X.

     REAL FUNCTION LONG(A,B)

defines a function named LONG which returns a real value and has two real arguments represented by A and B. If the type REAL had not been present, LONG would have returned an integer value in accordance with the type convention. In order to use this function statement, a type statement specifying LONG to be REAL must be included in the calling program unit.

     INTEGER FUNCTION COUNT(I,J,Y)

defines a function named COUNT which returns an integer value and has two integer arguments represented by I and J and one real argument represented by Y. In order to use this function statement, a type statement specifying COUNT to be INTEGER must be included in the calling program unit.

     FUNCTION NCHECK()

defines a function named NCHECK which returns an integer value and does not have any arguments. It should be noted that the brackets must still be included.

  The general form of the function definition statement is:

     type FUNCTION name (argument-list)

where "type" and "argument-list" may be omitted where appropriate. Only functions of type REAL and INTEGER are considered in this chapter. Functions of other types are described in later chapters.

  If the type convention is inappropriate for the function name, it is also possible to specify the type by omitting the type specification in the function statement and including a type statement in the function definition, for example,

     REAL FUNCTION LONG(A,B)

could be replaced by the pair of statements:

     FUNCTION LONG(A,B)
     REAL LONG

7.2.3 Other Statements in a Function Definition

The function definition always starts with the FUNCTION statement as defined in the previous section and it must be terminated with an END statement. In between these two statements are all the other statements which perform the calculation. These will use the names of the variables in the argument list and may also use variables that are purely LOCAL to the subprogram. Local variables are used inside the subprogram and are not usually related to any other variables used in the main program or other subprograms, even those with the same name. In program EX71, the variables ROOTR, THETA, A and B are

local variables used in the function subprogram PHI. The local
variables A and B used in PHI are not related in any way to the
variables A and B used in the main program. These temporary local
variables normally lose their values when a return is made and must
be re-assigned values when the subprogram is used again. This
concept of local variables is very useful because it means that when
a library subprogram is used, it is not necessary to check whether
there is a clash of names between variables used in the main program
and the library subprogram.

There must be at least one statement where the function name is
treated like an ordinary variable and assigned a value, such as

        PHI = A-B

in program EX71. In fact, there may be several such statements if
the structure of the subprogram has several branches. The RETURN
statement is used to transfer control back to the program unit at the
point from which the function was called. If there are several
branches in the structure of the subprogram, each branch might
terminate with a RETURN statement. The END statement also acts as a
RETURN, as well as indicating the end of the subprogram. Thus in
program EX71, the RETURN statement immediately before the END is
redundant, since the return would be caused by the END statement. It
can be seen that the RETURN statement in a subprogram is analogous to
the STOP statement in a main program in that it indicates a logical
end to a branch in the subprogram.

7.2.4 Simple Variables as Function Arguments

The number and type of arguments required is usually fairly obvious
from the nature of the calculation that has to be performed. For
example, in program EX42, which was discussed in section 4.1, it was
shown how to compare two values and assign the larger to BIG. This
can be written as a function subprogram called BIG which has two
arguments. These are the names of the two real variables that are to
be compared. The function can be written as follows:

```
FUNCTION BIG(A,B)
IF (A .GT. B) THEN
    BIG=A
ELSE
    BIG=B
ENDIF
END
```

Here, because there are two branches in the structure, there are two

statements of the form
        BIG=.....
At this stage, a most important point about the arguments should be
noted. The names of the arguments in the function definition are
purely DUMMY NAMES. This means that they do not relate in any way to
the names of existing storage locations but are used merely to show
where the information supplied by the calling program unit is to be
inserted into the function subprogram instructions. The term DUMMY
ARGUMENTS is used to describe the dummy names used in the function
definition and the term ACTUAL ARGUMENTS is used to describe the
arguments that are provided when the function is called.

7.2.5 Using a Function Subprogram

The name of the function subprogram is used at the appropriate place
in an expression in exactly the same way as the name of an intrinsic
function. It can be used anywhere that an expression of the same
type would be valid. In the following program, four values are read
as data and the function BIG is used to find which is the largest.

```
        PROGRAM EX72
  CCCC  PROGRAM TO USE THE FUNCTION BIG
        READ *,A,B,C,D
        X=BIG(A,B)
        Y=BIG(C,D)
        Z=BIG(X,Y)
        PRINT *,´THE 4 VALUES CONSIDERED ARE ´,A,B,C,D
        PRINT *,´THE LARGEST IS ´,Z
        END
  CCCC  DEFINITION OF FUNCTION BIG
        FUNCTION BIG(A,B)
        IF (A.GT.B) THEN
           BIG=A
        ELSE
           BIG=B
        ENDIF
        END
```

The following points about this program should be noted:
   (i)   BIG is used first to compare the values of A and B. It
should be noted that although the same names are used for the ACTUAL
ARGUMENTS in the main program and the DUMMY ARGUMENTS in the function
definition, the dummy and actual arguments are regarded as being
quite different. In the second and third calls of BIG, the actual

arguments used   (C,D) and (X,Y) have different names to those of the
dummy arguments.

(ii) The following process occurs when BIG is used.

First, the actual arguments are evaluated.   If a constant is
provided, the value given is used in the subprogram; if a variable is
provided, its associated value is used; if an expression is provided,
its value is calculated and used. In addition, any other FORTRAN 77
construction which produces a single value can be provided as an
argument and its value used.

Next, the value produced from the first actual argument is
associated with the first dummy argument, which in the case of BIG is
A, and its value is used wherever the first dummy argument occurs in
a statement in the subprogram. Similarly, the value produced from
the second actual argument is associated with the second dummy
argument, and so on. In the case of BIG, because the dummy arguments
are real, the values provided by the actual arguments must also be
real, otherwise a failure will be caused.

Finally, a value is calculated from the statements in the
subprogram and assigned to the name BIG. This value is then inserted
in the statement in the main program that called the function BIG,
replacing the name BIG and its arguments. The association between
the actual and dummy arguments is then terminated.

(iii) Since all that is required of an actual argument of BIG is
that it produces a real value, the argument itself may be the call of
a real valued function. Thus, the three statements

       X=BIG(A,B)
       Y=BIG(C,D)
       Z=BIG(X,Y)

in program EX72 could be replaced by the single statement

       Z=BIG(BIG(A,B),BIG(C,D))

In this case, BIG(A,B) and BIG(C,D) are both obeyed and the values
they return are used as arguments for the third call of BIG.

(iv) It was mentioned in note (ii) that the type of value produced
by the actual arguments must correspond exactly with the type
indicated by the dummy arguments. It is also necessary for there to
be the same number of actual arguments as dummy arguments. Thus, in
the statement

       Q = BIG(3,X) + BIG(X,Y,Z)

both calls of BIG are invalid, the first because the first argument
is an integer and the second because there are three actual
arguments. Conversely, all three calls of BIG in the statement

       Q = BIG(2.0,3.5) + BIG(A*B,SQRT(C)) + BIG(X(I,J),Y(2))

are valid, assuming the normal type convention. It should be noted
that in the third call of BIG, real array elements are used as actual

arguments.   This is different from using the name of the whole array
as an argument, which is discussed later.

(v)   There is in fact an intrinsic function MAX, described in
appendix 1, which will perform the task for which BIG was written.
The purpose of writing BIG was to provide a relatively simple example
of a function subprogram.

7.3 SUBROUTINE SUBPROGRAMS

It was mentioned in section 7.1 that a subroutine is usually used to
perform a   task involving more than just calculating a single value.
One of the more common tasks is to calculate a whole array of values.
The subroutine is brought into use by a special CALL statement and
information is usually returned by means of arguments. Many of the
detailed features of subroutines are similar to those previously
described for functions and will be covered briefly below.

7.3.1 The SUBROUTINE Statement

The subroutine is given a name and details of its arguments are
provided by the SUBROUTINE STATEMENT which is of the form:
        SUBROUTINE name (argument-list)
The following are examples of SUBROUTINE statements.
        SUBROUTINE SORT(X,N)
        SUBROUTINE MATADD(A,B,C,M,N,M1,N1)
        SUBROUTINE OUTPUT
In the last example, the subroutine OUTPUT has no arguments. Unlike
a function in these circumstances, it does not need any brackets.

It should be noted that the name of the subroutine is used purely
for identification purposes and never has a value associated with it.
Hence the name need not conform to the type convention.

7.3.2 Other Statements in the Subroutine Definition

As with function subprograms, the definition of a subroutine must
terminate with an END statement and a RETURN statement may be used
where appropriate. However, in contrast to a function, a subroutine
must never contain a statement which assigns a value to the
subroutine name.

7.3.3 Simple Variables as Subroutine Arguments

The number and type of arguments required is usually fairly obvious
from the nature of the task to be performed. As with functions, the

arguments specified in the definition are DUMMY ARGUMENTS. ACTUAL ARGUMENTS are substituted when the subroutine is called. When simple variables are used to bring information from the calling program unit, the association set up between the dummy arguments and the actual arguments is as described in section 7.2.4.

However, the arguments are normally the mechanism for the transfer of information back from a subroutine to the calling program unit. In these circumstances, some of the dummy arguments will appear on the left-hand side of assignment statements in the subprogram and so have values assigned to them. An association is again set up between the actual and dummy arguments and, when a value is assigned to a dummy argument, that value is transferred to the storage location specified by the actual argument. Thus the type of actual argument that can be used under these circumstances is restricted and must be a variable, array element or array name. It cannot be a constant, an expression or the name of another subprogram. An important consideration is whether it would make sense to have the actual argument on the left-hand side of an assignment statement.

As an example, suppose that the actual arguments were A*B (an expression) or 2.5 (a constant). Then assignments of the form

$$A*B = \ldots\ldots\ldots$$
$$2.5 = \ldots\ldots\ldots$$

would clearly be incorrect and would cause a failure. An example where arguments are used correctly to transfer information back to the main program is given in section 7.3.5.

It is also possible to use arguments of a FUNCTION SUBPROGRAM to transmit information back to the calling program unit in a similar way to that just described for subroutines. This is in addition to the value which is transmitted in association with the name of the function. However, this rather obscure use of a function is <u>not recommended</u>.

7.3.4 Using a Subroutine - the CALL Statement

When a subroutine is called, a special statement of the form

          CALL name (argument-list)

is used. Examples of the CALL statement are

          CALL SORT(X,N)
          CALL MATADD(A,B,C,M,N,M1,N1)
          CALL OUTPUT

When a CALL statement is encountered, control passes to the subprogram and the instructions there are executed. The RETURN or END statements in the subprogram transfer control back to the statement immediately after the CALL statement.

7.3.5 Example of a Subroutine Subprogram

In program EX410 (section 4.5.3) the solution of the quadratic equation $ax^2 + bx + c = 0$ was described. A program which includes a subroutine for solving this equation is now described. The following points were considered when writing the program:

(i)   A suitable name for the subroutine has to be chosen.   In   the program it is called QUADEQ.

(ii) The number and type of arguments needs consideration. Firstly, the question of what information should be brought across into the subprogram has to be answered. Obviously values for "a", "b" and "c" are required to specify the particular equation. It is noted in section 4.5.3 that the nature of the solution changed when various quantities were zero. The question of how small a value should be before it is treated as zero is of great practical importance in computing. In order to make the subroutine flexible, a variable EPS is used as an argument and values numerically smaller than EPS are treated as zero. Secondly, consideration must be given to the information that has to be returned to the main program. The obvious answer is the value of the roots, but there are a number of different cases that can occur. An integer argument INDIC (an indicator) is used to identify the particular case that has occurred and two real arguments R1 and R2 are used to bring across the information from which the roots are determined. The various cases are given in the table below, with an indication of the values given to R1, R2 and INDIC.

Condition	INDIC	R1	R2	Roots
$a \neq 0$ $b^2 \geq 4ac$	1	$\dfrac{-b}{2a}$	$\dfrac{\sqrt{b^2-4ac}}{2a}$	ROOT1=R1+SIGN(R2,R1) ROOT2= C/(A*ROOT1)
$a \neq 0$ $b^2 < 4ac$	2	$\dfrac{-b}{2a}$	$\dfrac{\sqrt{4ac-b^2}}{2a}$	R1+iR2 , R1-iR2
$a=0$ $b \neq 0$	3	$\dfrac{-c}{b}$	not assigned	R1
$a=b=0$ $c \neq 0$	4	not assigned	not assigned	invalid equation
$a=b=c=0$	5	not assigned	not assigned	used to terminate the program

However, it should be noted that the calculation has been modified for the case of real roots to take into account the effect of subtractive cancellation errors that occur when "4ac" is very small, as discussed in section 4.5.3. The numerically larger root is calculated from the quadratic equation formula, then the numerically smaller root is calculated from it. As can be seen from the table, for this case

$$R1 = -b/2a \text{ and } R2 = \sqrt{b^2 - 4ac}/2a$$

and so the numerically larger root will be R1+R2 or R1-R2 according to whether R1 is positive or negative. This can be programmed very neatly as

    ROOT1=R1+SIGN(R2,R1)

The intrinsic function SIGN is described in appendix 1. The smaller root can then be calculated from the relationship

    ROOT1*ROOT2=c/a

given in section 4.5.3. In the program, the test for "a", "b" or "c" being zero is carried out by testing whether the absolute value of the quantity is less than EPS. Program EX410 has been rewritten as follows, to include use of the subroutine QUADEQ and the formatted output given in program EX67 (section 6.6.1).

```
      PROGRAM EX73
CCCC  QUADRATIC EQUATION PROGRAM USING SUBROUTINE QUADEQ
      PRINT 100
      READ *,EPS
   11 READ *,A,B,C
CCCC  USE OF THE SUBROUTINE
      CALL QUADEQ(A,B,C,EPS,R1,R2,INDIC)
      IF (INDIC .EQ. 5) STOP
      IF (INDIC .EQ. 1) THEN
         ROOT1=R1+SIGN(R2,R1)
         ROOT2=C/(A*ROOT1)
         PRINT 101,A,B,C,ROOT1,ROOT2
      ELSEIF (INDIC .EQ. 2) THEN
         PRINT 102,A,B,C,R1,R2,R1,R2
      ELSEIF (INDIC .EQ. 3) THEN
         PRINT 104,A,B,C,R1
      ELSE
         PRINT 103,A,B,C
      ENDIF
      GOTO 11
  100 FORMAT(6X,'THE FOLLOWING TABLE GIVES THE ROOTS OF',
     1     ' THE EQUATION'/25X,'A*X**2+B*X+C=0'//6X,'A',6X,'B',
     2     6X,'C',21X,'ROOTS')
```

```
  101 FORMAT(2X,3(1X,F6.3),13X,F6.3,´ AND ´,F6.3)
  102 FORMAT(2X,3(1X,F6.3),4X,F6.3,´+´,F6.3,´*I AND ´,F6.3,
    1    ´-´,F6.3,´*I´)
  103 FORMAT(2X,3(1X,F6.3),18X,´INVALID´)
  104 FORMAT(2X,3(1X,F6.3),18X,F6.3)
      END
CCCC  DEFINITION OF SUBROUTINE QUADEQ
      SUBROUTINE QUADEQ(A,B,C,EPS,R1,R2,INDIC)
      IF (ABS(A) .GT. EPS) THEN
CCCC  GENUINE QUADRATIC EQUATION
        DISCR=B**2-4.0*A*C
        TWOA=2.0*A
        R1= -B/TWOA
        IF (DISCR .GT. 0.0) THEN
CCCC  REAL ROOTS
          R2=SQRT(DISCR)/TWOA
          INDIC=1
        ELSE
CCCC  COMPLEX ROOTS
          R2=SQRT(-DISCR)/TWOA
          INDIC=2
        ENDIF
      ELSEIF (ABS(B) .GT. EPS) THEN
CCCC  LINEAR EQUATION WITH ONE ROOT
        R1= -C/B
        INDIC=3
      ELSEIF (ABS(C) .GT. EPS) THEN
CCCC  INCONSISTENT LINEAR EQUATION
        INDIC=4
      ELSE
CCCC  ALL COEFFICIENTS ZERO
        INDIC=5
      ENDIF
      END
```

The following points about the program should be noted:

(i)   The subroutine is brought into use by the CALL statement in
line 7 of the main program.

(ii) Although the dummy arguments and actual arguments for QUADEQ
have the same names, it must be remembered that they are   treated   as
different entities, with an association being set up between them.

(iii) The arguments A, B, C, EPS are used to carry information from
the main program into the subroutine. The arguments R1, R2, INDIC
are used to carry information back from the subprogram   to   the   main

program, so they occur on the left-hand side of assignment statements
in the subprogram.

(iv) The results obtained by using program EX73 with EPS given the
value 1E-12 and the same data as used in program EX67 are identical
to those given in section 6.6.1.

(v)   The body of the subprogram, that is the   instructions
contained between the SUBROUTINE statement and the END statement, has
a fairly complicated logical structure. However, the actual use of
the subprogram is simple enough.   Thus, provided the name of the
subroutine and details of the various arguments are well documented,
a subroutine like QUADEQ could be incorporated into a standard
library. It could then be used in programs without the programmer
requiring a detailed knowledge of the logical structure.

(vi) In the main program, a fairly complicated BLOCK IF statement
is used to associate the appropriate PRINT statement with the value
of INDIC. Comments indicate the various cases. A much neater way of
implementing a multiple branch like this is provided by the computed
GOTO statement which is considered in chapter 10.

7.4 USE OF ARRAYS AS ARGUMENTS OF A SUBPROGRAM

It is often necessary to communicate information about a whole set of
array elements between program units.   An example of this is a
subroutine which sorts an array into ascending or descending order.
In these circumstances, the names of arrays in the calling program
unit will quite naturally be used as actual arguments in the call of
the subprogram.   In consequence, dummy array names will be included
in the argument list of the subprogram definition. However, since an
array cannot be distinguished from a simple variable by its name
alone, a DIMENSION statement indicating all the dummy arguments that
are arrays has to be included in the subprogram.

A complete statement of the way FORTRAN 77 handles array arguments
is quite complicated and inappropriate at this stage. A basic set of
rules will be given which will enable array arguments in a subprogram
to be handled correctly.   These rules apply to both functions and
subroutines. A more detailed account of the mechanism involved is
given in appendix 2.

7.4.1 General Considerations and Example Program

In a function, arrays are usually only used to bring information into
the subprogram, so that the values of array elements are not changed
as a result of the instructions in the subprogram. In a subroutine,
information may be returned to the calling program unit by the actual

arguments, when the values of the array elements have been changed as a result of instructions in the subprogram. The use of an array as an argument is illustrated by the following example, where for simplicity only a one-dimensional array is used.

Suppose that a function AVRGE is required to find the average of the values stored in an array. This is to be used in a main program which reads in an integer N, to indicate the number of array elements which hold data values, with $N \le 100$, followed by the N data values. The average of these values is to be calculated and the data values, together with the average, is to be printed out.

The following program fits the given specification:

```
      PROGRAM EX74
CCCC  DRIVER PROGRAM FOR FUNCTION AVRGE
      DIMENSION X(100)
      READ *,N
      READ *,(X(I),I=1,N)
CCCC  USE OF THE FUNCTION AVRGE
      AV=AVRGE(X,N,100)
      PRINT *,´ARRAY VALUES´
      PRINT *,(X(I),I=1,N)
      PRINT *
      PRINT *,´AVERAGE = ´,AV
      END
CCCC  DEFINITION OF AVRGE
      FUNCTION AVRGE(A,N,LU)
      DIMENSION A(LU)
      SUM=0.0
      DO 10 I=1,N
         SUM=SUM+A(I)
   10 CONTINUE
      AVRGE=SUM/N
      END
```

The following points were considered when writing the program:

(i)   The problem of averaging a set of values held in an array has already been considered in programs EX51, EX52 and EX53 and the program logic is based on these examples.

(ii) If the function were only to be used in a main program as specified, then there would be little point in using a function (or indeed an array) since program EX51 does all that is required. However, the main program specified is really just constructed to test the function subprogram, which would probably be used as part of a more sophisticated program. Such a simple main program is often called a DRIVER PROGRAM since its purpose is to "drive" the subprogram for testing purposes.

(iii) The name of the function is AVRGE. The arguments required are the name of the array holding the values, its size specified in the DIMENSION statement in the main program and an integer N to indicate the number of elements of the array which hold values.

(iv) It should be noted that the DUMMY ARGUMENT A refers to an array and so must appear in a DIMENSION statement in the function definition. The ACTUAL ARGUMENT array used is X, which has its own DIMENSION statement in the main program. In a subprogram, but <u>not</u> a main program, the array bounds for a dummy argument may be specified in the DIMENSION statement by integer variables or integer expressions, provided that the integer variables are included in the argument list. Thus, in the definition of AVRGE an integer argument LU, standing for <u>L</u>imit of the <u>U</u>pper bound, has been included to convey the size of the actual array to be used. This is used in the DIMENSION statement in AVRGE. When AVRGE is called in the main program, the value 100 is provided for LU.

7.4.2 Variable Size Bounds for DIMENSION Statements in Subprograms

Since the dimension statement in a subprogram may have an integer dummy argument, instead of a constant, as an array bound for a dummy argument, a subprogram which uses this is capable of accepting different size arrays from the main program as arguments. For example, program EX75 gives the outline of a driver program which calls the function AVRGE using two different size arrays.

```
        PROGRAM EX75
        DIMENSION X(100),Y(10)
        ..........
        AV1=AVRGE(X,N1,100)
        AV2=AVRGE(Y,N2,10)
        ..........
        END
CCCC    DEFINITION OF AVRGE
        FUNCTION AVRGE(A,N,LU)
        DIMENSION A(LU)
        SUM=0.0
        DO 10 I=1,N
            SUM=SUM+A(I)
     10 CONTINUE
        AVRGE=SUM/N
        END
```

The definition of AVRGE in this program means that the function can
be used with a one-dimensional array of any size, provided that the
first subscript starts at 1.   It is possible that the DIMENSION
statement in the main program may specify a lower limit other than
unity for the array. Under these circumstances, two arguments (for
example, LL and LU) would be used to convey this information to the
subprogram. In this case the definition of AVRGE would be modified
as follows

```
      FUNCTION AVRGE(A,N,LL,LU)
      DIMENSION A(LL:LU)
      SUM=0.0
      DO 10 I=LL,LL+N-1
         SUM=SUM+A(I)
   10 CONTINUE
      AVRGE=SUM/N
      END
```

A call of AVRGE in the main program might then be of the form
```
      AV=AVRGE(Z,N,0,50)
```
It can be seen that the use of a single one-dimensional array can
require up to four arguments to specify the elements involved.   In
principle, for each dimension of an array to be used as an actual
argument in a subprogram, three arguments may be required; the first
to specify the lower limit of the dimension, the second to specify
the upper limit and the third to specify how much of the array
actually holds values. Thus, for a single two-dimensional array
there are potentially 7 arguments required; the name of the array and
three arguments for each of the two dimensions.

In FORTRAN 77, the UPPER LIMIT OF THE LAST DIMENSION in an array
need not be specified explicitly in the dimension statement in a
subprogram but may be replaced by an asterisk (*). This means that
subprograms which use one-dimensional arrays can be written in a
simple way and still be of general use. It is strongly recommended
that subprograms be written in this way. Thus, AVRGE may be written

```
      FUNCTION AVRGE(A,N)
      DIMENSION A(*)
      SUM=0.0
      DO 10 I=1,N
         SUM=SUM+A(I)
   10 CONTINUE
      AVRGE=SUM/N
      END
```

This is the form that would normally be used, provided that the lower limit of the array to be used is unity. If the lower limit cannot always be guaranteed to be unity, the appropriate modification would be

```
      FUNCTION AVRGE(A,N,LL)
      DIMENSION A(LL:*)
      SUM=0.0
      DO 10 I=LL,LL+N-1
         SUM=SUM+A(I)
   10 CONTINUE
      AVRGE=SUM/N
      END
```

It should be noted that an asterisk may not be used in the dimension statement in place of LL because only the upper limit may be specified in this way.

The limits for dummy arrays in a dimension statement in a subprogram may also contain arithmetic expressions involving integer arguments and integer constants. The following outline is valid FORTRAN 77.

```
      FUNCTION FRED(A,B,M,N)
      DIMENSION A(M:*),B(2*N-1,M*N)
      ..........
      END
```

Naturally, any arithmetic expression used must produce an integer result, otherwise the limits in the DIMENSION statement would be invalid. The two different uses of the asterisk in the DIMENSION statement should be noted.

It should be noted that only dummy arrays, that is arrays whose names appear in the argument list, may have their array bounds specified by integer variables or asterisks in the DIMENSION statement. Any other arrays used in the subprogram must have their bounds specified by constants. For example, in the function definition

```
      FUNCTION BILL(A,M)
      DIMENSION A(M,*),B(0:4)
      ..........
      END
```

A is a dummy array whose bound is specified by the dummy integer

argument M and the asterisk. In contrast, B is a local array and so
its bounds must be specified by constants, as shown.

7.4.3 A Set of Rules for the use of Array Arguments

It has been seen that there can be complications in the use of arrays
as arguments in subprograms. The following set of rules have been
designed to try to simplify the situation for inexperienced
programmers and should ensure that arrays are handled correctly. A
more complete description of the mechanism involved in the use of
array arguments is given in appendix 2.

(i)   Where possible, use arrays whose lower limits for each
dimension are unity in the calling program unit. This avoids the
necessity of including lower limits in the argument list.

(ii) If several arrays are to be used as arguments, try to ensure
that they are all the same size.   This reduces the number of
arguments needed to carry dimension information.

(iii) Use arrays with as few dimensions as possible.

(iv) For each array, the array name and, for each dimension, a
lower limit, upper limit and an indication of the range of values
occupied may be required. If the lower limits can be assumed to be
unity, they may be omitted. An asterisk may be used instead of a
specific value for the upper limit of the last dimension.

The following examples illustrate the use of these rules.

(1)   A one-dimensional array with N elements occupied is to be
sorted. Assuming that the lower limit is unity, the only arguments
needed are the name of the array and the value of N. The subroutine
definition might then be

```
      SUBROUTINE SORT(X,N)
      DIMENSION X(*)
      ..........
      END
```

If the lower limit of the array has to be specified, an extra
argument is required and the definition becomes

```
      SUBROUTINE SORT(X,N,LL)
      DIMENSION X(LL:*)
      ..........
      END
```

(2)   All elements of a two-dimensional array are to be added
together and the sum returned to the main program.   Since only a

single value is returned, this could be written as a function
subprogram. The arguments required are the name of the array, the
number of rows and columns occupied (M and N respectively) and
details of the lower and upper limits of each dimension. The
subroutine definition is

```
FUNCTION SUMMAT(A,M,N,LU1)
DIMENSION A(LU1,*)
..........
END
```

where only the upper limit of the first dimension is provided.
Alternatively, if lower limits are included, it then becomes

```
FUNCTION SUMMAT(A,M,N,LL1,LU1,LL2)
DIMENSION A(LL1:LU1,LL2:*)
..........
END
```

(3)   An LxM matrix is to multiply a MxN matrix to produce the LxN
matrix product. Here there are three arrays involved - two to bring
information from the main program and the third to indicate the name
of the array in the main program in which the result is to be placed.
In principal, the name, number of rows and columns occupied and three
dimension parameters are required for each array - making a total of
18 arguments. This seems rather excessive and obviously thought
should be given to reducing this number. If rules (i) and (ii) are
heeded, a considerable simplification can be made. Assuming that the
arrays in the main program are all of the same size with lower limits
of unity, the number of arguments can be reduced to 7 - the names of
the three arrays, the number of rows and columns occupied (L, M and
N) and the common upper limit of the first dimension of each matrix.
Then the subroutine definition becomes

```
SUBROUTINE MATMLT(A,B,C,L,M,N,LU)
DIMENSION A(LU,*),B(LU,*),C(LU,*)
..........
END
```

7.5 A FUNCTION OR SUBROUTINE USED AS AN ARGUMENT OF A SUBPROGRAM

There are occasions when it is useful to have a function or, less
commonly, a subroutine as an argument of a subprogram.

In the case of a function, a suitable DUMMY NAME is included in the argument list in the usual way and the name is used in the subprogram instructions in accordance with the rules for a function. This function is termed a DUMMY FUNCTION. When the subprogram is called, the actual function argument used in the calling program unit must be the name of an intrinsic function, external function or other dummy function. The type of the actual function must be the same as the dummy function. The arguments associated with the dummy and actual functions must agree in number and type.

When a subprogram is to have a subroutine as an argument, similar rules apply and the argument is termed a DUMMY SUBROUTINE. The actual argument used must be the name of an external subroutine or another dummy subroutine. The arguments associated with the dummy and actual subroutines must agree in number and type.

All functions or subroutines that are to be used as arguments to other subprograms must be listed in an EXTERNAL or INTRINSIC statement in the calling program unit. These statements are described in section 7.5.2. They enable the calling program unit to recognise that the actual argument used is not an ordinary variable.

7.5.1 Example Program using a Function as an Argument of a Subprogram

The subroutine described in this section illustrates the use of a function as an argument. It tabulates a given function over a specified range. The name of the function "f" is specified and the function is to be evaluated at the points x0, x0+h, x0+2h, ... , x1=x0+nh, where the values x0,x1 and h are provided as data. The value of n=(x1-x0)/h is calculated in the subroutine and returned. The n+1 values of x and f(x) are placed in two arrays X and Y respectively. It is assumed in the subroutine that the arrays X and Y have general lower and upper bounds LL and LU respectively. Hence,

    X(LL)=x0,   X(LL+1)=x0+h,   ... , X(LL+n)=x0+nh;
    Y(LL)=f(x0),   Y(LL+1)=f(x0+h), ... , Y(LL+n)=f(x0+nh);

It is possible that the values of x0, x1 and h provided will result in the number of function values (n+1) being greater than the size of the arrays (LU-LL+1), so a check is made to see whether n > LU-LL. If this is the case, "n" is reset to the value LU-LL. Since the upper bound LU is used in the subroutine (other than just in the DIMENSION statement where it could be replaced by *), it must be included as an argument, as well as the lower bound LL. The subroutine will have dummy arguments F, X0, X1, H, N, X, Y, LL, LU and can be written as follows

```
      SUBROUTINE TAB(F,X0,X1,H,N,X,Y,LL,LU)
      DIMENSION X(LL:LU),Y(LL:LU)
      N=(X1-X0)/H+0.5
      M=LU-LL
      IF (N .GT. M) N=M
      DO 10 I=0,N
         XX=X0+I*H
         J=LL+I
         X(J)=XX
         Y(J)=F(XX)
   10 CONTINUE
      END
```

Here X0, X1, XX, H, N, M, LL, LU, I and J are simple variables and X
and Y are arrays which are specified in the DIMENSION statement.   The
value 0.5 is added to the expression (X1-X0)/H so that when
truncation occurs before assignment to the integer N, a correctly
rounded value is stored.   F can be identified as a function because
it appears on the right-hand side of an assignment statement and is
used with a pair of brackets.   Only arrays or functions occur like
that and, since F is not named in the dimension statement, it must be
a function.

   The subroutine TAB can be used in a program to tabulate Gould's
Function as follows

```
      PROGRAM EX76
      PARAMETER (LL=0,LU=100)
      EXTERNAL PHI
      DIMENSION X(LL:LU),Y(LL:LU)
      READ *,R0,R1,DR
      CALL TAB(PHI,R0,R1,DR,N,X,Y,LL,LU)
      PRINT *,'TABULATION OF GOULD''S FUNCTION'
      PRINT *
      PRINT *,(X(I),Y(I),I=LL,LL+N)
      END
CCCC  DEFINITION OF TAB
      SUBROUTINE TAB(F,X0,X1,H,N,X,Y,LL,LU)
      ..........
      END
CCCC  DEFINITION OF GOULD'S FUNCTION
      FUNCTION PHI(R)
      ..........
      END
```

The full definition of TAB is given earlier in this section and the
definition of PHI is given in section 7.2.1. The following points
about the program should be noted:

(i)   The subroutine TAB is called from the main program with the
ACTUAL FUNCTION ARGUMENT PHI. The name of this actual argument is
placed in an EXTERNAL statement which informs the compiler that PHI
is the name of an external subprogram.

(ii) A PARAMETER statement is used to define LL and LU (the lower
and upper bounds of the arrays). This makes the program slightly
more versatile since only the PARAMETER statement need be changed if
the arrays X and Y are not big enough for a particular set of data.

(iii) The order in which the DIMENSION, EXTERNAL and PARAMETER
statements occur in the main program is immaterial, as described in
appendix 3.

(iv) The order in which the subprograms TAB and PHI are positioned
is also immaterial.

7.5.2 EXTERNAL and INTRINSIC Statements

Whenever the name of a function or subroutine is to be used as an
actual argument, it must be specified in an EXTERNAL or INTRINSIC
statement in the calling program unit, as appropriate. An EXTERNAL
statement specifies that the actual argument is an external function
or subroutine and is of the form

        EXTERNAL list
where "list" is a list of names separated by commas. An INTRINSIC
statement specifies that the actual argument is an intrinsic function
and is of the form

        INTRINSIC list
where "list" is a list of names, separated by commas. There are
restrictions on the use of intrinsic functions as actual arguments.
The name used for the intrinsic function must be its SPECIFIC NAME
and not its GENERIC NAME, and certain functions may not be used as
arguments. Full details are given in appendix 1.

As an example, suppose that the subroutine TAB is used to tabulate
sin(x). Since SIN is an intrinsic function, the complete program
will be of the form shown on the next page. It should be noted that
the definition of SIN is not provided since SIN, being an intrinsic
function, is already part of the language.

The EXTERNAL statement may also be used when the name of an
external subprogram is identical to that of an intrinsic function.
The intrinsic function will always be used unless the name is
included in an external statement in the calling program unit, in
which case the external subprogram will be used and the intrinsic

function will not be available. This rule holds whether the name is
used   as   the   actual   argument   in the call of a subprogram or used
independently.   It is strongly recommended that the names of external
subprograms   are   chosen   to   be   <u>different</u>   from   those of intrinsic
functions.

```
PROGRAM EX77
INTRINSIC SIN
PARAMETER(LL=0,LU=100)
DIMENSION X(LL:LU),Y(LL:LU)
..........
CALL TAB(SIN,R0,R1,DR,N,X,Y,LL,LU)
..........
END
SUBROUTINE TAB(F,X0,X1,H,N,X,Y,LL,LU)
..........
END
```

7.6 COMMON BLOCKS AND BLOCK DATA SUBPROGRAMS

Under   normal   circumstances,   all   variables are purely LOCAL to the
program unit in which they are declared and used.   Arguments are used
to pass information from one program unit to another.   However, it is
possible to make information available to several, or all, program
units by means of COMMON BLOCKS. A variable stored in a common block
becomes GLOBAL to all program units which have access to that common
block.

   There are two types of common block. These are the NAMED COMMON
BLOCK, which has a name by which it is known in all program units
which specify it, and the BLANK COMMON BLOCK, which does not have a
name.   There may be several named common blocks in a complete program
but only one blank common block. The differences between the two
types of common block are considered in section 7.6.4. Both types
are specified by a COMMON statement, which is a non-executable
statement that must appear at the start of a program unit before any
executable statements.   A complete list of the order in which
statements may appear is given in appendix 3.

7.6.1 The COMMON Statement

This is of the form:
```
COMMON/name1/list1, /name2/list2, /.....
```
where "name1" and "name2" are the names given to the common blocks.
These must obey the usual rules for names but do not have a type

associated with them and must not be used for any other purpose in the program. Whenever a name is omitted, the blank common block is associated with the list. For example

COMMON /name1/list1, //list2, /...

associates "list2" with the blank common block. If "name1" is to be omitted, the statement may be abbreviated to

COMMON list1, /name2/list2, /...

where the two initial slashes have also been omitted. The commas in front of the slashes in the statement are optional and may be omitted. Each list may contain variable names and array names (with or without array bounds) each separated by commas. Dummy arguments and function names may not appear in a list. The common statement declares that the items in "list1" are in the common block with name "name1" and so on. In general, items of any type can appear in the same common block, with the important exception that CHARACTER variables are restricted to common blocks which only contain character variables, as described in chapter 8.

The following examples illustrate the use of COMMON statements.

COMMON /CB1/X,Y,Z /CB2/I,J,A(10,20) //P(100),Q(100),R(100)

specifies three common blocks, CB1, CB2 and blank common. CB1 contains three variables X, Y, Z and is of size 3 elements. CB2 contains two integer variables I, J and the array A. It is of size 202 elements. Blank common contains three arrays P, Q, R and is of size 300 elements. Although the array dimensions have been included in the COMMON statement, they could have been included in a type statement or DIMENSION statement. However, the array dimensions may not be specified in more than one statement. Thus the single COMMON statement could be replaced by the three statements

REAL A(10,20),Q(100)
COMMON /CB1/X,Y,Z /CB2/I,J,A //P,Q,R
DIMENSION P(100),R(100)

which may be in any order. However, it is probably easier for anyone reading the program if the REAL and DIMENSION statements occur before the COMMON statement.

COMMON X,Y,B(0:20),Z

specifies only blank common with three variables X, Y, Z and an array B. The common block is of size 24 elements.

COMMON I,J,A(10,20) /DATA/D1,D2,D3,D4,DAT(-5:100)

specifies that blank common contains I, J and the array A and is of size 202 elements; DATA contains variables D1, D2, D3, D4 and the array DAT and is of size 110 elements.

The name of a common block may appear more than once in a statement and the lists following successive occurrences are treated as continuations of each other. Thus the first example could be replaced by

      COMMON /CB1/X,Y/CB2/I,J/CB1/Z//P(100),Q(100)/CB2/A(10,20)//R(100)
which has the same effect. However, it is clear that this form of
statement is more confusing for someone reading the program and it is
not recommended! A program is easier to read if a separate COMMON
statement is used for the definition of each common block.

7.6.2 Association of Variables in COMMON BLOCKS

Any program unit which uses a variable contained in a common block
must specify the name of the block (or specify blank common) in a
COMMON statement in the program unit. If a named common block is
used, all COMMON statements that include that particular name must
contain lists associated with that name which imply the same number
of elements. However, the names given to the elements need not be
the same from one program unit to another. For example, the
statement

         COMMON/CB1/X,Y,A(100)
may occur in the main program, and the statement

         COMMON/CB1/Z(5),A(97)
may occur in the subprogram. Both references to the common block CB1
imply a size of 102 elements, but in the main program the first
element is called X, the second Y, the third A(1) and so on; whilst
in the subprogram the first element is called Z(1), the second Z(2),
the third Z(3) and so on. This means that A(1) in the main program
refers to the same storage location as Z(3) in the subprogram and
A(4) in the main program is referred to as A(1) in the subprogram.

     The names given to the elements of the common block are purely
local to the program unit, but the values are available to all
program units referencing common block CB1. Thus it is not the name
of the variable that is really important but the position in the list
in the COMMON statement. Obviously the elements have to be assigned
initial values before these values can be used anywhere else. This
can be done by ordinary assignment statements in the program units
referencing the common block or by means of a BLOCK DATA SUBPROGRAM,
as described in section 7.6.5. For blank common, the list in the
COMMON statement in different program units may imply a different
size, but the sequence of the elements is still determined by the
position in the list. For example, if the statement

         COMMON X,Y,A(100),B(50)
appears in the main program and the statement

         COMMON A,B,X(100)
appears in the subprogram, only the first 102 elements of blank
common, associated with the names A, B, X(1), ... , X(100), are

available for use in the subprogram.

Although the names used to reference the elements in a common block are local to the program unit, they must not imply a different type from one program unit to another. For example, the first element may not be referenced as an integer in one program unit and as a real number in another. It should be noted that the same variable may not be included in more than one common block within a program unit.

7.6.3 Example Program using a COMMON BLOCK

Here, program EX74 from section 7.4.1 is re-written so that the information for the function AVRGE is passed from the main program by means of a common block named INFO instead of by arguments, as in program EX74. The modified program is

```
        PROGRAM EX78
  CCCC  DRIVER PROGRAM FOR FUNCTION AVRGE
        COMMON /INFO/ N,X(100)
        READ *,N
        READ *,(X(I),I=1,N)
        AV=AVRGE()
        PRINT *,´ARRAY VALUES´
        PRINT *,(X(I),I=1,N)
        PRINT *
        PRINT *,´AVERAGE = ´,AV
        END
  CCCC  DEFINITION OF AVRGE, USING A COMMON BLOCK
        FUNCTION AVRGE()
        COMMON /INFO/ N,A
        DIMENSION A(100)
        SUM=0.0
        DO 10 I=1,N
           SUM=SUM+A(I)
     10 CONTINUE
        AVRGE=SUM/N
        END
```

The following points about the program should be noted:

(i)   In the main program the array is called X, whilst in the function definition the array is called A. Both names refer to the same storage space in the common block INFO. The DIMENSION statement in the subprogram could be absorbed into the COMMON statement as

```
        COMMON /INFO/N,A(100)
```

(ii)   The results produced by program EX78 are identical   to   those from program EX74.

(iii) There is no reason why blank common should not be used instead of named common for passing the information. If this were done, the statement in the main program would be modified to

COMMON N,X(100)

and the statement in the subprogram altered accordingly.

(iv) There is one important disadvantage to passing array information by means of common storage instead of by arguments. Variable size arrays are <u>not permitted</u> in a common block. Thus the flexibility of writing a subprogram which can be used with any size array in the calling program unit is lost.

7.6.4 Differences between NAMED and BLANK Common Blocks

Named and blank common blocks have the following differences:

(i) Execution of a RETURN or END statement sometimes causes elements in a named common block to become undefined, so that the values are not retained for the next reference to the common block. However this never causes elements in blank common to become undefined. Elements may become undefined when the named common block is specified in several subprogram units but not in the main program. In this case, the variables in the named common block are only preserved on exit from the subprogram if the common block name appears in a SAVE statement (described in chapter 10) in the subprogram or the subprogram is currently being referenced, directly or indirectly, by another program unit which also specifies this named common block. Since the main program references all subprograms, either directly or indirectly, all elements in named common blocks declared in the main program can never become undefined between calls of a subprogram.

(ii) All COMMON statements in different program units which refer to a particular named common block must imply the same size for the common block. The blank common block may be implied to have a different size by different program units.

(iii) No elements in any common block may be given initial values by means of a DATA statement in a main program unit, function subprogram or subroutine subprogram. However, elements in a named common block may be given initial values by means of a DATA statement in a BLOCK DATA SUBPROGRAM, whereas elements in blank common may not.

7.6.5 BLOCK DATA Subprograms

A BLOCK DATA SUBPROGRAM is used solely to initialise the elements in NAMED common blocks. It may not contain any executable statements.

The only statements permitted are IMPLICIT, PARAMETER, DIMENSION, COMMON, SAVE, EQUIVALENCE, DATA, END and type statements like INTEGER and REAL. The IMPLICIT, SAVE and EQUIVALENCE statements are described in chapter 10.

The first statement in a BLOCK DATA subprogram must be a BLOCK DATA STATEMENT. This is of the form

          BLOCK DATA name

where "name" is the name of the BLOCK DATA subprogram. As with any other subprogram, the name is global and should not be used for any other purpose in the program. The name may be omitted if desired, but there may be only one unnamed BLOCK DATA subprogram in a program. The subprogram must be terminated with an END statement. Each common block which is to have elements initialised must be declared in a COMMON statement in the subprogram. It is not necessary to initialise all elements in a common block but of course the COMMON statement must refer to all elements, since all references to the same named common block must imply the same size. A particular named common block may not be referred to in more than one BLOCK DATA subprogram.

Examples of BLOCK DATA subprograms are:

```
BLOCK DATA BD1
COMMON /CB1/A(100,100)
DATA (A(I,I),I=1,100)/100*1.0/
END
```

which has the name BD1 and sets all the diagonal elements of the two dimensional array A in the common block CB1 to 1.0 and leaves all other elements undefined.

```
BLOCK DATA
PARAMETER (N=100)
DIMENSION P(N),Q(N),R(N)
COMMON /CB2/X,Y,Z/CB3/P,Q,R
DATA X,P,(Q(I),I=1,N)/1.4142,N*0.0,N*-1.0/
END
```

is an unnamed BLOCK DATA subprogram which initialises some elements of common blocks CB2 and CB3. It should be noted that that N is the symbolic name of a constant which is given a value by the PARAMETER statement and which is used in both the DIMENSION and DATA statements. The array P is given initial values by just mentioning its name, whereas the array Q appears in an implied DO loop – both constructions have the same effect here.

7.6.6 Example Program with a BLOCK DATA Subprogram

With big programs, it is fairly common to have some data which does not change for different runs of the program within a given project, such as the data specifying a complicated body shape or structure. This data is usually held in arrays which may be initialised by a BLOCK DATA subprogram.

A rather simple example can be developed from the salesman problem discussed in programs EX59 and EX68. Instead of reading the coordinates of the towns as data, it will be assumed that the distances between the towns are already known so that the distance matrix DIST can be initialised in an unnamed BLOCK DATA subprogram. The data for any particular run of the program will consist only of the towns to be visited, this information being stored in the array ROUTE as before. The total number of towns is held by the constant DIM which is used to set the array bounds in the DIMENSION statements. The arrays DIST and ROUTE are held in a common block called CBLOCK. The total distance travelled is calculated in a subroutine SUMDIS which accesses CBLOCK and also has arguments K (the number of different towns on the specified route), TDIST (the total distance of the specified route) and FLAG (which is set to zero before the call of SUMDIS and is reset to 1 within the subroutine if the specified route is invalid). TDIST and FLAG are used to carry information back to the main program.

The complete program is given below

```
      PROGRAM EX79
 CCCC  DISTANCES TRAVELLED BY A SALESMAN
      INTEGER ROUTE,DIM,FLAG
      PARAMETER (DIM=4)
      COMMON /CBLOCK/ DIST(DIM,DIM),ROUTE(DIM+1)
   15 READ *,K
      IF (K .EQ. 0) STOP
      READ *,(ROUTE(I),I=1,K)
      K1=K+1
      ROUTE(K1)=ROUTE(1)
      PRINT 100,(ROUTE(I),I=1,K1)
      FLAG=0
      CALL SUMDIS(K,TDIST,FLAG)
      IF (FLAG .EQ. 1) THEN
         PRINT 101
         GOTO 15
      ENDIF
      PRINT 102,TDIST
```

```
          GOTO 15
  100 FORMAT(' ROUTE IS FROM ',I2,17(' TO ',I2:))
  101 FORMAT(' THIS ROUTE IS NOT VALID.')
  102 FORMAT(' TOTAL DISTANCE TRAVELLED IS ',F10.4,
     1   ' KILOMETRES.')
      END
CCCC  SUBPROGRAM TO CALCULATE THE TOTAL DISTANCE
      SUBROUTINE SUMDIS(K,TDIST,FLAG)
      INTEGER DIM,ROUTE,FLAG
      PARAMETER (DIM=4)
      COMMON /CBLOCK/ DIST(DIM,DIM),ROUTE(DIM+1)
      DO 10 I=1,K
         IF (ROUTE(I) .LT. 1 .OR. ROUTE(I) .GT. DIM) THEN
            FLAG=1
            RETURN
         ENDIF
   10 CONTINUE
      TDIST=0.0
      DO 11 I=1,K
         TDIST=TDIST+DIST(ROUTE(I),ROUTE(I+1))
   11 CONTINUE
      END
CCCC  SUBPROGRAM TO INITIALISE THE DISTANCE MATRIX
      BLOCK DATA
      INTEGER DIM,ROUTE
      PARAMETER (DIM=4)
      COMMON /CBLOCK/ DIST(DIM,DIM),ROUTE(DIM+1)
      DATA ((DIST(I,J),J=1,4),I=1,4) /
     1   0.0, 7.211103, 9.486833, 2.236068,
     2   7.211103, 0.0, 7.615773, 9.219544,
     3   9.486833, 7.615773, 0.0, 10.04988,
     4   2.236068, 9.219544, 10.04988, 0.0 /
      END
```

The results obtained are the same as those from program EX68.

7.7 LIBRARY SUBPROGRAMS

It is common practice for computer systems to have available
libraries of subroutines and functions which perform many of the
standard calculations in mathematics, numerical analysis, statistics
and other specialist fields. The library subprograms have usually
been designed by experts in the particular field and have been
rigorously tested to ensure that they perform as expected. Two

commonly available libraries are NAG (produced by Numerical
Algorithms Group Ltd, Oxford) which contains a comprehensive set of
numerical and statistical routines and GINO (produced by the Computer
Aided Design Centre, Cambridge) which contains graphical routines.

When a program to carry out a particular task has to be written,
the programmer can consult the library manuals to find whether there
are any subprograms which perform some of the required operations.
The library manual should contain a detailed description of what a
particular subprogram is designed to do, together with details of all
arguments required and possibly test data and results. The method by
which library subroutines are made available to the program depends
on the implementation, but once available, any library subprogram is
used in the program in exactly the same way that a subprogram
provided by the programmer would be used. Full details of what
libraries are available and how they may be used should be obtainable
from the advisory service of the computer installation.

7.7.1 Example using a Library Subprogram

As an example of the use of a LIBRARY SUBPROGRAM, a NAG library
subprogram called C05ADF is used to find a root of the equation
$$\cos(x) - x = 0$$
which lies in the interval (0.7,0.8). The specification of the
subprogram states that there are 7 arguments, given the dummy names
A, B, EPS, ETA, F, X, IFAIL. A and B are the endpoints of the
interval in which the root is known to lie and F is the name of the
external function which defines the equation whose root is to be
found, in this case
$$F(X)=COS(X)-X$$
The method for finding the root is based on a simple iterative
process, but incorporates some refinements to ensure that convergence
occurs within a limited number of iterations (provided that the
function does indeed have a root in the given interval and that the
computer works to sufficient precision to achieve the requested
accuracy). The process is terminated when either two successive
approximations differ by an amount less than EPS or when the absolute
value of F at the approximate root is less than ETA. Values for EPS
and ETA are provided as data and determine the accuracy to which the
root is to be found. The argument X is used to return the value of
the root. IFAIL is the standard NAG error-handling argument. In
this example it is initially set to 1 which indicates that the
subprogram must return control to the calling program if an error
occurs. If the computation in the subprogram is successful, IFAIL is
set to 0. However, if something is wrong, it is set to the value 1,

2, 3 or 4, depending upon the nature of the error.   The subprogram
specification gives a description of the conditions which give rise
to the different failure numbers.   For instance, a value of 1
indicates that either EPS $\leq$ 0, or A = B or that the value of F at the
two ends of the interval (A,B) has the same sign.
   A driver program to run the NAG library subprogram C05ADF is

```
          PROGRAM EX710
    CCCC  DRIVER PROGRAM FOR NAG LIBRARY SUBPROGRAM C05ADF
          EXTERNAL F
          READ *,A,B,EPS,ETA
          PRINT 100,A,B,EPS,ETA
          IFAIL=1
    CCCC  USE OF LIBRARY SUBROUTINE
          CALL C05ADF(A,B,EPS,ETA,F,X,IFAIL)
    CCCC  CHECK WHETHER THE ROUTINE HAS WORKED
          IF (IFAIL .NE. 0) THEN
              PRINT *,´ AN ERROR CONDITION HAS OCCURRED IN C05ADF´
              PRINT *,´ THE VALUE OF IFAIL IS ´,IFAIL
              STOP
          ENDIF
    CCCC  OUTPUT THE ROOT AND THE VALUE OF F AT THE ROOT
          F1=F(X)
          PRINT 101, X,F1
      100 FORMAT(´ ROOTFINDING PROGRAM USING C05ADF´//
         1    ´ THE ROOT LIES IN THE INTERVAL´,F10.4,´ TO´,F10.4/
         2    ´ THE PROCESS WILL STOP WHEN EITHER´/´ X(N+1)-X(N)<´,F12.8,
         3    ´ OR F(X(N+1))<´,F12.8/)
      101 FORMAT(´ ROOT X=´,F12.8,5X,´F(X)=´,F12.8)
          END
    CCCC  FUNCTION DEFINING THE EQUATION WHOSE ROOT IS REQUIRED
          FUNCTION F(X)
          F=COS(X)-X
          END
```

When run with the data values A = 0.7, B = 0.8, EPS = 0.5E-6 and
ETA = 0.5E-6 the results were

```
ROOTFINDING PROGRAM USING C05ADF

THE ROOT LIES IN THE INTERVAL   0.7000 TO     0.8000
THE PROCESS WILL STOP WHEN EITHER
X(N+1)-X(N)<  0.00000050 OR F(X(N+1))<  0.00000050
ROOT X=  0.73908505     F(X)=  0.00000015
```

7.8 EXERCISES

1.   FORTRAN 77 contains the intrinsic function SQRT but does not
contain an intrinsic function for calculating the cube root. Write a
function subprogram called CUBRT, having a single real argument X.
The method used for the calculation of the cube root should be that
described in section 4.5.2.

2.   In many experiments it is necessary to find the equation of the
straight line that most closely fits a set of data points. The usual
technique is to use the method of least squares, which states that
the best straight line fit, in the least squares sense, to the set of
data points $(x_1,y_1),\ldots,(x_n,y_n)$ is $y = ax + b$, where

$$a = \frac{N\sum(x_iy_i) - \sum x_i\sum y_i}{N\sum x_i^2 - (\sum x_i)^2} \qquad b = \frac{\sum x_i^2\sum y_i - \sum x_i\sum(x_iy_i)}{N\sum x_i^2 - (\sum x_i)^2}$$

the summations being taken over all "n" data points.

   (i)   Write a function subprogram called SUMX(X,N) where X is a
one-dimensional array, with lower limit 1, and N is the number of
elements occupied. SUMX returns the sum of all the occupied elements
of X, that is
   SUMX(X,N) = X(1) + X(2) + ... + X(N)
   (ii) Write a function subprogram SUMXY(X,Y,N) where X and Y are
one-dimensional arrays, both with lower limit 1, which have N
elements occupied.   SUMXY produces the scalar product of the
elements, that is
   SUMXY(X,Y,N) = X(1)*Y(1) + X(2)*Y(2) + ... + X(N)*Y(N)
   (iii) Use these functions in a main program which
   (a) Reads an integer N and N pairs of real numbers (x_i,y_i) which
are stored in the one-dimensional arrays X and Y respectively. It
may be assumed that $N \leq 200$.
   (b) Calculates the coefficients "a" and "b" in the least squares
straight line approximation y = ax + b to the set of data points. It
should be noted that in the equations for "a" and "b", a number of
quantities appear more than once: it would be inefficient to
calculate them more than once.
   (c) Prints the values of "a" and "b" (correct to six decimal
places) with suitable captions and a table with four columns X, Y, Z,
E.   X and Y are the original data values, Z=aX+b is the approximation
to Y produced from the straight line fit and E is the error in this
approximation, that is E=Y-Z. Suitable headings should be printed
and each number in the table should be printed correct to six decimal

places, with the exception of the entries in the E column which should be printed in E format with four significant digits.

Specimen Data: N=11, (0,0.047) (0.1,0.270) (0.2,0.476) (0.3,0.702) (0.4,0.910)   (0.5,1.106)   (0.6,1.350)   (0.7,1.560)   (0.8,1.742) (0.9,1.994) (1.0,2.182)

3.   The   path   of a satellite describing a plane elliptic orbit round the earth may be plotted from the coordinates (x,y) of its position at equal time intervals.   The   coordinates of the next position (x_{n+1},y_{n+1}) may be calculated from the coordinates of the present position (x_n,y_n) and the previous position (x_{n-1},y_{n-1}) by the formulae:

$$x_{n+1} = 2x_n + x_{n-1}d \qquad y_{n+1} = 2y_n + y_{n-1}d$$

$$\text{where } d = (x_{n-1}^2 + y_{n-1}^2)^{-1.5} - 1$$

Write a subroutine called SATPSN which will calculate the coordinates of the next position from those of the present and previous positions.

Incorporate the subroutine into a main program which reads an integer N and two sets of successive position coordinates (x_1,y_1) and (x_2,y_2) and which calculates and prints these original two   positions and the N subsequent ones.

Specimen Data: N=20, (x_1,y_1)=(7.5,0), (x_2,y_2)=(7.35,0.0136)

4.   (i) Write a subroutine called POLY which has as input arguments an integer N, a one-dimensional array   A   (holding   the   coefficients $a_0,a_1,\ldots,a_N$ of a polynomial of degree N) and a real value X and as output arguments FX (the value of the polynomial at X) and FDASH (the value of the first derivative of the polynomial at X).   The method used to calculate FX and FDASH may be based on program EX55,   section 5.6.3.

(ii) Use the subprogram POLY with a main program which

(a) Reads an integer N and the coefficients of an N-th degree polynomial, to be stored in a one-dimensional array with lower limit zero.

(b) Reads a real value X (an approximation to a root of the polynomial), a real value EPS (to specify the accuracy with which the root should be found) and an integer NMAX (to specify the maximum number of iterations that may be used to find the root).

(c) Calculates a sequence of successive approximations to the root of the polynomial, using the relationship that if XO is an approximation to a root of f(x)=0 then, in general, a better approximation is:

X1 = X0 - DX0   where   DX0 = f(X0)/f´(X0).

The sequence of approximations should be stopped when either
|DX0|<EPS or NMAX iterations have been made. In the first case, the
value of the root is taken to be the last approximation produced and
in the second case a message indicating that the root has not been
found should be output.

(d) Prints a list of the polynomial coefficients, the values used
for EPS and NMAX and either the value of the root or the message that
the root has not been found.

Specimen Data: $x^3 - 3x+1$, X=2.0, EPS=0.000005, NMAX=50

5. In section 5.6.2 a method of sorting an array of values into
descending order was described and implemented in program EX54.

(i) Write a subroutine called SORTD which has two arguments N (an
integer) and A (a one-dimensional array with lower limit 1) and which
sorts the N elements of A into descending order.

(ii) Write a second subroutine SORTA with the same arguments as
SORTD but which sorts the array into ascending order.

(iii) Write a driver program to test your subroutines. It should
read an integer N and N values into an array. These values should be
copied into a second array and the two identical arrays should be
sorted, one by SORTA and the other by SORTD. The original order of
the data and the two sorted orders should be printed.

(iv) Write a subroutine SORT(K,N,A) which combines the effects of
both SORTA and SORTD. The argument K is an integer which is set to
+1 if the elements are to be sorted in ascending order and to -1 if
the elements are to be sorted in descending order.

(v) Write a driver program to test SORT(K,N,A).

Specimen Data: N=6, array values 47.18, 64.42, 21.06,
19.98,-4.36,21.06

6. (i) Two MxN matrices A and B may be added together to produce a
MxN matrix C, where the elements of C are defined by

C(I,J)=A(I,J)+B(I,J)   where I=1,2,...,M and J=1,2,...,N

Write a subroutine called MATADD(A,B,C,M,N,LU) which will perform
matrix addition, where A, B, C are two-dimensional arrays all of the
same size with lower limits 1 and upper limit for the first dimension
LU. In each array, M rows and N columns are occupied.

(ii) In section 7.4.3, example 3, the construction of a subroutine
MATMLT to multiply two matrices was discussed. Write the complete
subroutine given the following definition of matrix multiplication:

An LxM matrix A multiplies an MxN matrix B to produce an LxN matrix
C, where the elements of C are given by

$$C(I,J)=A(I,1)*B(1,J)+A(I,2)*B(2,J)+\ldots+A(I,M)*B(M,J)$$

$$= \sum_{K=1}^{M} A(I,K)*B(K,J) \qquad I=1,2,\ldots,L \qquad J=1,2,\ldots,N$$

(iii) Write a driver program, to test the subroutines, which

(a) Reads three integers L, M, N and then an LxN matrix X, an LxM matrix Y and an MxN matrix Z. These matrices should be stored in two-dimensional arrays in the main program of size 10x10. Output the elements of the matrices X, Y, Z for reference purposes.

(b) Uses the subroutines to calculate the matrix P=X+YZ and then prints the elements of P.

Specimen Data:

$$X=\begin{bmatrix} 7 & -4 & 7 \\ 3 & 9 & -9 \end{bmatrix} \qquad Y=\begin{bmatrix} 4 & -6 & 0 & -5 \\ 2 & 9 & -2 & 7 \end{bmatrix} \qquad Z=\begin{bmatrix} -6 & 9 & 7 \\ 1 & -5 & 8 \\ 6 & 1 & -9 \\ 2 & 7 & 3 \end{bmatrix}$$

7. (i) Write a function SIMINT(F,A,B,N) which approximates the integral of the function f(x) over the range A to B using Simpson's Rule with N intervals. Here, F is an external function subprogram which defines the integrand f(x). Simpson's Rule is as follows:

$$\int_{A}^{B} f(x)\,dx = \frac{H}{3}(f_0+4f_1+2f_2+\ldots+2f_{N-2}+4f_{N-1}+f_N)$$

where $f_i=f(A+iH)$ and $H=(B-A)/N$.

(ii) Write a driver program, to test the function, which

(a) Reads the limits of integration A and B and the number of intervals N for the Simpson integration. N must be even for Simpson's Rule, so a test should be incorporated which rejects an odd value.

(b) Prints the values of A, B and N and calculates and prints the approximate value of the integral.

It should be noted that the external function F, defining the integrand, will also have to be written and included as part of the complete program.

Specimen Data: $f(x)=\log_e(1+e^x)$ A=0, B=1.2, N=20

8. Repeat question 6 above, incorporating the arrays in a common block instead of passing them as arguments of the subroutines.

CHAPTER 8
CHARACTER MANIPULATION

Up to this point, the emphasis has been on the manipulation of numeric data. However, as was stated in chapter 1, a computer can store and manipulate character information stored in a suitably coded form. Most commercial applications involve information which is both numeric and non-numeric. For example, a simple personnel file will probably contain the name of each employee as well as a man number. Although FORTRAN was initially designed as a language for numerical work, FORTRAN 77 possesses in addition extensive character handling facilities. This makes it a more suitable language for character manipulation than its predecessors.

8.1 CHARACTER CONSTANTS AND VARIABLES

In chapter 2, three types of constant were introduced. These were the character constant, the real constant and the integer constant. Character constants have since been used only in connection with the output of text, either in PRINT statements or in FORMAT statements associated with PRINT statements.

In fact, character constants can be stored in a similar way to real and integer constants. To do this requires a special type of variable called a CHARACTER VARIABLE. All character variables must be declared at the start of a program unit by a CHARACTER STATEMENT, since there is no implicit type convention for them. In addition the statement indicates to the compiler the number of characters that are stored as the value of the character variable, that is, the LENGTH of the character variable.

8.1.1 Example Program

At this point, it is useful to consider a simple program which uses a character variable.

```
PROGRAM EX81
CHARACTER SIGN*8
DO 11 I=1,6
   READ *,NUMBER
   IF (NUMBER.GT.0) THEN
      SIGN='POSITIVE'
   ELSEIF (NUMBER.LT.0) THEN
      SIGN='NEGATIVE'
   ELSE
      SIGN='ZERO'
   ENDIF
   PRINT 100,NUMBER,SIGN
11 CONTINUE
100 FORMAT (1X,I6,' IS ',A)
   END
```

In this program, a character variable SIGN, which holds a maximum of 8 characters, is defined. A DO loop is performed six times and in each cycle an integer variable, NUMBER, is assigned a value read from an input record. The value of NUMBER is then checked to see if it is positive, negative or zero. If it is positive, the character string 'POSITIVE' is assigned to the character variable SIGN by means of the CHARACTER ASSIGNMENT STATEMENT

```
SIGN='POSITIVE'
```

If the value of NUMBER is negative, 'NEGATIVE' is assigned to SIGN; while if it is zero, 'ZERO' is assigned to SIGN. The values of the variables NUMBER and SIGN are then output in an appropriate format.
  When supplied with the data records

```
12
654321
-543
0
-1
7
```

the program produced the output

```
    12 IS POSITIVE
654321 IS POSITIVE
  -543 IS NEGATIVE
     0 IS ZERO
    -1 IS NEGATIVE
     7 IS POSITIVE
```

It should be noted that when SIGN is assigned the value 'ZERO' the extra four character positions are treated as blanks, so that the value assigned to SIGN is ´ZERO^^^^´.

This program includes a CHARACTER STATEMENT, a simple CHARACTER ASSIGNMENT STATEMENT and a statement which outputs a character variable. These statements are considered in detail in the following sections.

8.1.2 The CHARACTER Statement

Every name used for a character variable <u>must</u> be declared in a CHARACTER STATEMENT, which is a type statement similar to the REAL statement and the INTEGER statement described in chapter 2. However, the CHARACTER statement specifies not only the names of the character variables used by the program unit in which they appear, but also the length of the character string each is to hold.

The general form of a CHARACTER statement is

        CHARACTER list

where "list" consists of a list of character variables and character array names together with the number of characters which the character variable is to hold. This is normally attached to each element of the "list" by *n, as in program EX81, where "n" is an integer constant (or integer constant expression contained in brackets) indicating the number of characters the character variable is to hold. If no *n is present, a default value of 1 is assumed. When a number of character variables have the same length, the length can be specified by including *n after CHARACTER. This is then the default value. If a different length is required for any variable in the list, the length must be included explicitly.

For example, the statement

        CHARACTER*6 A,B,C*8

specifies that A and B are to have the "default" length of 6 and C is to have length 8, whereas the statement

        CHARACTER A,B,C*8

indicates that A and B are of length 1 and C is again of length 8.

Character array names are defined in a similar way to real and integer array names, except that the number of characters held by each element of the array must be specified in the character statement. All array elements have the same character length. As an example, the two statements

        DIMENSION ALPHA(3)

        CHARACTER ALPHA*6

allocate the three character array elements ALPHA(1), ALPHA(2) and ALPHA(3), each of which is of length six characters. As with the REAL and INTEGER type statements, the same effect can be produced by declaring the size of the array in the CHARACTER statement, that is

        CHARACTER ALPHA(3)*6

The *6 may alternatively be attached to CHARACTER, that is

        CHARACTER*6 ALPHA(3)

It should be noted that character arrays and character variables may
appear in the same CHARACTER statement. An example of this is

        DIMENSION A(-1:1)

        CHARACTER*4 X,Y,A*2,Z*8,B(0:2,-3:-2)

These statements declare three character variables X, Y and Z of
lengths four characters, four characters and eight characters
respectively; array elements A(-1), A(0) and A(1), each of which is
of length two characters; and array elements B(0,-3), B(1,-3),
B(2,-3), B(0,-2), B(1,-2) and B(2,-2), each of which is of length
four characters.

8.1.3 Character Assignment Statements

Program EX81 used the three simple CHARACTER ASSIGNMENT STATEMENTS

        SIGN='POSITIVE'

        SIGN='NEGATIVE'

        SIGN='ZERO'

The effect of these statements is to give the values 'POSITIVE',
'NEGATIVE' and 'ZERO^^^^' respectively to the character variable
SIGN, where ^ represents a blank character.

  The general form of a character assignment statement is

        character variable = character expression

The simplest form of a character expression is a character variable
or a character constant. More general character expressions are
described in section 8.3.

  It may happen that the number of characters specified for the
character variable on the left-hand side of a character assignment
statement is not the same as the number of characters which result
from the character expression on the right-hand side.   For   example,
assuming that the character variable SIGN has been specified to be of
length eight, as in program EX81, the right-hand side of the
statement

        SIGN='ZERO'

is shorter than the length of SIGN, while the right hand side of

        SIGN='OVER^ZERO'

is of length nine characters. This includes the blank character,
which is significant in a character string, and is thus longer than
the length of SIGN. In cases like this, the assignment takes place
character by character, starting from the left.   If the character
expression is too short for the character variable, blank characters

are stored in the extra positions. Conversely, if the character
expression is too long for the character variable, the expression is
truncated, so that successive characters are removed from the right-
hand end until the expression is the same length as the character
variable. Hence, in the above two examples, SIGN is given the value
´ZERO^^^^´ as a result of
        SIGN=´ZERO´
and the value ´OVER^ZER´ as a result of
        SIGN=´OVER^ZERO´
  As another example of this, the statements
        CHARACTER S,SIGN*8
        SIGN=´PLUS´
        S=SIGN
        SIGN=S
declare two character variables S of length one (by default) and SIGN
of length eight.   SIGN is given the value ´PLUS^^^^´, since the
character string is automatically padded out with blank characters.
In the second assignment, the character string now in SIGN is
truncated from the right to one character and S contains the string
´P´.   In the third assignment statement the character string in S is
padded out with blank characters when the assignment to SIGN is made,
so that the value of SIGN is ´P^^^^^^^´.

8.1.4 PARAMETER and DATA Statements

As described in section 2.7, a constant may be given a symbolic name
by means of a PARAMETER statement.   The only constants considered
then were real and integer numbers.   It is also possible for a
character string to be given a symbolic name.   For example, the
statements
        CHARACTER NAME*4,BLANK*3
        PARAMETER (NAME=´FRED´,BLANK=´^^^^´)
give the symbolic name NAME to the string ´FRED´ and the symbolic
name BLANK to the string ´^^^^´, where ^ represents a blank character.
  In section 2.8, it was shown how to initialise variables by means
of a DATA statement. Again, the only variables considered in that
section were numeric, but character variables may be initialised in a
similar way. Thus the statements
        CHARACTER ALFBET*26,NAME(6)*5
        DATA ALFBET,NAME / ´ABCDEFGHIJKLMNOPQRSTUVWXYZ´,
     1   6*´JAMES´ /
initialise the character variable ALFBET with the 26 characters of
the alphabet and each of the six elements of the character array NAME
with the string ´JAMES´.

8.2 INPUT AND OUTPUT OF CHARACTER VARIABLES

As with numeric data, character data can be input or output by either list-directed or formatted READ and PRINT statements. It is recommended that the formatted form, which uses the A-format edit descriptor, is used for output rather than the list-directed form. This is because the layout of list-directed output is dependent on the implementation. The form of input used depends on how the data is presented to the program, but it is to be expected that formatted input will be used in most cases.

8.2.1 Formatted Input and Output

Character data is input and output by statements which are similar to numeric input and output statements. The difference is that the A-format edit descriptor described in section 6.4.5 is used to describe the layout of the data. The normal form of this edit descriptor is

A

and the effect is that the number of characters specified by the length of the character variable is transferred to or from the store of the computer. As an example, the statements

        CHARACTER CHAR*4
        READ 100,CHAR
    100 FORMAT (A)

when used with the data record

    ABCDEFGH

result in CHAR being given the value ˊABCDˊ.

  Similarly, the statements

        CHARACTER CHAR*4
        PRINT 100,CHAR
    100 FORMAT (1X,A)

with CHAR having the value ˊABCDˊ produce the output

    ABCD

It should be noted that the edit descriptor 1X is used to provide the carriage control character at the start of the output record.

  In section 6.4.5, the alternative form of the A-format edit descriptor

    Aw

where "w" specifies the field width was described. In this case, if "w" is the same as the length of the character variable being input or output, the result of using this edit descriptor is the same as if "w" were not present. However, if there is incompatibility between "w" and the length of the character variable, the input or output is determined by the following rules.

On INPUT, if the receiving variable has length "n", the last "n" characters read are used. When there are less than "n" characters read, the string is padded out with blanks. That is, if "n" is GREATER than "w", "w" characters are read from the data record and then "n-w" blank characters are added at the right-hand end of the field to make up the full "n" characters. This is similar to what happens with an assignment statement, as described in section 8.1.3. For example, the statements

        CHARACTER CHAR*4

        READ 100,CHAR

   100 FORMAT (A2)

when used with the data record

   ABCDEFGH

result in CHAR being given the value ´AB^^´. However, if "n" is LESS than "w", the right-most "n" characters are taken from the data record and the first "w-n" characters are lost. It should be noted that this is the exact opposite to what happens with an assignment statement. For example, the statements

        CHARACTER CHAR*4

        READ 100,CHAR

   100 FORMAT (A6)

when used with the data record

   ABCDEFGH

result in CHAR being given the value ´CDEF´.

On OUTPUT, characters are inserted in the output field until it is full. If there are insufficient characters to fill the output field, additional blanks are used. That is, if the number of characters to be output is GREATER than "w", only the left-most "w" characters from the character string will be printed. It should be noted that this is the exact opposite of what happens on input. As an example of this, consider

        CHARACTER CHAR*4

        PRINT 100,CHAR

   100 FORMAT (1X,A2)

If the value of CHAR is ´ABCD´, the output will be

   AB

However, if "n" is LESS than "w", "w-n" blank characters are inserted before the character string to make up the "w" characters to be output. For example, the statements

        CHARACTER CHAR*4

        PRINT 100,CHAR

   100 FORMAT (1X,A6)

with CHAR having the value ´ABCD´, produce the output

    ^^ABCD

The discrepancy between input and output in the case where the number
of characters being transferred is greater than the number of
character positions available means that it is advisable to take
great care to make sure that the two quantities are the same.

When a number of values are to be read from the same data record,
the READ statement is similar to the corresponding numeric case. For
example, the statements

        CHARACTER*6 CH1,CH2,CH3,CH4*3,CH5
        READ 100,CH1,CH2,CH3,CH4,CH5
   100 FORMAT (5A)

when used with the data record

   ABCDEFGHIJKLMNOPQRSTUWXYZA

result in CH1, CH2, CH3, CH4 and CH5 being given the values ´ABCDEF´,
´GHIJKL´, ´MNOPQR´, ´STU´ and ´WXYZA´ respectively. Note that, even
though the character variables have different lengths, it is not
necessary to take account of this in the FORMAT statement. This is
because no field width is included in the A-format edit descriptor.

Character arrays are input and output in a similar way to numeric
arrays. For example, the statements

        CHARACTER TOWN(3)*8
        READ 100,(TOWN(I),I=1,3)
        PRINT 101,(TOWN(I),I=1,3)
   100 FORMAT (3A8)
   101 FORMAT (1X,A8)

when used with the data record

   SALFORD^HULL^^^^DERBY

will store the strings ´SALFORD^´, ´HULL^^^^´ and ´DERBY^^^´ in the
character array elements TOWN(1), TOWN(2) and TOWN(3) respectively.
The output will be

   SALFORD^
   HULL^^^^
   DERBY^^^

since the PRINT statement only specifies one A-format edit descriptor
per line. In this case, the field width specifier (8 in the example)
in the FORMAT statements is redundant, since exactly the same effect
would be produced if it were omitted. It should be noted that if the
data record had been

   SALFORD^HULL^DERBY

the values given to TOWN(1), TOWN(2) and TOWN(3) would have been
´SALFORD^´, ´HULL^DER´ and ´BY^^^^^^´ respectively. This illustrates
the necessity, when formatted input is being used, of character data
being precisely arranged on the data record.

Character data and numeric data may appear on the same data record

and be read by a single input statement. Likewise, character and
numeric data may be output by a single statement. The statements

```
      CHARACTER TOWN(2)*8
      INTEGER DIST
      READ 100,(TOWN(I),I=1,2),DIST
      PRINT 101,(TOWN(I),I=1,2),DIST
  100 FORMAT (2A,I4)
  101 FORMAT (1X,A,´ TO ´,A,´ IS ´,I4,´ MILES´)
```

when used with the input data record

    LONDON^^SALFORD^^197

produce the following line of output

    LONDON^^^TO^SALFORD^^IS^^197^MILES

As a further example of the way strings are truncated as a result of
including the field width in the A-format edit descriptor, consider
the statements

```
      CHARACTER TEXT*25
      READ 100,TEXT
      PRINT 101,TEXT
  100 FORMAT (A40)
  101 FORMAT (1X,A10)
```

In these statements, the character variable TEXT is defined to be of
length 25 characters. If the input data record is

    THIS^IS^A^STRING^OF^LENGTH^40^CHARACTERS

the character variable TEXT is given a value of

    ´G^OF^LENGTH^40^CHARACTERS´

as a result of the READ statement. This is because the discrepancy
between the field width specified in the FORMAT statement and the
length of the CHARACTER variable causes only the last 25 characters
to be stored. The PRINT statement then outputs the characters

    G^OF^LENGT

Again, this is because of the discrepancy between the field width and
the length of the character variable.

8.2.2 List-directed Input and Output

List-directed input is produced by a statement of the form

```
      READ *,list
```

where "list" is a list of variables or their equivalents as described
in earlier chapters. Character data on an input record which is   to
be read using list-directed input <u>must</u> be in the form of a character
string. This means that the apostrophes which precede and terminate
the string <u>must</u> be present. As an example, consider the statements

```
      CHARACTER*3 A,B
      READ *,A,I,B,Q
```

With the data record
     ´DOG´ 25 ´CAT´ 2.345
the effect is that A, I, B and Q are given values ´DOG´, 25, ´CAT´
and 2.345 respectively.   If the apostrophes were not present, a
failure would occur.

    As with formatted input, it is possible for the number of
characters in the string on the data record to be different from the
length of the character variable.   In the case of list-directed
input, the rule is precisely the same as for assignment.

    The list-directed output statement
          PRINT *,list
prints out a character string for each of the character variables
specified in the "list", no apostrophes being printed.
As an example of list-directed input and output, consider the
statements
          CHARACTER TOWN*7
          READ *,TOWN
          PRINT *,TOWN
When presented with the data record
     ´SALFORD´
these give the character variable TOWN the value ´SALFORD´ and print
     SALFORD
Character data may be read into and printed from character arrays
using list-directed input and output, as the following example
illustrates.   The statements
          CHARACTER TOWN(3)*8
          READ *,(TOWN(I),I=1,3)
          PRINT *,(TOWN(I),I=1,3)
when presented with the data record
     ´SALFORD´ ´HULL´ ´DERBY´
cause the variables TOWN(1), TOWN(2) and TOWN(3) to be given values
´SALFORD^^´, ´HULL^^^^^´ and ´DERBY^^^´. The output is
     SALFORD^^HULL^^^^^DERBY
It should be noted that, when a character constant is printed using
list directed output it is not enclosed within apostrophes.

8.3 CHARACTER EXPRESSIONS

The simplest form of character expression, as described in section
8.1.3, is a character constant or a character variable. These are
called CHARACTER PRIMARIES. Other character primaries are symbolic
names of character constants, character array elements, character
substrings and character function references.   Character expressions
may be constructed by combining character primaries by means of the

CHARACTER OPERATOR //.

The general form of a character expression is one of

character primary

character primary // character expression

where the character operator // indicates the CONCATENATION (or joining together) of the terms on either side of the operator.

The effect of concatenation can be illustrated by the following examples. The character expression

´AB´//´CD´

produces the character string ´ABCD´. Similarly, the character expression

´TH´//´REE´

produces the string ´THREE´. If the character variable FRED has the value ´ISTMAS´, the result of the character expression

´CHR´//FRED

is the string ´CHRISTMAS´.

In any character expression involving more than one character operator, the character primaries are combined from left to right to establish the interpretation of the expression. Thus the character expression

´CHR´//´IST´//´MAS´

also produces the string ´CHRISTMAS´. This character expression is considered equivalent to the character primary ´CHR´ concatenated with the character expression

´IST´//´MAS´

A character expression enclosed within brackets is regarded as a character primary. However, the brackets have no effect on the value of the character expression. Thus for example,

´CHR´//(´IST´//´MAS´) and (´CHR´//´IST´)//´MAS´

are both interpreted as ´CHRISTMAS´.

Character expressions may be stored in character variables by means of character assignment statements, as described in section 8.1.3. For example, the statements

          CHARACTER CH1*3

          CH1=´AB´//´CD´

result in the character expression ´ABCD´ being assigned to the character variable CH1. This has been specified to have length three characters, so that the character string ´ABCD´ is truncated and CH1 given the value ´ABC´. Similarly, the statements

          CHARACTER CH1*5,CH2*2,CH3*3

          CH2=´AB´

          CH3=´CDE´

          CH1=CH2//CH3

result in CH2 being given the value ´AB´, CH3 being given the value

´CDE´ and CH1 being given the value ´ABCDE´.

8.3.1 Example Program

The program described in this section reads a name and address as data, where the first character of each line is in the first position of each data record. It then prints out the name and address, with the start of each line of output indented three places more to the right than the previous line of output. It is assumed that the maximum length of any line is 60 characters and the maximum number of lines is 6.

```
        PROGRAM EX82
        CHARACTER Y*75,Z*75
        READ 100,N
        IF (N.GT.6) STOP
        DO 11 I=1,N
            READ 101,Y
            DO 12 J=1,I-1
                Z=´   ´//Y
                Y=Z
  12        CONTINUE
            PRINT 102,Y
  11    CONTINUE
 100    FORMAT (I1)
 101    FORMAT (A)
 102    FORMAT (1X,A)
        END
```

The program first reads into N the number of data records on which the name and address appear. The DO loop labelled 11 reads the records in turn and the DO loop labelled 12 ensures that the i-th data record has "i-1" groups of three spaces inserted at the beginning. With the input data

```
    4
    A.N.OTHER,ESQ.
    DEPARTMENT OF MATHEMATICS
    UNIVERSITY OF SALFORD
    SALFORD M5 4WT
```

the output produced by the program was

```
    A.N.OTHER,ESQ
        DEPARTMENT OF MATHEMATICS
            UNIVERSITY OF SALFORD
                SALFORD M5 4WT
```

It should be noted that the statements

        Z=´   ´//Y

        Y=Z

cannot be replaced by the single statement

        Y=´   ´//Y

because, unlike numeric variables, character variables cannot be assigned values defined by expressions that include themselves.

8.3.2 Character Expressions in a Parameter Statement

In section 3.2.4, a description was given of how constant arithmetic expressions can be used in PARAMETER statements. Constant character expressions may also be used in this way. As an example, consider the statements

        CHARACTER CH1*2,CH2*3,CH3*5

        PARAMETER (CH1=´AB´,CH2=´B´//CH1,CH3=CH1//CH2)

These statements result in the character strings ´AB´, ´BAB´ and ´ABBAB´ being given the symbolic names CH1, CH2 and CH3 respectively.

8.4 COMPARISONS OF CHARACTER EXPRESSIONS

As was seen in chapter 1, characters are held in the store of the computer as a coded pattern of bits. This means that it is possible to rank characters in order and say that one character is "greater than" another. To distinguish this from the corresponding numeric terminology, it is normal to use a phrase such as "lexicographically greater than" in connection with comparisons of characters thus leaving "greater than" to imply "numerically greater than".

The FORTRAN 77 standard requires that the letters should be ordered alphabetically and that the digits should be in an increasing sequence. This means, for example, that ´F´ must be before ´U´ and ´5´ must be less than ´9´. In addition the blank character must be less than both ´A´ and the character representation of zero, and the letters and numbers must be in two distinct sets, not mixed together. Apart from this, the ordering of the characters, called the COLLATING SEQUENCE, is dependent on the implementation.

Comparisons can be made between character expressions in a similar way to comparisons between arithmetic expressions. The same relational operators

    .LT.   .GT.   .EQ.   .NE.   .LE.   .GE.

are used with the same general construction, namely

    character expression relational operator character expression

An example of a conditional statement which uses this feature is

        IF (FRED.LT.´JIM´) M=1

The effect of this statement is that the variable M is assigned the value 1 if the value of FRED is before 'JIM' in the alphabetical order. Thus for example, M would be given the value 1 if FRED had the value 'ALF' and would be unchanged if FRED had the value 'LEN'.

Two strings are compared character by character from the left. As soon as two characters differ, the decision is made on these characters. Hence the logical expressions

   'ABCD'.LT.'DCBA'
   'ABCD'.LT.'ADCB'
   'ABCD'.LT.'ABDC'
   'ABCD'.LT.'ABCE'

are all "true".

If the character expressions are not of the same length, the comparison is still carried out, with the shorter character expression padded out with an appropriate number of blank characters. The blank character is always the first character in the collating sequence of "printable" characters. Thus, for example,

   'A'.LT.'AB'

is "true", since the comparison carried out is 'A^' with 'AB', where blank is assumed to have a null value. Likewise, the expression

   'HARRY'.LT.'JOHN'

is "true", since a comparison is made between the string 'HARRY' and the string 'JOHN^'.

8.4.1 Example Program

The following program reads a list of names in arbitrary order, sorts them into alphabetic order using the linear exchange sort described in section 5.6.2 and prints them in their new order. It illustrates the use of character comparisons.

The algorithm for sorting the names into alphabetical order is the same as that for sorting numbers into ascending order. The only fundamental differences between the following program and program EX54 are that the array is declared to be of type CHARACTER and .LT. is used in the conditional statement instead of .GT. to give an ascending order in this program rather than the descending order in program EX54.

Note that the program assumes that each name to be processed is at most six characters in length. If it is necessary to process longer names, the CHARACTER statement would be adjusted in an appropriate manner. Note also that the apostrophes on the data records are necessary, since list-directed input has been used in this program. The program is given on the following page.

```
        PROGRAM EX83
CCCC    SORTING A LIST OF NAMES INTO ALPHABETICAL ORDER
        PARAMETER (NDIM=100,LENGTH=6)
        DIMENSION NAMES(NDIM)
        CHARACTER*(LENGTH) NAMES,ALPHA
        READ *,N
        READ *,(NAMES(I),I=1,N)
CCCC    THE SORTING PROCESS
        DO 11 I=1,N-1
            ALPHA=NAMES(I)
            IALPHA=I
            DO 12 J=I+1,N
                IF (NAMES(J).LT.ALPHA) THEN
                    ALPHA=NAMES(J)
                    IALPHA=J
                ENDIF
    12      CONTINUE
            NAMES(IALPHA)=NAMES(I)
            NAMES(I)=ALPHA
    11  CONTINUE
        PRINT 100,(NAMES(I),I=1,N)
   100  FORMAT (1X,A)
        END
```

When the data records
```
   6
   ´GEORGE´ ´MARY´ ´ALBERT´ ´HENRY´ ´WENDY´ ´JAMES´
```
were used as data for this program, the output was
```
   ALBERT
   GEORGE
   HENRY
   JAMES
   MARY
   WENDY
```
   This type of algorithm can be used to create a dictionary, or to
make up a list of names and addresses. It should be noted that, in a
sorting program of this nature where the information is in the form
of character data, it is rather inefficient to move the data around
in the character array. Instead, a one-dimensional integer array,
called an indexing vector should be used. This array has its
consecutive elements initially set to 1, 2, 3, ..., which corresponds
to the order of the data in the character array. Then, instead of
interchanging the elements of the character array in the sorting
program, the appropriate two elements in the indexing vector are

interchanged. After the sort, the consecutive values in the indexing vector may be, for example, 3, 18, 1, 5, ... This would indicate that element 3 of the character array is the first in order, that element 18 is the second in order, and so on.

8.5 SUBSTRINGS

FORTRAN 77 enables the programmer to access SUBSTRINGS. These are individual characters or sequences of successive characters of a character string. This is achieved by referring to characters by their position in the character variable. Clearly, a substring can consist of any number of characters from 1 up to and including the length of the character variable.

As an example of a substring, suppose that CHAR1 is a character variable whose value is ´ABCDEFG´, and that it is necessary to access the substring ´BCDE´. This can be done by using the term

   CHAR1(2:5)

in the appropriate character expression. Similarly, the substring ´F´ from CHAR1 can be accessed by using the term

   CHAR1(6:6)

in the appropriate character expression.

In general, the substring which starts in position "p" and ends in position "q" is specified by the term

   CHAR1(p:q)

Substrings of character array elements are also defined. For example, if CHAR2 is a character array, a substring of the "i-th" element of CHAR2 is specified by

   CHAR2(I)(p:q)

The rules which govern the SUBSTRING EXPRESSIONS "p" and "q" are that

   $1 \leq p \leq q \leq$ length of CHAR1 (or an element of CHAR2)

where "p" and "q" can be integer constants, integer variables or integer arithmetic expressions; and that if "p" is omitted, a value of 1 is assumed, while if "q" is omitted, a value equal to the length of the character variable is assumed.

Substrings can be used in character expressions and on the left-hand sides of character assignments. Suppose that the character variable TEXT is of length six characters and has a value of ´ABCDEF´; and that the character variable CHAR is of length eight characters. The statements

        CHAR=TEXT(1:3)//´XY´//TEXT(4:6)

        TEXT(2:4)=CHAR(1:3)

result in CHAR being given the value ´ABCXYDEF´ and TEXT the value ´AABCEF´.

It should be noted that in a character assignment statement, no character positions involved on the left-hand side of the assignment symbol may be in the expression on the right-hand side. This means that as stated earlier a character variable cannot appear on both sides of an assignment. However, the assignment statement

TEXT(2:3)=TEXT(4:5)

is valid as this assigns one substring to another disjoint substring. On the other hand the character assignment

TEXT(2:4)=TEXT(3:5)

is invalid as character positions 3 and 4 are involved on both sides of the assignment.

8.5.1 Example Program

The program described in this section reads a number of lines of text and finds the number of times the word "THE" occurs. This is done by searching the beginning of each line of text for the character string ´THE^´, the end of the line for the character string ´^THE´ and the rest of the line for the character string ´^THE^´. Thus all strings of five characters on each line are examined. In addition, the first and last four characters are examined. The character variable TEXT is used to store a whole line of text and all substrings of TEXT of length five characters are compared to the character string ´^THE^´. Whenever the logical expressions are "true", a counter M is increased by 1. Should a sentence include the word THE immediately preceded or followed by a punctuation character or other non-alphabetic character (other than a space) the program will not count the word. This limitation could be overcome by removing all these types of character from the text first. A program EX85 which does this for one line of text is given in section 8.6.1.
Using the data records

9

THE OWL AND THE PUSSY-CAT WENT TO SEA
IN A BEAUTIFUL PEA-GREEN BOAT.
THEY TOOK SOME HONEY AND PLENTY OF MONEY
WRAPPED UP IN A FIVE-POUND NOTE.

THE OWL LOOKED UP TO THE STARS ABOVE
AND SANG TO A SMALL GUITAR,
´OH LOVELY PUSSY, OH PUSSY MY LOVE
WHAT A BEAUTIFUL PUSSY YOU ARE´.

the program EX84 produced the following output

THE WORD ´THE´ APPEARS   4 TIMES IN THE ABOVE TEXT.

```
          PROGRAM EX84
CCCC    PROGRAM TO COUNT THE OCCURRENCES OF ´THE´ IN A PIECE OF TEXT
          CHARACTER TEXT*80
          READ *,NREC
          M=0
          DO 11 I=1,NREC
             READ 100,TEXT
             IF (TEXT(1:4).EQ.´THE ´) M=M+1
             DO 12 J=1,76
                IF (TEXT(J:J+4).EQ.´ THE ´) M=M+1
     12      CONTINUE
             IF (TEXT(77:80).EQ.´ THE´) M=M+1
     11   CONTINUE
          PRINT 101,M
    100 FORMAT (A)
    101 FORMAT (´ THE WORD ´´THE´´ APPEARS,I3,
       1     ´ TIMES IN THE ABOVE TEXT.´)
          END
```

8.5.2 Initialising Substrings

A DATA statement may be used to initialise a substring as well as a
whole character variable. As an example, consider the statements

```
          CHARACTER CHAR*6
          DATA CHAR(3:5) / ´END´ /
```

These will result in the substring CHAR(3:5) being initialised with
the string ´END´, the remaining substrings CHAR(1:2) and CHAR(6:6)
being left undefined.

   It should be noted that even if the first part of a character
variable is the only part to have been initialised, it is still
possible to use it in an assignment statement provided the undefined
part is not involved. For example, the statements

```
          CHARACTER CH1*6,CH2*4
          DATA CH1(1:4) / ´ABCD´ /
          CH2=CH1
```

are valid. This is because CH2 is only of length 4 and so the
undefined substring CH1(5:6) is not used in the assignment statement.

8.6 THE INTRINSIC FUNCTIONS FOR CHARACTER VARIABLES

A number of intrinsic functions either have character arguments or
return a character result. Of these, the most important are LEN and
INDEX. Details of the remaining intrinsic functions for character
variables can be found in appendix 1.

(a) LEN

The intrinsic function LEN(c) returns an integer value representing the length of the character expression "c". If "c" is a character variable, LEN(c) is the length specified for "c" by its character statement. The contents of "c" need not be defined at the time the function reference is executed. The length of a character string must be greater than zero, since the blank character is counted. If the character CHAR has been specified by the CHARACTER STATEMENT

    CHARACTER CHAR*8

then LEN(CHAR) gives the value 8. This function is not normally used in main programs, but it is very useful in subprograms, when the length of a character variable is not specified explicitly.

(b) INDEX

The intrinsic function INDEX(a,b) returns an integer value which indicates the starting position within the character string "a" of a sub-string identical to the string "b". If "b" occurs more than once in "a", the starting position of the first occurrence is returned. If "b" does not occur in "a", the value zero is returned. The value zero is also returned if LEN(a) is less than LEN(b).

Examples of the results of using INDEX are given in the table below. In the fourth example, the result is 2 because the first occurrence of A in BANANA is in position 2.

FUNCTION	RESULT
INDEX(´ABCDEFG´,´DEF´)	4
INDEX(´ABCDEFG´,´H´)	0
INDEX(´ABC´,´ABCD´)	0
INDEX(´BANANA´,´A´)	2

As a further example, the values of CHAR1 and CHAR2 are ´FORTRAN 77´ and ´N 7´ respectively. The result of

    INDEX(CHAR1,´A´//CHAR2)

is then 6, since the search is for the string ´AN 7´, which starts in position 6 of FORTRAN 77.

8.6.1 Example Program

The use of the intrinsic function INDEX is illustrated in a program which replaces all the characters other than alphabetic and space characters in a piece of text, by space characters. Every character position of the character variable TEXT, which contains the text, is examined. The letters are referenced as one-character substrings and tested by using INDEX to compare the letter from the substring of TEXT with the letters of the alphabet which are stored in LETTER. If the character is not a letter or a space character, it is replaced by a space character.

```
      PROGRAM EX85
      CHARACTER TEXT*80,LETTER*27
      DATA LETTER/´ABCDEFGHIJKLMNOPQRSTUVWXYZ ´/
      READ 100,TEXT
      DO 11 J=1,80
CCCC     EACH CHARACTER IS COMPARED WITH THOSE IN LETTER
         IF (INDEX(LETTER,TEXT(J:J)).EQ.0) TEXT(J:J)=´ ´
   11 CONTINUE
      PRINT 101,TEXT
  100 FORMAT (A)
  101 FORMAT (1X,A)
      END
```

When this program was run with the data

HE SAID, ´SHE SAID, ´12 CHARACTERS´; NEVER´.

the results were

HE SAID   SHE SAID   CHARACTERS   NEVER

8.7 CHARACTERS IN SUBPROGRAMS AND COMMON BLOCKS

This section describes how subprograms are affected when character variables appear in them.

8.7.1 Subprograms with Character Arguments

Like other variables, character variables may be used as the arguments of a subprogram. This means that dummy character variables may be used in the subprogram definition but these variables must be declared by a CHARACTER type statement within the subprogram. Thus the length of each dummy character variable must be specified.

For simple character variables, the ANSI Standard states that the length of a dummy character argument must be less than or equal to the actual character argument which is used when the subprogram is called. If the length of the dummy argument is less than the length of the actual argument, the excess characters on the right-hand end of the actual argument will be lost. This means that only the appropriate number of characters from the left-hand end of the argument will be associated with the dummy argument. It will be noted that this is a similar effect to that of an assignment statement. To avoid a possible loss of characters and still make the subprogram flexible, there is a special facility provided whereby the length of the character argument in the subprogram is not given as a specific constant value, but is specified by an asterisk enclosed in brackets, (*). When this is done, the dummy character argument always assumes the same length as the actual character argument used. Naturally, any actual argument must be of type character but may be a character constant, variable, substring, array element or expression.

For example, the statements

```
FUNCTION LENGTH(STRING)
CHARACTER STRING*(*)
```

define an integer function named LENGTH which has one argument. This is a character variable whose length will be taken to be the length of whatever actual argument is used in place of STRING.

A similar, but rather more involved, rule holds for character array variables. The simplest way to handle these is to use the asterisk to specify the character length of the array elements. Thus for a one-dimensional character array, an asterisk can be used to specify the dimension of the array as described in section 7.4.2; and an asterisk can be used to specify the length of each array element. For example, the subroutine named FRED, which is specified by the statements

```
SUBROUTINE FRED(CHAR)
CHARACTER CHAR(*)*(*)
```

defines CHAR as a character array. The number of elements in CHAR is specified by the first occurrence of (*) and the length of each character array element is specified by *(*). Programmers may find it less confusing to use a separate DIMENSION statement. For example, the above could have been written

```
SUBROUTINE FRED(CHAR)
DIMENSION CHAR(*)
CHARACTER CHAR*(*)
```

Any actual argument used in the call of a subprogram must be of type character. In addition to using a character array, it is also possible to use a substring or character array element as an actual argument when the dummy argument is a character array, but the rules specifying what will happen are rather complicated. It is, therefore, not recommended. A more detailed discussion of character arguments in subprograms is given in appendix 2.

8.7.2 Example Program

The following program illustrates the use of a character function subprogram. A function subprogram LENGTH(STRING) which returns the length of the character argument STRING as the number of characters up to and including the last non-blank character is constructed. The function LENGTH operates by working backwards from the last character of STRING until the first non-blank character is found. Control is then returned to the calling program with LENGTH having been set equal to the length of STRING when trailing blanks are ignored.

The function LENGTH is used in program EX86 to find the maximum length of a specified number of lines of text. In the main program an integer variable MAX is initially set equal to zero and subsequently replaced by any count of the number of characters in a line of text given by the function LENGTH(STRING) which is greater than the current value of MAX.

```
      PROGRAM EX86
      CHARACTER TEXT*80
      READ *,NREC
      MAX=0
      DO 11 J=1,NREC
          READ 100,TEXT
          I=LENGTH(TEXT)
          IF (I.GT.MAX) MAX=I
          PRINT 101,TEXT
   11 CONTINUE
      PRINT 102,MAX
  100 FORMAT (A)
  101 FORMAT (1X,A)
  102 FORMAT (´ THE LONGEST LINE OF TEXT HAS ´,I2,´ CHARACTERS´)
      END
      FUNCTION LENGTH(STRING)
      CHARACTER STRING *(*)
      DO 11 I=LEN(STRING),1,-1
          IF (STRING(I:I).NE.´ ´) THEN
              LENGTH=I
              RETURN
          ENDIF
   11 CONTINUE
      LENGTH=0
      END
```

The output consists of the eight lines of the poem as given by

program EX84 and listed in section 8.5.1 followed by the statement
THE LONGEST LINE OF TEXT HAS 40 CHARACTERS

8.7.3 Common Blocks holding Character Variables

As described in section 7.6, common blocks may be used instead of
arguments to transfer information between subprograms. The handling
of character variables is similar to that of numeric variables except
that character variables must occur in their own common block or
blocks and they may not be mixed in a common block with other types
of variable. They may be initialised in a BLOCK DATA subprogram
provided that a named common block is used for the character
variables.

8.7.4 Character Function Subprograms

A function subprogram can be defined to return a character value to
the calling program unit in a similar way to a function subprogram
which returns a numeric value, as was described in section 7.2. The
function is specified to be of type CHARACTER by using the function
definition statement in the form
          CHARACTER*length FUNCTION function-name (arguments)
or by using it in the form
          FUNCTION function-name (arguments)
in conjunction with a CHARACTER statement in the subprogram which
defines the name of the function to be of type CHARACTER and which
specifies its length. The length specification in either case should
normally be an unsigned non-zero integer constant or the expression
(*).
   In addition to stating in the subprogram that the name of the
function is a character variable, any program unit that uses the
function must also include its name in a CHARACTER statement and
specify its length. The length specification in the function
definition and in the calling program unit must agree. This will
happen automatically if the specification (*) is used in the function
definition. This is analogous to a character variable being
similarly defined when used as a dummy argument in a subprogram.
   The following program outlines illustrate the points made above

```
PROGRAM FIRST
CHARACTER*6 CHFUN1,A

.........
A=CHFUN1(...)

.........
END
```

```
      CHARACTER*(*) FUNCTION CHFUN1(...)
      .........
      CHFUN1=...
      END
```

In this case, the character definition is part of the FUNCTION statement and (*) ensures a character length of 6 is used for CHFUN1.

```
      PROGRAM SECOND
      CHARACTER*3 CHFUN2,B
      .........
      B=CHFUN2(...)
      .........
      END
      FUNCTION CHFUN2(...)
      CHARACTER CHFUN2*3
      .........
      CHFUN2=...
      END
```

In this case, the character definition in the subprogram is separate from the FUNCTION statement and specifically defines the character length of CHFUN2 to be 3.

8.7.5 Example Program which uses a Character Function

In this program, a two-dimensional character array named DETAIL with 100 rows and two columns holds names of students in the first column and details of their courses in the second column. A character function COURSE, when provided with the array DETAIL and a student name as the value of the character variable NAME, searches the array for the given name and returns with either the course details or, if the name is not found, the message "ERROR". A driver program sets up the array DETAIL, reads a value for NAME, calls the character function COURSE, and prints the value of NAME and either the course details or an error message as appropriate.

It should be noted that the name of the character function COURSE appears in the CHARACTER statement in the main program, and that it is stated to be of length 20 characters. The FUNCTION statement specifies the length of COURSE by (*) which automatically guarantees a match for the length specification.

The function COURSE has two character arguments. The dummy character array A and the dummy character variable NAME both have the length specification (*), which guarantees agreement in length with any actual argument that is used.

```
      PROGRAM EX87
      CHARACTER*20 NAME,COURSE,CSE,DETAIL(100,2)
      READ 100,N
      READ 101,((DETAIL(I,J),J=1,2),I=1,N)
      READ 101,NAME
      CSE=COURSE(DETAIL,100,N,NAME)
      IF (CSE.EQ.'ERROR') CSE='NOT FOUND'
      PRINT 102,NAME,CSE
  100 FORMAT (I4)
  101 FORMAT (2A20)
  102 FORMAT (1X,2A20)
      END
      CHARACTER*(*) FUNCTION COURSE(A,N1,N,NAME)
      CHARACTER*(*) A(N1,2),NAME
      DO 11 I=1,N
         IF (A(I,1).EQ.NAME) THEN
            COURSE=A(I,2)
            RETURN
         ENDIF
   11 CONTINUE
      COURSE='ERROR'
      END
```

The program represents a solution of a very simple data processing
problem, that of searching an array for a required item. Even in a
simple problem like this, the data for each student is likely to be
much more extensive in practice than that given in the example. It
would probably be stored in a file in the backing store of the
computer. Methods of accessing information stored like this are
discussed in chapter 9.

8.8 EXAMPLE PROGRAMS USING CHARACTERS

Programs illustrating some of the features of data processing and
text analysis are given in the following two sections.

8.8.1 Some Features of a Data Processing Program

Matching of character strings and searching for data is a common
problem in data processing. The following example is chosen to
illustrate how these tasks can be performed using the character
handling features of FORTRAN 77.

The problem is simply to read in a date and print the Zodiac sign
for this date. The date is to be given in the form month day, where

month is a three character representation of the month and day an up to two digit integer indicating the day of the month. Typical examples would be JAN10 FEB28

According to one astrologer the signs of the Zodiac are as follows:

AQUARIUS	Jan20–Feb18	LEO	Jul22–Aug21
PISCES	Feb19–Mar20	VIRGO	Aug22–Sep21
ARIES	Mar21–Apr20	LIBRA	Sep22–Oct22
TAURUS	Apr21–May20	SCORPIO	Oct23–Nov21
GEMINI	May21–Jun20	SAGITTARIUS	Nov22–Dec20
CANCER	Jun21–Jul21	CAPRICORN	Dec21–Jan19

The signs of the Zodiac do not change and hence the data for the Zodiac signs and the corresponding dates can be set up using a DATA statement. When the program reads in a date, it must be validated and any illegal dates are printed with an appropriate message. First the three characters assigned to MONTH are checked, by finding their position in a character variable KEY using the intrinsic function INDEX. This returns an integer value which is assigned to I. This integer gives the position of the first character in MONTH in KEY. If I+2 is not exactly divisible by 3 the string match, if any, is not a valid representation for a month and an error message "CHARACTERS FOR MONTH INVALID" is printed. For a genuine month the value J=(I+2)/3 will be the number of the month. For example, if the month is DEC, J will be 12.

The integer J is used in a subscript to find the maximum number of days in the "j"-th month by selecting MAXDAY(J) and a check is made that the integer value of DAY lies in the range 1 to MAXDAY(J), if not an error message "INVALID DAY IN MONTH" is output.

If the input date is valid, the day in the "j"-th month on which the Zodiac sign changes is selected from the integer array STARTS, that is, the integer value of STARTS(J). When the value of DAY is less than the value of STARTS(J), J is decreased by 1 to indicate the previous sign. However, if the new value of J is zero, J is set to 12, so that the required sign CAPRICORN is obtained.

Finally, the appropriate sign is obtained from a character array SIGN and the date and corresponding Zodiac sign are printed.

Program EX88 takes a set of dates terminated by "END" and either gives the date and corresponding Zodiac sign or an appropriate error message. When run with the following data

    JUN13
    DEC20
    JAN 1
    JON13
    OCT32
    END

```
      PROGRAM EX88
      CHARACTER KEY*36, SIGN(12)*11, MONTH*3
      INTEGER MAXDAY(12), STARTS(12), DAY
CCCC  SET UP DATA DEFINING THE SIGNS OF THE ZODIAC
      DATA KEY /´JANFEBMARAPRMAYJUNJULAUGSEPOCTNOVDEC´/
     1     SIGN /´AQUARIUS´,´PISCES´,´ARIES´,´TAURUS´,
     2            ´GEMINI´,´CANCER´,´LEO´,´VIRGO´,´LIBRA´,
     3            ´SCORPIO´,´SAGITTARIUS´,´CAPRICORN´/
     4       MAXDAY /31,29,31,30,31,30,31,31,30,31,30,31/
     5       STARTS /20,19,21,21,21,21,22,22,22,23,22,21/
   10 READ 100,MONTH,DAY
CCCC  CHECK FOR END OF DATA MARKER
      IF (MONTH.EQ.´END´) STOP
CCCC  FIND MONTH INDEX
      I=INDEX(KEY,MONTH)
      I=I+2
      J=I/3
CCCC  CHECKS IF I IS A MULTIPLE OF 3
      IF (J*3.EQ.I) THEN
         IF (DAY.LT.1 .OR. DAY.GT.MAXDAY(J)) THEN
CCCC        INVALID DAY OF THE MONTH
            PRINT 101,MONTH,DAY
            GOTO 10
         ELSE
CCCC        FIND ZODIAC SIGN
            IF (DAY.LT.STARTS(J)) THEN
               J=J-1
CCCC           ZERO IMPLIES 12-TH MONTH
               IF (J.EQ.0) J=12
            ENDIF
            PRINT 102,MONTH,DAY,SIGN(J)
            GOTO 10
         ENDIF
      ELSE
CCCC     INVALID CHARACTERS FOR MONTH
         PRINT 103,MONTH
         GOTO 10
      ENDIF
  100 FORMAT(A3,I2)
  101 FORMAT(1X,A3,2X,I2,´  INVALID DAY IN MOUTH´)
  102 FORMAT(1X,A3,2X,I2,2X,A)
  103 FORMAT(1X,A3,´  CHARACTERS FOR MONTH INVALID´)
      END
```

The program produced the following output

```
JUN   13   GEMINI
DEC   20   SAGITTARIUS
JAN    1   CAPRICORN
JON   CHARACTERS FOR MONTH INVALID
OCT   32   INVALID DAY IN MONTH
```

8.8.2 A Text Analysis Program

The program described in this section reads an integer N followed by
N lines of text. The number of times each letter of the alphabet
occurs in the text is found and tabulated in the form of a histogram.

In the program twenty-six integer elements of the array HSTGRM are
used to count the number of times each letter of the alphabet
appears. The elements are set to zero initially by a DATA statement,
which also fills the character variable HGM, which is used to store
each line of the histogram, with blank characters.

The number of records of text to be analysed is read into NREC.
This is used to control a DO loop which reads each record into a
character variable TEXT. The subprogram LENGTH described in section
8.7.2 is used to find the last non-blank character on each line of
text.   The   remaining   characters   in TEXT are then examined
individually. If the character is a letter, the appropriate element
of HSTGRM is increased by one.

Next the histogram is printed. The maximum value in HSTGRM, which
represents the number of times the most frequent letter appears in
the text, is found. This gives the maximum number of lines, MK,
required to display the histogram.

It is necessary to determine when the top of each column of the
histogram begins to appear, as it is printed line by line from the
top. A counter I is set initially to MK and decreased by 1 for each
line of the histogram printed.

The columns in the histogram are separated by a space, so pairs of
characters of HGM represent each letter in a column of the histogram.
A check is made to see if the corresponding value of HSTGRM is equal
to I. If it is, this is the top of that column of the histogram, and
the characters ^* are inserted at those two positions of HGM.   Once
set these characters remain for subsequent lines of the histogram.
This is repeated for each element of HSTGRM, after which a complete
line of the histogram is output. The process is repeated for each
line of the histogram. It should be noted that only a single blank
character is specified for HGM in the DATA statement but this is
padded out automatically with other blanks to fill the variable.

```
      PROGRAM EX89
      CHARACTER TEXT*80,LETTER*26,HGM*52
      INTEGER HSTGRM(26)
      DATA LETTER,HSTGRM,HGM/´ABCDEFGHIJKLMNOPQRSTUVWXYZ´,26*0,´ ´/
      READ *,NREC
      DO 11 I=1,NREC
         READ 100,TEXT
CCCC     FINDS THE CONTRIBUTIONS OF EACH LINE TO THE HISTOGRAM
         DO 12 J=1,LENGTH(TEXT)
            K=INDEX(LETTER,TEXT(J:J))
            IF (K.NE.0) HSTGRM(K)=HSTGRM(K)+1
   12    CONTINUE
   11 CONTINUE
      PRINT *
CCCC  FIND THE MAXIMUM NUMBER OF OCCURRENCES OF ANY LETTER
      MK=0
      DO 13 I=1,26
         IF (HSTGRM(I).GT.MK) MK=HSTGRM(I)
   13 CONTINUE
CCCC  PRINT THE HISTOGRAM
      DO 14 I=MK,1,-1
         DO 15 J=1,26
            JJ=J*2
            IF (HSTGRM(J).EQ.I) HGM(JJ-1:JJ)=´ *´
CCCC        ONCE A STAR HAS BEEN SET IT REMAINS SET
   15    CONTINUE
         PRINT 101,HGM
   14 CONTINUE
      PRINT 102,(LETTER(I:I),I=1,26)
  100 FORMAT (A)
  101 FORMAT (1X,A)
  102 FORMAT (1X,26(1X,A1))
      END
CCCC  FUNCTION LENGTH IS DESCRIBED IN SECTION 8.7.2
      FUNCTION LENGTH(STRING)
      CHARACTER STRING *(*)
      DO 11 I=LEN(STRING),1,-1
         IF (STRING(I:I).NE.´ ´) THEN
            LENGTH=I
            RETURN
         ENDIF
   11 CONTINUE
      LENGTH=0
      END
```

When the program was run using the first verse of the poem used as
data for program EX84, the results were

```
            *
            *
            *
            *
            *
            *                   * *           *
 *          *                   * *           *
 *          *                   * *           *
 *          *                   * *           *
 *          *                   * * *         *
 *          *                   * * *         *
 *          *                   * * *     * *       *
 *      * *      * *            * * *   * * *       *
 *      * * *    * *        *   * * *   * * *   *   *
 * *    * * *    * *      * * * * *   * * * *   *   *
 * * * * * * * *    * * * * * *   * * * * * *     *
 A B C D E F G H I J K L M N O P Q R S T U V W X Y Z
```

8.9 EXERCISES

1. Write a program which reads the address in section 8.3.1 on one
record, the lines of the address being separated by /, and then
prints it in the normal off-set form. Thus for the input data
A.N.OTHER,ESQ./DEPARTMENT OF MATHEMATICS/
UNIVERSITY OF SALFORD/SALFORD M5 4WT/
the output should be

```
        A.N.OTHER,ESQ.
          DEPARTMENT OF MATHEMATICS
           UNIVERSITY OF SALFORD
             SALFORD M5 4WT
```

2. Write a function subprogram REVERS(STRING) that returns a
character string which is the reverse of the argument. Any trailing
blanks of the argument should remain at the right-hand end of the
string. Thus, for example, the result of
    REVERS('IN SIDE OUT ') is 'TUO EDIS NI '

3. Write a program which finds the number of four-letter words in a
piece of text. As sample data use the poem given in section 8.5.1.

4. Write a function subprogram SEARCH(DLIST,STRING,N) to search the first N elements of a one-dimensional character array DLIST for the element equal to the name defined by the character string STRING and return the value of the subscript expression for this element. Incorporate it in a test program.

Give a more efficient algorithm that could be used if the words in DLIST were in alphabetical order, by adapting the binary search technique described in Exercise 6, section 5.9.

5. Write a program which extends Exercise 3, section 5.9, by producing a histogram of the form shown below, where xxx represents a candidate who has obtained a particular grade.

```
            xxx
            xxx
        xxx xxx
    xxx xxx xxx         xxx
    xxx xxx xxx xxx xxx
    xxx xxx xxx xxx xxx
    xxx xxx xxx xxx xxx
     A   B   C   D   E
```

6. Rewrite program EX83 using an indexing vector as described in section 8.4.1.

7. Use the intrinsic function INDEX in an extension of program EX85 which replaces all the characters other than letters and space characters by space characters in a piece of text. Use the poem given in section 8.5.1 as test data.

8. Write a program which takes the date in the form day/month/year and prints out the day of the week for any date in the twentieth century given that 1/1/1900 was a Monday.
Hints: (a) Test if the date is valid.
       (b) How is the day of the week calculated?
       (c) What facts about each month and leap years affect these calculations?

CHAPTER 9
FILE CONTROL

In the programs written so far, there has been no explicit indication
of the source of the input data. It has simply been assumed that data
is available to the program in some way whenever a READ statement
appears. The data is therefore only available from one source and
has to be read sequentially. Also, it has been assumed that all
results are printed on the line printer. This need not be the case.
Frequently data is held on some form of backing store such as discs,
drums or magnetic tapes as described in chapter 1. The results from
the program are often returned to backing store, only a small
proportion of the results being printed on the line printer. To
allow access to data stored on some auxiliary medium, FORTRAN 77
provides nine input/output statements. The nine statements can be
classified into two groups. The first group consists of the data
transfer statements READ, WRITE and PRINT; while the second group
consists of the auxiliary input/output statements OPEN, CLOSE,
INQUIRE, BACKSPACE, ENDFILE and REWIND. In this chapter, the
function and scope of all but one of these are examined. The
exception is the INQUIRE statement, which is discussed in chapter 10.

9.1 EXTERNAL FILES AND RECORDS

As was described in chapter 1, data can be held on backing store as a
collection of records which constitute one or more files. A sequence
of characters or values make up a FORMATTED or UNFORMATTED record.
Records in a file are either all FORMATTED or all UNFORMATTED.

9.1.1 Formatted Records

A FORMATTED RECORD consists of a sequence of characters that are
capable of representation in the processor. To interpret the meaning
of the characters requires a FORMAT statement. For example, the

characters 100 can be interpreted as the characters representing one, zero and zero, or the value one hundred, or the values ten and zero. Which of these interpretations is correct depends on the FORMAT statement which describes the data. The length of a formatted record is measured in characters and depends primarily on the number of characters put into the record when it is written. These records can be written to a file using some form of system input command not directly associated with FORTRAN 77, or they can be written by a FORTRAN 77 program using FORMATTED output.

9.1.2 Unformatted Records

When data is processed, it is stored internally in the form most suitable for processing. Thus although INTEGER, REAL and CHARACTER variables will have different representations in the processor, they will all be represented internally by some form of binary pattern, because the machine works in binary. When these binary patterns are stored as the record of values the record is said to be UNFORMATTED. Obviously, if a binary pattern for a character is subsequently read as the value for an integer, errors may occur.

The formal definition of an UNFORMATTED record states that "an UNFORMATTED RECORD consists of a sequence of values in a processor-dependent form and may contain a mixture of character and non-character data, or even no data".

Since the internal binary format is processor-dependent and is different for the different types of value represented, it follows that the length of an unformatted record is measured in processor-dependent units and is governed by the output list used when the record is written. The only way of creating an unformatted record is by means of a FORTRAN 77 unformatted output statement.

9.1.3 The Endfile Record

A special record is used to mark the end of a file. This record is called an ENDFILE RECORD. It is normally inserted automatically when a file is created, although it can be written to the file by an ENDFILE statement, as described in section 9.8.1. Endfile records have no length property, so they can appear at the end of any file.

9.2 FILE ACCESS

Input and output statements must specify the source and destination respectively of the data to be transferred. When a program reads data from a file, the source of the data is indicated by a unit number and

the locations into which the data is to be copied are indicated by a
list of variables. The reverse is true when a program writes records
to a file. When the program is run, this unit number must be
associated with a particular file; that is, a connection between the
unit number and the required file must be established. This
connection can be made outside the FORTRAN 77 program using a system
macro-command or the appropriate commands in the Job Control Language
of the operating system in use, thus preconnecting the units with the
required files. Alternatively, the files can be connected to the
FORTRAN 77 program when the program is running by means of an OPEN
statement as described later in this chapter.

There are two basic modes of access to the records in an external
file. The first is when the records are read sequentially in the
same order in which they were written. This is called SEQUENTIAL
ACCESS. Some terminology used when referring to sequential files
seems a little odd at first sight and a few words of explanation are
desirable. Files held on magnetic tapes are always sequential files.
To read a record from a magnetic tape, the tape (and hence the file)
has to be positioned with the required record under the read head.
This leads to the notion of a file being positioned prior to reading
data. Thus when the phrase "position the file" is used this is
synonymous with "move to the correct position in the file". The
second mode of access is when records are read directly from any
known position in the file. This is called DIRECT ACCESS. The mode
of access used is defined in the program by means of an OPEN
statement.

The notion of a preconnected file has already been encountered,
since the PRINT statement assumes a predefined connection, normally
to a line printer. This connection is made automatically by the
system. Similarly, when no unit number is given in a READ statement,
a default connection is made.

9.2.1 Simple Programs that use Files

In section 5.8.1, a program to transpose the elements of an array was
discussed. This program was modified in sections 6.2 and 6.6 to use
formatted input and output. Suppose now that the data required by
this program is stored in a file whose name is MYDATA.

How the data came to be stored in this file is irrelevant to the
program. The file may have been created as a result of system
commands, or it may have been the output from a FORTRAN 77 program,
as described later in this chapter, or it may have been the output
from a program written in another language. All that the program
requires is that the records in the file shall be arranged in the

same way as the data records given in section 6.6.

The program needs some modification to obtain the data from the file MYDATA. The modified program is:

```
      PROGRAM EX91
      DIMENSION A(20,20)
CCCC  THIS PROGRAM CONNECTS AN EXISTING FILE 'MYDATA' TO UNIT 5
CCCC  READS THIS DATA INTO AN ARRAY A AND PRINTS THE TRANSPOSE
CCCC  ON THE STANDARD OUTPUT UNIT
      OPEN (5,FILE='MYDATA',STATUS='OLD')
      READ (5,100) M,N
      DO 11 I=1,M
         READ (5,101) (A(I,J),J=1,N)
   11 CONTINUE
      PRINT 102,N,M
      DO 12 J=1,N
         PRINT 103,(A(I,J),I=1,M)
   12 CONTINUE
      CLOSE (5)
  100 FORMAT (2I2)
  101 FORMAT (8F10.0)
  102 FORMAT (' THE ',I2,' BY ',I2,' MATRIX IS')
  103 FORMAT (20(1X,F5.2))
      END
```

In this program, the OPEN statement is used to connect unit 5 to the file whose name is MYDATA. Subsequent references to unit 5 will then automatically refer to the file named MYDATA until this file is released from the program. The STATUS parameter is described in section 9.3.3. The READ statement has been modified to include a parameter that specifies which unit is to be used for the data. It should be noted that this parameter and the format specifier have both been enclosed in brackets. It is the presence of these brackets that indicates to the compiler that the first parameter specifies which unit to use. When these brackets are absent, the first parameter is assumed to specify the format of the input data as described in earlier chapters. Note also that there is no comma after the brackets. The other statement in this program that has not been used previously is the CLOSE statement, which releases the file connected to unit 5.

The program can be further modified to write the results to a second file. To do this, the file to which the results are to be sent must first be connected to a unit. Next the PRINT statements in the program must be changed to WRITE statements, which allow the program to specify the unit to be used for the output. This is because the PRINT statement refers to a predefined unit. The program becomes

```
      PROGRAM EX92
      DIMENSION A(20,20)
      OPEN (5,FILE='MYDATA',STATUS='OLD')
      OPEN (3,FILE='FILERES',STATUS='NEW')
      READ (5,100) M,N
      DO 11 I=1,M
          READ (5,101) (A(I,J),J=1,N)
   11 CONTINUE
      WRITE (3,102) N,M
      DO 12 J=1,N
          WRITE (3,103) (A(I,J),I=1,M)
   12 CONTINUE
      CLOSE (3)
      CLOSE (5)
  100 FORMAT (2I2)
  101 FORMAT (8F10.0)
  102 FORMAT (' THE ',I2,' BY ',I2,' MATRIX IS')
  103 FORMAT (20(1X,F5.2))
      END
```

It should be noted that this program creates the file named FILERES in which the results are stored.

9.3 THE OPEN STATEMENT

Within a FORTRAN 77 program, a file is connected to a unit by means of an OPEN statement, which is described in this section. Before discussing the general form of the OPEN statement, it is instructive to consider some simple examples.

9.3.1 Simple examples of the OPEN Statement for Sequential files

In its simplest form the OPEN statement only requires two ancillary pieces of information, one to specify the unit number and one to specify the file. For example, the statement

```
      OPEN (5,FILE='MYFILE')
```

causes the file named MYFILE to be connected to unit 5 for formatted sequential access. Subsequent references to unit 5 will automatically access this file. The statement

```
      OPEN (6,FILE=A)
```

connects the file whose name is the value of the character variable A

to unit 6 for formatted sequential access. The name stored in A could
be set up at run time by reading the name from a data file, which may
be in the form of data records supplied with the program. An
equivalent form of this statement is

        OPEN (UNIT=6,FILE=A)

If the file is required for temporary use only, that is a work file,
then the file will have no name and the appropriate form of the OPEN
statement is

        OPEN (5, STATUS='SCRATCH')

This will cause a temporary file to be created and subsequent
references to unit 5 will access this temporary file. The file will
only exist while the program is being executed.

  The STATUS specifier can be used to indicate whether the file being
connected exists or is to be created. For example,

        OPEN (5, FILE='MYFILE', STATUS='OLD')

indicates that the file MYFILE already exists (because the STATUS is
OLD). If the file does not exist then an error will occur. Errors of
this kind can be checked by the program using the error specifier.
For example,

        OPEN (5, FILE='MYFILE', STATUS='OLD', ERR=999)

will cause the statement labelled 999 to be obeyed next if the file
MYFILE does not exist. There are other errors that can occur, any of
which will cause the statement labelled 999 to be obeyed next, but
these will be discussed later.

9.3.2 Simple examples of the OPEN Statement for Direct Access files

The simplest form of the OPEN statement for direct access files
requires four specifiers. These are needed to specify the unit
number, the file to be used, the length of each record and that the
file is to be used for direct access and not sequential access. For
example,

        OPEN (5,FILE='MYFILE', ACCESS='DIRECT', RECL=10)

causes the file MYFILE to be connected to unit 5 for unformatted
direct access. All of the records in the file have length 10 as
indicated by the specifier RECL=10. Note that in this case the
records are unformatted, whereas for sequential files they were
assumed to be formatted. Also all of the records on the file must
have the same length.

  In order to use a work file for direct access, it is necessary to
create it and to associate a unit number with it. If the chosen unit
number is 5 and the record length is 10, the appropriate OPEN
statement is of the form

        OPEN (5,STATUS='SCRATCH',ACCESS='DIRECT',RECL=10)

If a file named MYFILE is to be used for input and output using
direct access with records of length 30, the OPEN statement for
UNFORMATTED records might be

        OPEN (8,FILE='MYFILE',ACCESS='DIRECT',RECL=30,ERR=99)

This causes unit 8 to be connected to the file named MYFILE for
direct access. Should the file not exist, a new file is created. If
an error occurs, the statement labelled 99 is obeyed. Reference to
unit 8 in subsequent input or output statements will cause the file
named MYFILE to be accessed. The STATUS specifier is not present in
this example of the OPEN statement, so the default value 'UNKNOWN is
given. The meaning of this depends on the implementation; a
reasonable interpretation of the ANSI Standard in the case of direct
access files being that it allows both READ and WRITE access. This
should be checked with the advisory service of the site at which the
program is to be run. Since, when omitted, the status is UNKNOWN and
hence processor dependent it is recommended that the status specifier
is always included.

Once the connection between a file and a unit has been established,
data transfers to or from that file can take place. The transfer is
achieved by either a READ or a WRITE statement. Both of these
statements use a unit number to determine the external source or
destination of the data. Changing the connection changes the file
being used.

9.3.3 The General Form of the OPEN Statement

The OPEN statement can be used to connect an existing file to a unit,
to create a file, or to change certain specifiers of a connection
between a file and a unit. Because the facilities and conventions
for handling files will differ from one system to another, this
statement is unlikely to be portable. Although the ANSI Standard lays
down the general rules for the OPEN statement, it does permit
extensions and thus leaves a lot of scope to the implementor. Anyone
wishing to use this statement should check beforehand to make sure
that their use of the OPEN statement is compatible with the
facilities available at the installation on which the program is to
be run.

The general form of the OPEN statement is

        OPEN (list of specifiers)

The ANSI Standard defines nine specifiers and allows the implementor
to decide whether or not any additional specifiers are to be made
available. With so many options, the full definition looks a little
formidable. However, not all specifiers are needed each time the OPEN
statement is used, as can be seen by the examples given in sections

9.3.1 and 9.3.2. In fact, the only specifier that must always be present is the unit number, which should always be first in the list of specifiers. The order of the other specifiers is immaterial. The ordering of the definitions of the various specifiers that follow is an attempt to reflect the needs of the average user. The nine defined specifiers and their significance are

(i) A UNIT SPECIFIER written as
     n   or   *
where "n" is a non-negative integer expression and * indicates the default unit. The value of "n" will be restricted to a limited range of values which will be site dependent and must be checked by the programmer. This specifier must always be present and is the first in the list. It can be written in the alternative forms
     UNIT=n   or   UNIT=*

(ii) A STATUS SPECIFIER written as
     STATUS=type
where "type" is a character expression whose value is 'OLD', 'NEW', 'SCRATCH' or 'UNKNOWN'. Trailing blanks are not significant. If 'OLD' is specified, the file must exist. If 'NEW' is specified, the file must not exist. In this case, a new file is created and the status becomes 'OLD', although the file may not physically exist until the first WRITE statement has been obeyed. If 'SCRATCH' is specified, the file specifier as described in (iii) must be omitted, and the unit is connected to a WORK FILE. This is a file that is created for the duration of the job. When the file is disconnected, it is automatically deleted from the system. If 'UNKNOWN' is specified, the status is processor dependent. When the status specifier is omitted, 'UNKNOWN' is assumed. It is recommended that the status specifier should always be included in any OPEN statement.
     The ANSI Standard permits extra facilities to be built in to an implementation so as to take advantage of any features of the system that might be desirable. Care should be taken to check how this feature of FORTRAN 77 has been implemented.

(iii) A FILE SPECIFIER written as
     FILE=name
where "name" is a character expression defining the file to be connected. Trailing blanks in the name are not significant. This specifier must be present unless a status of 'SCRATCH' has been specified, in which case it must not be present.

(iv) An ACCESS SPECIFIER written as

ACCESS=acc

where "acc" is a character expression whose value is either ´SEQUENTIAL´ or ´DIRECT´. The mode of access requested must be compatible with that of the file being connected. If this specifier is omitted, SEQUENTIAL access is assumed.

(v) A RECORD LENGTH SPECIFIER written as

RECL=re

where "re" is an integer expression whose value must be positive and which indicates the length of a record. For FORMATTED data, "re" is equal to the number of characters in a record. For UNFORMATTED data, the record length is processor-dependent. This specifier must be given when DIRECT access is specified and must not be given when SEQUENTIAL access is specified.

It should be noted that either both the access and record length are required (for DIRECT access) or neither are required (for SEQUENTIAL access).

(vi) A FORMAT SPECIFIER written as

FORM=fm

where "fm" is a character expression whose value is either ´FORMATTED´ or ´UNFORMATTED´. If this specifier is omitted, a default value is assumed, which depends on the access mode requested. In the case of DIRECT access the default is ´UNFORMATTED´ and for SEQUENTIAL access the default is ´FORMATTED´.

(vii) An ERROR SPECIFIER written as

ERR=s

where "s" is the statement label of an executable statement that appears in the same program unit as the specifier. If an error condition exists, the next instruction to be obeyed will be the one labelled "s".

(viii) An INPUT/OUTPUT STATUS SPECIFIER written as

IOSTAT=ios

where "ios" is an integer variable used to convey the status of the file to the program. If no error condition exists, "ios" is set to zero; otherwise it is given a positive value corresponding to a particular entry in an error table. The values given are processor dependent.

(ix) An EDITING SPECIFIER written as

BLANK=bl

where "bl" is a character expression whose value is either ´NULL´ or

´ZERO´. This can only be used with FORMATTED input and output. It determines the way blank characters are treated in numeric fields. If "bl" has the value ´NULL´, all blanks in edited numeric fields are ignored unless the complete field is blank, when the number is treated as zero. If "bl" has a value ´ZERO´ then, except for leading blanks, all blanks in edited numeric fields are treated as zeros. When the specifier is omitted, a value of ´NULL´ is assumed.

In all the above cases, the character expressions are those obtained when trailing spaces are removed. Hence, ´ZERO´ and ´ZERO ´ are treated as being equivalent. The only obligatory specifier is the unit number, the others being optional and sometimes omitted. A unit can be connected to only one file at any one time and vice versa.

9.3.4 Summary of Specifier Default Values

As was mentioned earlier, the only mandatory specifier in the OPEN statement is the UNIT specifier. All other specifiers may be omitted under certain circumstances, in which case default values are assumed. The following table gives a summary of these values.

SPECIFIER	VALUE ASSUMED IF OMITTED	COMMENTS
STATUS=	´UNKNOWN´	It is recommended that this specifier is always used
FILE=		This specifier can only be omitted for ´SCRATCH´ files
ACCESS=	´SEQUENTIAL´	This must be compatible with the file being connected
RECL=		MUST be given for DIRECT access files and must NOT be given for SEQUENTIAL access
FORM=	´UNFORMATTED´ for DIRECT access files and ´FORMATTED´ for SEQUENTIAL access files	
BLANK=	´NULL´	

The IOSTAT= and ERR= specifiers have no effect unless errors occur, in which case their omission will cause a run-time failure.

9.4 WRITING DATA TO A FILE

A FORTRAN 77 program sends records to a file by means of WRITE statements. These can be used to write formatted or unformatted records to both sequential and direct access files.

9.4.1 Examples of Write Statements

The following simple examples illustrate the various ways in which the WRITE statement is used. As a first example, consider
          WRITE (2) X,I
This statement writes an unformatted record to unit 2. The record consists of the binary representation of one real and one integer value. This could not have been achieved by a PRINT statement, since this always requires a format to be specified, either explicitly (the formatted PRINT statement) or implicitly (the list-directed PRINT statement). However, the values in X and I could have been written in character form (formatted) using the WRITE statement
          WRITE (2,100) X,I
where 100 is the label used to reference a suitable FORMAT statement.
   The above examples are suitable for writing records sequentially to a file. The WRITE statement can also be used to state the position in the file that a record is to be stored. In this case the file must be connected for direct access and the WRITE statement would then be used in the form
          WRITE (5,100,REC=N) A,B,C
This will cause the content of the variables A, B and C to be written as the "N"-th record on the file connected to unit 5 in the format specified by statement 100. "N" must be a positive integer specifying a position within the file.

9.4.2 The General form of the Write Statement

The WRITE statement has the general form
          WRITE (control-information-list) output-list
The "control-information-list" specifies the location and format of the data record when stored. The "output-list" specifies the values that are to be stored. The form of the output list is the same as that for the PRINT statement and has been discussed in previous chapters. The control information list can contain up to 5 specifiers. These specifiers are used to convey information

concerning the unit to use, the format in which the record is to be
written, the position to store the record within the file, the status
of the file and the instruction to be obeyed when an error occurs.

Not all these specifiers need be given, as can be seen from the
following example program. Suppose that data is presented in a known
order suitable for list-directed input and that it is to be written
to an unformatted sequential file. If the data is presented on the
default unit, the program to transform the character data into binary
form and store it on a new file named MYDATA might be

```
      PROGRAM EX93
CCCC THIS PROGRAM CREATES AN UNFORMATTED SEQUENTIAL FILE OF
CCCC RECORDS READ FROM THE STANDARD INPUT UNIT
      OPEN (5,FILE='MYDATA',STATUS='NEW',FORM='UNFORMATTED')
      READ *,N
      DO 10 I=1,N
         READ *,A,B,C,I,M
         WRITE (5) A,B,C,I,M
   10 CONTINUE
      CLOSE (5)
      END
```

In this program, the only information given in the control
information list for the WRITE statement is the unit number. This is
all that is required, since the other specifiers are all optional.
The file was opened for unformatted sequential access, so neither a
format nor a position specifier is needed. Since no error label or
variable for the file status is given, an output error will terminate
the program. The CLOSE statement in this program simply releases the
file connected to unit 5. It should be noted that the only way for a
FORTRAN 77 program to read the data in the file named MYDATA is by
means of an unformatted READ statement.

9.4.3 Control Information for the Write Statement

The complete list of specifiers that can appear in the control list
of a WRITE statement are as follows

(i) A UNIT SPECIFIER written as
      n   or   *
where "n" is a non-negative integer expression and * indicates the
default unit. It specifies the unit used by the WRITE statement, and
must be the first item in the list. It can also be written
      UNIT=n   or   UNIT=*

(ii) A FORMAT SPECIFIER written as

   n   or   *

where "n" is a positive integer specifying the FORMAT statement that defines the required layout and * indicates list directed output. When present, this must be the second item in the list. It can also be written

   FMT=n   or   FMT=*

or it can be inserted explicitly, as described in section 10.7.6 .

(iii) A RECORD SPECIFIER written as

   REC=rn

where "rn", the record number, is an integer expression indicating the relative position of the record in the file. The file must have been connected for direct access to the unit cited. This specifier must not be used for sequential access files.

(iv) A STATUS SPECIFIER written as

   IOSTAT=ios

as in the corresponding specifier for the OPEN statement. It is used to indicate the status of the file at any time during output (or input).

(v) An ERROR SPECIFIER written as

   ERR=s

This has the same significance as when used in the OPEN statement.

9.4.4 Sequential Output

In its simplest form, the WRITE statement can be used in exactly the same way as the PRINT statement, except that the required output unit must be specified. This allows several output files to be used instead of only one, as was the case when using the PRINT statement. If the default unit for output is unit 2, the statements

       PRINT 100,A,B,C
       WRITE (2,100)A,B,C
       WRITE (*,100)A,B,C

are equivalent; as are the statements

       PRINT *,A,B,C
       WRITE (2,*)A,B,C
       WRITE (*,*)A,B,C

Both these are examples of FORMATTED output. The first format is given explicitly by the FORMAT statement labelled 100. The second is in a format determined by the output list. The output need not be formatted, in which case no format specifier is given.

The additional features available when using the WRITE statement for sequential output instead of PRINT are that any appropriate file can be used for the output, that unformatted data can be used, and that an error label can be specified to aid recovery if an output error occurs.

When access to a file is sequential, records are written in sequence and the record just written becomes the last record on the file. To attempt to read the next record on the file is therefore meaningless. This means that at any one time a sequential file is being used either for input or for output. To read data from the file, the file must first be repositioned by means of the REWIND statement, which is described in section 9.8.2.

9.4.5 Direct Output

The other feature that the WRITE statement possesses which the PRINT statement does not is the ability to specify the location, within the file, where a record must be stored. This feature can only be used with files that are connected for direct access. To write a record contained in an array A, say, as the tenth entry in a direct access file, all that is needed is the statement

        WRITE (5,REC=10) A

This will write a copy of the contents of the array A as the tenth record on unit 5. If unit 5 is connected to a file named MYFILE, then A becomes the tenth record of MYFILE.

It should be noted that this is an unformatted WRITE statement and so all the records on MYFILE must be unformatted and the file must have been opened with ´UNFORMATTED´ as the format specifier. If A is not the same length as the record defined in the OPEN statement, either A defines a record that requires more space than that allocated for a record on the file and an error will occur, or the record defined by A is shorter than the records on the file, which will leave part of the record on the file undefined. Thus records should normally be chosen to have the same length as specified in the OPEN statement.

9.4.6 Example Program which Creates a Direct Access File

A class of students has up to 200 members. The students are each given a class number in the range 1 to 200 when they register. The enrolling officer does not allocate the numbers sequentially, but attempts to estimate the number each student will have when the class list is in alphabetical order. The student records are batched in the order of arrival. These records are then copied to a direct

access file in class number order. The record for a student consists
of a three digit class number; a name occupying 24 characters; an
address occupying 60 characters; and a list of options being taken
which occupies 20 characters. Assuming the records are preceded by a
single integer indicating the total number of records to be
processed, the program to create this file could be written

```
          PROGRAM EX94
   CCCC   CREATION OF A DIRECT ACCESS FILE
          CHARACTER VAL*104
          OPEN (5,FILE='MYDIRECT',FORM='FORMATTED',STATUS='NEW',
         1    ACCESS='DIRECT',RECL=107)
          READ *,N
          DO 10 J=1,N
             READ 100,I,VAL
             WRITE (5,100,REC=I) I,VAL
       10 CONTINUE
          CLOSE (5)
      100 FORMAT (I3,A)
          END
```

In this program, no sorting is necessary because the WRITE statement
automatically inserts the record in the correct position as defined
by the specifier REC=I. If the only information on the input file is
the list of records to be processed, the value for N is not needed,
since the information necessary to terminate the processing can be
determined from the READ statement, as indicated in the next section.

9.5   THE READ STATEMENT

The READ statement has already been encountered in its simplest form.
It was first introduced in chapter 2 and further developed in chapter
6.   In both of these chapters, the form used was
          READ f,output-list
where "f" represents either an asterisk in the case of list-directed
input, or the label of the FORMAT statement which describes the
layout of the data on the default input unit.

9.5.1 THE GENERAL FORM OF THE READ STATEMENT

The more general form of the READ statement is
          READ (control-information-list) input-list
The "control-information-list" is the same as that for the WRITE
statement given in section 9.4.3, with one additional optional

specifier. This is the END SPECIFIER, which is written
    END=label
This specifies that if the end of the file is reached   and   no   error
has occurred, the next statement to be obeyed is the one indicated by
the given label. For example, the statement
        READ (6,100,END=210) A,B,C
states that if the end of the file connected to   unit   6   is   reached
without   an   error   occurring, the next statement to be obeyed is the
one   labelled   210.   The   significance   of   the   "input-list"   is   as
described   in   chapter   6.   Using this extra facility when reading a
file sequentially, program EX94 can be rewritten

```
      PROGRAM EX95
CCCC CREATION OF A NEW FILE WHEN AMOUNT OF INPUT DATA ISN´T KNOWN
      CHARACTER VAL*104
      OPEN (5,FILE=´MYDIRECT´,FORM=´FORMATTED´,STATUS=´NEW´,
    1    ACCESS=´DIRECT´,RECL=107)
   10 READ (*,100,END=99) I,VAL
      WRITE (5,100,REC=I) I,VAL
      GOTO 10
   99 CLOSE (5)
  100 FORMAT (I3,A)
      END
```

Note the * in the READ statement which specifies   the   default   input
unit.   This   is   automatically   preconnected   and   therefore no OPEN
statement for this unit is required.   Note also that   the   number   of
records   to   be   read need not be read as data, since on reaching the
end of the file a jump   will   automatically   be   made   to   the   CLOSE
statement.

9.5.2 Sequential Input

All   of the input used so far in this book has been sequential.   This
means that the READ statement has always been used to read   the   next
record   from   the   (default)   input   unit.   The READ statement in its
simplest form always implies sequential   data.   The   only   difference
when   the   more   general   form   of   the   READ   statement   is used for
accessing data in a sequential file is the increased   flexibility   it
provides.   This   extra   flexibility   allows more than one file to be
read by the program, referencing each file by a unit number.   It also
means   that   the end of a file can be recognised without producing an
error, that unformatted data can be used for input   and   that   errors
can be detected using the file status specifier.

9.5.3 Direct Input

When using direct input, records can be read from any part of a file without having to read all of the preceding data, as would be necessary with sequential input. To do this, it is necessary to know the relative position of the required record on the file. For example, to read the tenth record from the file connected to unit 5 requires the single statement

        READ (5,100,REC=10,ERR=99) A,B,C,D

where the FORMAT statement labelled 100 indicates the layout of the record that is to be transferred. Sequential input would have required nine additional READ statements to read records one to nine from the file before the tenth record could be accessed.

9.6 EXAMPLE PROGRAMS

This section contains two programs which illustrate the use of sequential and direct access files.

9.6.1 Example Using Sequential Files

A file contains a sequence of records for transactions as they occurred. Each transaction is given as a 58-character record in which the first six characters indicate the date of the transaction. The seventh character indicates the type of transaction and is one of I, E, B or F, representing income, expenditure, bank transfer of funds and brought forward respectively. The eighth character indicates the account involved in the transaction, for example G represents the general account. The next two characters indicate the form in which the funds were received or given, for example by cheque, postal order or cash. The characters in positions eleven to sixteen give the amount involved in pence. The next twenty-four characters give a description of the giver or receiver, and the last twenty-four characters indicate the reason the funds were given or received. This file is used as input to a program that is designed to produce a summary file for the general account. The form of the summary is an income/expenditure table in which all of the transactions carried out for the same reason and of the same type are accumulated to form one entry in the table. The following program produces the required summary report.

The logic of the program is as follows. The type of transaction is first checked and is then entered into either the income or expenditure table as required. To enter an item into either table, a check is made to see if there is a transaction for the same cause

already in the table. If there is such an entry, the entry is
updated, otherwise a new entry is created in the table. The totals
are updated, and this process is repeated for all transactions. When
all transactions have been completed, the summary table is printed.

```
      PROGRAM EX96
      CHARACTER FIL1*6,TYPE*2,ONE*2,FIL2*24,TRDESC*24,
     1    INDESC(50)*24,OUTDES(50)*24
      DIMENSION TOTIN(50),TOTOUT(50)
      NIN=0
      NOUT=0
CCCC  INITIALISE THE COUNTS FOR THE NUMBER OF INCOME (NIN) AND
CCCC  THE NUMBER OF OUTGOING RECORDS (NOUT) IN THE TABLE
      OPEN (5,FILE='TRANSACTION',STATUS='OLD',FORM='FORMATTED')
      OPEN (6,FILE='FILETESR',STATUS='NEW')
   10 READ (5,100,END=99) FIL1,TYPE,ONE,AMOUNT,FIL2,TRDESC
      IF (TYPE.EQ.'IG') THEN
CCCC      ENTER THIS BLOCK IF INCOME FOR GENERAL ACCOUNT. MUST
CCCC      CHECK THE INCOME TABLE TO SEE IF INCOME FOR THE SAME
CCCC      CAUSE HAS BEEN PROCESSED.  IF SO UPDATE RECORD,
CCCC      OTHERWISE CREATE A NEW RECORD
          DO 20 I=1,NIN
             IF (TRDESC.EQ.INDESC(I)) THEN
                TOTIN(I)=TOTIN(I)+AMOUNT
                GOTO 10
             ENDIF
   20     CONTINUE
CCCC      FALL THROUGH IF FIRST OF ITS KIND. MUST UPDATE
CCCC      COUNTERS AND TABLE
          NIN=NIN+1
          INDESC(NIN)=TRDESC
          TOTIN(NIN)=AMOUNT
      ELSEIF (TYPE.EQ.'EG') THEN
CCCC      ENTER THIS BLOCK IF EXPENDITURE FOR GENERAL ACCOUNT.
CCCC      MUST PROCEED AS FOR INCOME TABLE, USING EXPENDITURE
CCCC      TABLE
          DO 30 I=1,NOUT
             IF (TRDESC.EQ.OUTDES(I)) THEN
                TOTOUT(I)=TOTOUT(I)+AMOUNT
                GOTO 10
             ENDIF
   30     CONTINUE
          NOUT=NOUT+1
          TOTOUT(NOUT)=AMOUNT
```

```
            OUTDES(NOUT)=TRDESC
         ELSEIF (TYPE.EQ.´FG´) THEN
CCCC        ENTER THIS BLOCK IF BROUGHT FORWARD. MUST CREATE NEW
CCCC        RECORD
            NIN=NIN+1
            INDESC(NIN)=TRDESC
            TOTIN(NIN)=AMOUNT
         ENDIF
         GOTO 10
     99 WRITE (6,110)
CCCC   SET UP THE HEADING
         CASHIN=0.0
         DO 40 I=1,NIN
            CASHIN=CASHIN+TOTIN(I)
     40 CONTINUE
         CASHOU=0.0
         DO 50 I=1,NOUT
            CASHOU=CASHOU+TOTOUT(I)
     50 CONTINUE
CCCC   HAVE COMPUTED TOTAL INCOME AND TOTAL EXPENDITURE
CCCC   AND STORED THEM IN CASHIN AND CASHOU RESPECTIVELY
         BALANC=CASHIN-CASHOU
         M=MIN(NIN,NOUT)
CCCC   M IS MIN(NIN,NOUT) AND INDICATES THE NUMBER OF ENTRIES
CCCC   WITH TWO COLUMNS. THE REST WILL ONLY HAVE INCOME OR
CCCC   EXPENDITURE
         DO 60 I=1,M
            WRITE(6,120) INDESC(I),TOTIN(I),OUTDES(I),TOTOUT(I)
     60 CONTINUE
         IF (M.LT.NOUT) THEN
CCCC        WE STILL HAVE SOME EXPENDITURE TO TABULATE
            DO 70 I=M+1,NOUT
               WRITE (6,130) OUTDES(I),TOTOUT(I)
     70     CONTINUE
         ELSE
CCCC        WE HAVE SOME MORE INCOME TO TABULATE
            DO 80 I= M+1,NIN
               WRITE (6,140) INDESC(I),TOTIN(I)
     80     CONTINUE
         ENDIF
         WRITE (6,150) CASHIN,CASHOU,BALANC
         CLOSE (5)
         CLOSE (6)
    100 FORMAT (A6,A2,A2,F6.2,A24,A24)
```

```
110 FORMAT (14X,´INCOME´,26X,´EXPENDITURE´)
120 FORMAT (1X,A24,F9.2,2X,A24,F9.2)
130 FORMAT (36X,A,F9.2)
140 FORMAT (1X,A,F9.2)
150 FORMAT (1X,33(´-´),2X,33(´-´),/,1X,
  1  ´TOTAL INCOME´,12X,F9.2,2X,
  2  ´TOTAL EXPENDITURE´,7X,F9.2,/,1X,33(´-´),2X,
  3  ´BALANCE CARRIED FORWARD ´,F9.2,/,36X,33(´-´),/)
    END
```

The results obtained when this program was run with an input file containing some 200 entries are listed at the end of this section. The logic of the program should be clear from the comments, but the following points should be noted. When no transactions have been processed both NIN and NOUT are zero, and whichever table is searched, the DO list will be empty and so the DO loop will not be obeyed. The descriptions of the transactions must be in exactly the same format, any incorrect spelling or positioning of the description will cause a new entry to be created in the output table. This means that, if data is input from terminals, tabs should be set and used. On most systems it is possible to define the width of each field when data is being input. When the TAB key is depressed this is a signal to move to the start of the next field.

INCOME		EXPENDITURE	
BALANCE BROUGHT FORWARD	64.29	CHURCH ADMINISTRATION	128.96
COVENANT REFUNDS	333.27	PRESENT	1.00
SUNDAY COLLECTIONS	1155.97	SOCIAL RESPONSIBILITY	5.00
SALE OF PLANTS	2.58	METH. INT. HOUSE	5.50
COFFEE MORNING	7.16	RETIREMENT FUND	5.50
DONATION INDIVIDUAL	7.00	TRAINING FUND	5.00
COLLECTION N.C.H.	10.09	GIFT WEEKEND MEAL	6.00
GIFT DAY	442.13	CIRCUIT ASSESSMENTS	790.00
REFUND	6.00	ORGANISTS HONORARIA	104.00
SELF DENIAL SCHEME	9.02	OVERSEAS MISSIONS	35.35
DONATION	3.00	SUNDAY SCHOOL PARTIES	12.71
CAROL SINGING	5.67	LOCAL PREACHERS MUT. AID	17.50
RETIREMENT COLLECTION	17.64	ASSOCIATION OF CHURCHES	5.00
W.W. EASTER OFFERINGS	1.50		
-------------------------------		-------------------------------	
TOTAL INCOME	2065.32	TOTAL EXPENDITURE	1121.52
-------------------------------		BALANCE CARRIED FORWARD	943.80

9.6.2 Example of a Simple Program using Direct Access

As an example of a simple update of a file consider the following
program:

```
      PROGRAM EX97
      CHARACTER NAME1*30,NAME2*30,OPTS*20,CODE*6
      CHARACTER*60 HOMADD,LOCADD,NEWADD,OLDADD
      OPEN (5,FILE='CLASSLIST',FORM='FORMATTED',
     1    STATUS='MODIFY',ACCESS='DIRECT',RECL=176)
CCCC  'MODIFY' IS A SITE DEPENDENT SPECIFIER NEEDED AT SALFORD
CCCC  WHEN THE FILE IS TO BE ALTERED AS WELL AS READ
      OPEN (6,FILE='UPDATES',FORM='FORMATTED',STATUS='OLD')
   10 READ (6,100,END=999) I,NAME1,OLDADD,NEWADD
      READ (5,101,REC=I,ERR=99) CODE,NAME2,HOMADD,LOCADD,
     1    OPTS
CCCC  CHECK AMENDMENT RECORD AGAINST CURRENT RECORD
      IF (NAME1.EQ.NAME2 .AND. OLDADD.EQ.LOCADD) THEN
          WRITE(5,101,REC=I) CODE,NAME2,HOMADD,NEWADD,OPTS
CCCC  HAVE UPDATED RECORD TO INDICATE THE NEW ADDRESS
      ELSE
          PRINT 102,I,NAME1,OLDADD,NEWADD
          PRINT 103,I,NAME2,LOCADD
CCCC  HAVE PRINTED ERROR MESSAGE TO INDICATE INVALID DATA
      ENDIF
      GOTO 10
   99 PRINT *,'ERROR READING CLASSLIST RECORD       ',I
      PRINT *
      GOTO 10
  999 CLOSE (5)
      CLOSE (6)
  100 FORMAT (I3,3A)
  101 FORMAT (5A)
  102 FORMAT (1X,'INVALID UPDATE: ',I6,3A)
  103 FORMAT (1X,'RECORD IN : ',I6,' IS  ',2A)
      END
```

In this example a master file called CLASSLIST contains formatted
records 176 characters long. Each record has 5 fields containing
values of code, name, home address, local address and options being
taken, occupying 6, 30, 60, 60 and 20 character positions
respectively. A second file named UPDATES contains records used to
update the master file. Each record in the update file has 4 fields
– a class number, name, old local address, new local address. The

class number is a 3 digit integer and indicates the relative position
of the record on the master file that is to be altered, the other
fields are 30,60 and 60 characters long respectively. To update a
record the record is first read and checked to see if it is
consistent with the update record. This is done by checking that the
name and local address contained on the master file are the same as
the name and old local address given in the update file. Should the
data for the update be inconsistent with that on the master file
(CLASSLIST) an error message is printed and the update does not take
place; otherwise the master file is updated.

It should be noted that at all sites there will be a default buffer
size available for the transfer of records to or from files. If this
size is not sufficient the computing advisory service should be
consulted.

9.7 DISCONNECTING FILES - THE CLOSE STATEMENT

It will have been noticed that whenever a file that has been opened
by a program is no longer required, the file is released by a CLOSE
statement. When a file is released, it is possible that the file will
never be required again and can be deleted from the system. The file
can be deleted at the time it is released by using one of the
specifiers permitted with the CLOSE statement. If the file connected
to unit 5 is no longer required and is to be deleted from the system
all that is needed is the statement
          CLOSE (5,STATUS='DELETE')
This statement will not only release the file connected to unit 5
from the program but it will also delete that file from the system,
provided the program has the right to delete the file. To prevent
unauthorised programs from deleting, or, altering files without the
owners consent, the access rights are restricted to those specified
by the owner of the file. Should a program attempt to delete a file
without permission an error will occur. This is also true if a
program attempts to open a file without permission or attempts to
write to a file for which the program only has read access rights.
Errors of this nature can be detected by the program using the error
specifier. In the case of the CLOSE statement this is achieved by
writing the statement in the form
          CLOSE (5,STATUS='DELETE',ERR=99)
Should an error occur, instead of the program terminating with an
error condition, the next instruction to be obeyed will be that
labelled 99.

More sophisticated users may wish to check for the cause of the
error. This can be done using the input/output status specifier. For

example, in th statement
>   CLOSE (5,STATUS=´DELETE´,ERR=99,IOSTAT=I)
the value in I indicates the cause of the error. The values given for
various errors are implementation dependent and a copy of the error
codes must be obtained for the particular implementation in use.

9.8 TRUNCATION AND REPOSITIONING OF SEQUENTIAL FILES

There are three statements for this purpose, namely ENDFILE,
BACKSPACE and REWIND. The last two are used to reposition the file,
and the first is used to mark the logical end of a file.

9.8.1 THE ENDFILE STATEMENT

In the discussion so far, the end of a file has always been
recognised by its physical end. However, it may happen that a file is
to be truncated after a certain point and records beyond that point
discarded. This can be achieved by writing the endfile record,
mentioned in section 9.1.3, using the ENDFILE statement. In its
simplest form this is
>   ENDFILE n
where "n" is the unit number associated with the file. This will
cause the endfile record to be inserted at the next position in the
file. The file is then positioned after the endfile record. There
are two optional specifiers that can be used with the ENDFILE
statement. These are the input/output specifier and the error
specifier, which have the same significance as described in section
9.3.3 for the OPEN statement. An example of the ENDFILE statement in
its most general form is
>   ENDFILE (5,IOSTAT=ISTAT,ERR=999)
If an ENDFILE statement has been obeyed, the file must be
repositioned before the endfile record using the REWIND or BACKSPACE
statement, before any data transfer statement can be obeyed.

9.8.2 THE REWIND STATEMENT

When data has been written to a sequential file, it cannot be read
back from the file without first repositioning the file. Nor can a
record be read for a second time without "turning back" to that
record. To start at the beginning of a file requires that the file be
first repositioned at the start. This is done using the REWIND
statement. As a simple example, consider the statement
>   REWIND 5
This will reposition the file connected to unit 5 at the beginning of

that file. If no file is connected to unit 5 an error will occur and
the program will fail. To permit the programmer the option of taking
remedial action, the two additional specifiers available with ENDFILE
are also available. The general form of the REWIND statement is thus
        REWIND (5,IOSTAT=IO,ERR=99)
If the file is already at the beginning, this statement has no
effect. After a successful REWIND the records on the file can be read
using the sequential form of the READ statement.

9.8.3 THE BACKSPACE STATEMENT

Sometimes only the preceding record is required and not the entire
file. In this case, the file can be positioned one position earlier
than its current position using the BACKSPACE statement.   To move
back one record on the file connected to unit "n" for sequential
access, all that is required is the statement
        BACKSPACE n
If the file is at the beginning this has no effect, but if there is
no file connected to unit "n", a failure will occur. A failure will
also occur if an attempt is made to perform a BACKSPACE over a record
that has been written using list directed formatting. Again there are
the two optional specifiers (IOSTAT and ERR) available to help detect
these situations and take any necessary remedial action.

    From the foregoing it will be obvious that files can be created and
erased by FORTRAN 77 programs, but to do this in a satisfactory
manner requires some means of checking the file store for the
existence and status of files.   This can be done by the INQUIRE
statement which is described in section 10.8.

9.9 EXERCISES

1. The records held in a sequential file named MYFILE are each 100
characters long. The first 15 character positions of each record
contain a name, the records being ordered so that the names are in
alphabetical order. A set of data cards containing amendment records
are presented with the name fields in alphabetical order.

    Write a program which reads an amendment record from the cards and
then scans through MYFILE copying records to an updated file
MYNEWFILE until the name of the record read from MYFILE is
alphabetically greater than or equal to the name field of the
amendment record. The amendment record is then written to MYNEWFILE
and, if the record from MYFILE has the same name field, another
record is taken from MYFILE. The next amendment record is now read
and the process repeated until all amendment records have been

processed. The remaining records from MYFILE are then copied to MYNEWFILE. Should MYFILE be exhausted first, the remaining amendment records are copied to MYNEWFILE.

2. A file AERO contains numerical data that describes the shape of an aeroplane body. The data consists of a number of two-dimensional arrays representing 200 equidistant coordinate positions on the perimeter of a cross-section through the body. The cross-sections are taken at positions distant dz, 2dz, 3dz, ... from the nose and at right angles to the length of the body. The points on the cross-section are assumed to be sufficiently close for the body shape to be considered to consist of the straight lines joining adjacent points.

Write a program to determine the position at which the perimeter divided by the cross-sectional area is a minimum, and the position at which it is a maximum. The program should then read the coordinates defining these cross-sections from the file AERO and print them, with suitable comments, on the line printer.

3. A wholesaler holds the details of his stock-in-hand in a sequential file. Each record in this file contains the stock number, item description, quantity in stock, reorder level, normal stock level, minimum reorder quantity and reorder quantum for each stock item. Each day the wholesaler creates another sequential file of customers' orders. In this file each record contains a stock number, customer description and the quantity ordered. In both files the stock number is a six digit unsigned integer, the descriptions are twenty characters long and all other fields consist of four digit unsigned integers. Both files are ordered with the stock number in increasing order.

Write a program to produce three separate listings

(i)   For orders that can be supplied, this should consist of the stock number, item and customer descriptions and the quantity ordered.

(ii) For orders that cannot be supplied, this should consist of the same information as in (i).

(iii) For items whose quantity in stock is less than the reorder level, the listing should include the stock number, item description and the reorder quantity. The reorder quantity is the smallest amount that can be ordered to bring the stock level above the normal stock level.

4. Modify your solution to question 3 so that your program uses a direct access file for the stock-in-hand and the update records are in an unordered sequential file.

CHAPTER 10
ADDITIONAL FEATURES OF FORTRAN 77

This chapter describes some additional features of FORTRAN 77 which, in general, are used less frequently than those discussed in the earlier chapters. The descriptions given are usually quite brief. The full definitions may be obtained from the ANSI Standard.

10.1 LOGICAL EXPRESSIONS, CONSTANTS AND VARIABLES

The construction of simple logical expressions was described in chapter 4. This section describes how to construct more complicated logical expressions, how logical variables can be given values by means of logical assignment statements, and how logical variables can be used in conditional statements.

10.1.1 Relational Expressions

A RELATIONAL EXPRESSION is used to compare the values of two arithmetic expressions or two character expressions. The general form of a relational expression is

    expression1   relational operator   expression2

where the relational operators allowed by FORTRAN 77 are

    .EQ.   .NE.   .GT.   .LT.   .GE.   .LE.

as described in chapter 4. Note that "expression1" and "expression2" must be either both numeric or both character. The comparison of a numeric expression with a character expression is not allowed.

10.1.2 Logical Expressions

A LOGICAL EXPRESSION normally consists of one or more relational expressions connected, if there is more than one relational expression, by LOGICAL OPERATORS. The general form of a logical expression is

relational expression   logical operator   relational expression
where the relational expressions can be replaced by logical constants
as   described   in   section   10.1.4,   logical   constant   names,   logical
variable names as described in section 10.1.3, logical array   element
names, logical function references or other logical expressions.   The
simplest   form   of   logical   expression   is   merely   a   relational
expression,   which   is   usually   called   a simple logical expression.
This was described in   chapter   4.   The   result   of   evaluating   any
logical expression is either "true" or "false".

The logical operators allowed by FORTRAN 77 are

.NOT.   .OR.   .AND.   .EQV.   .NEQV.

Of these, .OR. and .AND. were introduced briefly in chapter 4;   .NOT.
represents logical negation; .EQV. represents logical equivalence and
.NEQV. represents logical non-equivalence.   If   R   and   S   represent
relational   expressions,   .NOT.R   has the reverse value to R; R.AND.S
has the value "true" if both R and S have the   value   "true";   R.OR.S
has   the   value   "true"   if   either of R and S have the value "true";
R.EQV.S has the value "true" if R and S   have   the   same   value,   and
R.NEQV.S   has the value "true" if R and S have different values.   The
following table gives a summary of this.

	R="true" S="true"	R="true" S="false"	R="false" S="true"	R="false" S="false"
.NOT. R	"false"	"false"	"true"	"true"
R .OR. S	"true"	"true"	"true"	"false"
R .AND. S	"true"	"false"	"false"	"false"
R .EQV. S	"true"	"false"	"false"	"true"
R .NEQV. S	"false"	"true"	"true"	"false"

In   the   following examples of logical expressions, brackets are used
to separate the relational expressions from   the   logical   operators.
The   brackets   are   not   strictly   necessary,   but   they make logical
expressions easier to follow.   The logical expression

M.GT.´FRED´

is "true" if the character variable M has a   value   lexicographically
greater   than   ´FRED´,   and   is   "false"   otherwise.   The   logical
expression

(N.GT.1234) .AND. (N.LT.4321)

is "true" if the value of N lies between 1234 and 4321 and   is   false
otherwise.   The logical expression

(M.LT.´FRED´) .OR. (M.EQ.´GERT´)

is   "true" if the value of M is lexicographically less than ´FRED´ or
if its value is   ´GERT´.   It is   "false"   otherwise.   The   logical

expression
    (.NOT. (M.LT.´FRED´)) .AND. (M.LT.´GERT´)
has the same result as the logical expression
    (M.GE.´FRED´) .AND. (M.LT.´GERT´)
It is "true" if the value of M lies between ´FRED´ and ´GERT´ or if
it is equal to ´FRED´; and is "false" otherwise. The logical
expression
    (M.LT.´FRED´) .EQV. (M.LT.´GERT´)
is "true" if M is less than ´FRED´ or if M is greater than or equal
to the value of ´GERT´, since (M.LT.´FRED´) and (M.LT.´GERT´) are
both "true" in the former case and both "false" in the latter. The
logical expression
    ((A.GT.0.1) .NEQV. (A.GT.0.2))
is "true" if the value of the real variable A lies between 0.1 and
0.2 and "false" otherwise. This is because the two relational
expressions A.GT.0.1 and A.GT.0.2 have different values if A lies
between 0.1 and 0.2. The logical expression
    ((M.LT.´FRED´) .AND. (M.GT.´BERT´)) .OR. (M.EQ.´GERT´)
is "true" if the value of M lies between ´BERT´ and ´FRED´ or if it
is ´GERT´, and is "false" otherwise.

The logical operators described in this section are subject to an
order of precedence or hierarchy similar to that for the arithmetic
operators described in chapter 3. This is summarised in the
following table.

OPERATOR	LEVEL OF PRECEDENCE
.NOT.	level 1
.AND.	level 2
.OR.	level 3
.NEQV. or .EQV.	level 4

As an example, consider the logical expression
    (A.LT.0.0 .OR. B.LT.0.0 .AND. C.LT.0.0)
Since the operator .AND. has a higher level of precedence than the
operator .OR. in the hierarchy, this logical expression is treated
in the same way as
    (A.LT.0.0 .OR. (B.LT.0.0 .AND. C.LT.0.0))
Note that logical expressions inside brackets are always evaluated
before the hierarchy is brought into effect.

Even more complicated logical expressions can be constructed, but
their use is not recommended for the inexperienced programmer. One
reason for this is that it is very easy to construct them
incorrectly. In addition, unless they are constructed very carefully

indeed, redundant comparisons are often built into them. This
reduces the efficiency of the program.

10.1.3 Logical Variables

The type of all the variables used up to this point has been real,
integer or character. FORTRAN 77 permits the use of other types of
variable, one of which is called LOGICAL. Logical variables can be
given values by means of logical assignment statements, and they can
be used in conditional statements in place of logical expressions.

All logical variables used by a program must be declared at the
start of the program unit by a LOGICAL STATEMENT. The general form
of this statement is

        LOGICAL list

where, as with the other type statements, the "list" contains the
names of the logical variables used by the program. The names of the
variables in the list are constructed according to the normal rules
described in chapter 2. The "list" may also contain array names with
or without their dimensions, function names and the symbolic names of
constants.

An example of a LOGICAL statement is

        LOGICAL K9,FRED,HILDA(0:3)

which defines the variables K9, FRED, HILDA(0), HILDA(1), HILDA(2)
and HILDA(3) to be of type logical.

10.1.4 Logical Assignment Statements

Logical variables can be given values by means of LOGICAL ASSIGNMENT
STATEMENTS. These have the general form

        logical variable = logical expression

where the logical expression can be a relational expression as
described in section 10.1.1, a logical variable, one of the LOGICAL
CONSTANTS .TRUE. or .FALSE., or a logical expression involving
logical variables as described in section 10.1.5. Note that the only
values that a logical variable can take are .TRUE. and .FALSE.

As with other types of variable, the initial value of a logical
variable can be set by a DATA statement. For example, the statements

        LOGICAL K9,FRED

        DATA K9,FRED / .TRUE.,.FALSE. /

declares the variables K9 and FRED to be of type LOGICAL and gives
them initial values .TRUE. and .FALSE. respectively.

In the following examples of logical assignment statements, the
variables K9 and FRED are assumed to be of type LOGICAL. As a result
of

```
        K9=.TRUE.
```
K9 is given the value .TRUE.   As a result of
```
        FRED=I.EQ.J
```
FRED is given the value .TRUE. or the value .FALSE. depending on the
values of the integer variables I and J at the time the statement is
obeyed. For example, if I has the value 1 and J the value 2 at that
time, FRED is given the value .FALSE.; whereas if I and J both have
the value 1, FRED is given the value .TRUE. As a result of
```
        K9=(CHAR.GT.´JAMES´) .AND. (CHAR.LT.´KEITH´)
```
K9 is given the value .TRUE. if the value of the   character   variable
CHAR lies between ´JAMES´ and ´KEITH´ when the assignment statement
is obeyed, otherwise K9 is given the value .FALSE. As a result of
```
        FRED=K9
```
FRED is given the same logical value as K9.

10.1.5 The Use of Logical Variables in Logical Expressions

A logical variable that has previously been given a value can be used
in a logical expression. Thus the result of
```
        K9=FRED .OR. (I.EQ.0)
```
is that the logical variable K9 is given the value .TRUE. if the
logical variable FRED has the value .TRUE. or if the value of the
integer variable I is 0. K9 is given the value .FALSE. otherwise.
The statement
```
        K9=.NOT. K9
```
reverses the value of the logical variable K9.

   Logical variables can be used in conditional statements in place of
logical expressions.   For example, suppose that   the   logical
assignment statement
```
        K9=I.EQ.0
```
appears at some point in a program. As a result of this statement,
K9 is given the value .TRUE. or .FALSE.   depending on whether the
value of I is or is not zero at that point. A subsequent BLOCK IF
statement
```
        IF (K9) THEN
           J=1
        ELSE
           J=2
        ENDIF
```
will result in J being given the value 1 if K9 has the   value   .TRUE.
and the value 2 if K9 has the value .FALSE. Note that the value of I
at the time the conditional statement is obeyed does not affect K9,
since its value is set by the logical assignment statement. Hence
the statements

```
          I=0
          K9=I.EQ.0
          I=1
          IF (K9) THEN
              J=1
          ELSE
              J=2
          ENDIF
```

will result in J being given the value 1, since the logical assignment statement sets K9 to .TRUE. and the IF statement tests K9, not I.EQ.0.

10.1.6 Input and Output of Logical Data

Logical data can be input and output by list-directed READ, PRINT and WRITE statements. For example, if K9 is a logical variable, the statement

```
          READ *,I,K9,R
```

will, if the data record being read is

```
     21 .TRUE. 16.6
```

result in the integer variable I being given the value 21, K9 being given the value .TRUE. and the real variable R being given the value 16.6. Note that the same value is read into K9 if the characters .TRUE. on the data record are replaced by any character string which does not contain a space, a comma or a slash character and which starts with .T, such as .TIME. The input of .FALSE. is treated similarly.

  The corresponding PRINT statement

```
          PRINT *,I,K9,R
```

results in the output

```
          21  T   16.600000
```

  Formatted input and output uses the L-format edit descriptor, which has the general form

```
     Lw
```

where "w" is the field width. On input, the leading non-blank characters in the field must be .T or .F depending on whether the value to be read is .TRUE. or .FALSE. The output is "w-1" space characters followed by a T or an F as appropriate in position "w".

10.1.7 Logical Functions

A function subprogram which returns a logical value to its calling program unit must have its type declared in the same way as a function subprogram which returns a character value, as described in chapter 8. This can be done either by including the type of the function in the FUNCTION statement or by including in the function a type statement which declares the function name to be of type LOGICAL.

As an example, consider a function EVEN(N) which returns the value .TRUE. if N is an even number and the value .FALSE. if N is an odd number. This could be written as

```
LOGICAL FUNCTION EVEN(N)
EVEN=N.EQ.N/2*2
END
```

It could also be written as

```
FUNCTION EVEN(N)
LOGICAL EVEN
EVEN=N.EQ.N/2*2
END
```

It should be noted that the function EVEN must be declared to be of type LOGICAL in any program unit that calls it.

10.2 DOUBLE PRECISION AND COMPLEX VARIABLES

FORTRAN 77 allows a total of six types of variable. The two which have not yet been described are DOUBLE PRECISION and COMPLEX. As with variables of type CHARACTER and LOGICAL, DOUBLE PRECISION and COMPLEX variables must be declared by appropriate type statements. These appear with the other specification statements at the start of a program unit. Both DOUBLE PRECISION and COMPLEX variables are used for particular specialised tasks.

10.2.1 Double Precision Variables

Round-off errors can cause incorrect results to be produced by a program which solves a numeric problem. When this happens, programmers should first consider whether the numerical method being used is appropriate for the problem being solved, or whether the use of a different method will avoid the difficulty.

When use of a different method is not feasible, FORTRAN 77 allows accuracy to be improved by letting one variable use two words of storage. Such a variable is called a DOUBLE PRECISION VARIABLE. All double precision variables used must be declared by a DOUBLE PRECISION TYPE STATEMENT, which has the form

```
DOUBLE PRECISION list
```

where the "list" contains the names of the double precision variables. These are constructed according to the normal rules detailed in chapter 2. The "list" may also contain array names with or without their dimensions, function names and symbolic names of constants.

Double precision variables can be used in arithmetic expressions in the same way as real variables. They can appear in the same arithmetic expression as real or integer quantities, the result of the expression being of type double precision. Hence, if either X or Y are double precision, the result of

X+Y

is double precision. It should be noted that mixed real, integer and double precision expressions are evaluated in a similar way to mixed real and integer expressions, as described in chapter 3. For example, if D is a double precision variable and the values of D, R, I and J are 4.0, 2.0, 5 and 3 respectively, the result of

D-R+I/J

is the double precision number 3.0. Following the normal rules, I/J is evaluated first, resulting in the integer quantity 1. After this, D-R+1 is evaluated, resulting in the double precision version of 3.0.

Double precision constants may be used in FORTRAN 77 programs in the same way as real constants such as 1.0E-8, although for most purposes the corresponding real constant is sufficient. The form of a double precision constant is similar to the exponential form of a real constant, with D replacing E. Examples of double precision constants are 1.0D-8, 1.23456789D10 and 22D2.

An intrinsic function is available to transform real or integer quantities into double precision form. The general form of this function is

DBLE(X)

where X can be replaced by any numeric expression. Similarly, a double precision quantity D can be converted to single precision by using REAL(D). Full details of functions which accept double precision arguments are given in appendix 1.

Assignments to double precision variables are carried out in the same way as those to real or integer variables. For example, if D is double precision, the result of the statement

D=X

is that the double precision equivalent of X is stored in D, where X can be replaced by any numeric quantity.

The input and output of double precision quantities can be achieved either by normal list-directed statements; or by formatted input and output. When the latter alternative is taken, F-format and E-format edit descriptors may be used in the same way as for real quantities, as described in chapter 6; or a special edit descriptor can be used. This has the form

Dw.d

the result being the same as that of using the E-format edit
descriptor except that D replaces E in the output.

Finally, it should be noted that a function may be declared to be
double precision if the function statement is written in the form

DOUBLE PRECISION FUNCTION name (arguments)

The effect is that a double precision quantity is returned to the
calling program unit. It should be noted that "name" must be
declared to be of type DOUBLE PRECISION in any program unit that
calls it.

10.2.2 Complex Variables

The type statement

COMPLEX list

reserves two words of storage for each variable in the "list", one
for the real part of the complex number and the other for the
imaginary part. FORTRAN 77 also defines COMPLEX CONSTANTS, which
consist of a bracketed pair of real numbers separated by a comma.
Examples are $(1.4, 3.5)$, which represents the complex number $1.4+3.5i$,
and $(-1.4, -3.5)$, which represents the complex number $-1.4-3.5i$.
Complex variables can be given values in the same way as real
variables. The only constraint is that complex and double precision
quantities must not appear in the same arithmetic expression. An
operation which involves a complex quantity will have a complex
result. It should be noted that the normal algebraic rules for
manipulating complex quantities are obeyed, so that

C=(1.0,2.0)*(3.0,4.0)

where C is of type COMPLEX, results in C being given the value
$(-5.0, 10.0)$. In addition it should be noted that, when a mixed
expression is being evaluated, a real quantity R is regarded as being
equivalent to the complex quantity $(R, 0)$.

When complex constants are read using list-directed input, they
must appear explicitly on the data record. For example, suppose that

READ *,R,C

appears in a program, where R and C are of type REAL and COMPLEX
respectively. A data record containing

1.2 (2.3,3.4)

could be read by this statement. The results when list-directed
output is used are printed in a similar way, with the arguments of
the complex number in brackets. When formatted input and output is
used, two adjacent real edit descriptors must be specified for each
complex quantity.

Very few FORTRAN 77 programs require the use of complex quantities
since mathematical manipulation can usually reduce the problem to one

involving real quantities. Although provision is made for their use in the language, complex variables are normally detrimental to program efficiency, so they should be avoided.

10.3 ADDITIONAL SPECIFICATION STATEMENTS

Most of the specification statements allowed by FORTRAN 77 have been described in earlier chapters. Those remaining are the IMPLICIT statement, the SAVE statement and the EQUIVALENCE statement, which are described in this section.

10.3.1 The IMPLICIT Statement

This statement allows the normal convention for naming real and integer variables to be overridden. For example, the statement
        IMPLICIT REAL (A-Z)
imposes the convention that all variables are of type REAL unless they are declared otherwise by a type statement. Similarly, the statement
        IMPLICIT LOGICAL (A-Z)
states that all variables are of type LOGICAL unless a type statement declares them otherwise. The normal convention is confirmed by the statement
        IMPLICIT REAL (A-H,O-Z), INTEGER (I-N)
The general form of the IMPLICIT statement is
        IMPLICIT type (range), type (range), ...
where the "type" is any that can appear in a type statement and the "range" consists of sets of single letters or pairs of letters connected by a hyphen, each member of the set being separated from the next by a comma. The sets must be in alphabetic order. The effect is that all variables used by the program with names starting with a letter in the range will be of the type specified unless this is overridden by a type statement.

10.3.2 The SAVE Statement

Variables used in a subprogram which are neither dummy arguments nor variables in a common block are purely local to the subprogram. They may lose their values when a return is made unless they appear in the list of a SAVE statement. Those local variables mentioned in the list are guaranteed to have their values saved for use the next time the subprogram is called.

The SAVE statement is non-executable. It has the general form
        SAVE list

where "list" is a list of variable names, array names and common block names. The names of the common blocks must be preceded and followed by slash characters. When a particular common block name is specified in a SAVE statement in a subprogram, it must be specified in a SAVE statement in every subprogram accessing that common block. Dummy argument names, subprogram names and individual items in a common block may not be included in the save list. If the list is omitted, it is assumed that all permitted entities in the subprogram are to be saved.

As an example, consider a subroutine named FRED which has the form

```
SUBROUTINE FRED(A,N,X,Y)
DIMENSION A(N),B(10)
COMMON /INFO/ C(100),D(100)
SAVE SUM,K,B,/INFO/
 . . . . . . . . . .
END
```

The local variables SUM and K, the local array B and the common block INFO are all included in the SAVE statement, which means that their values are retained between calls of the subprogram.

10.3.3 The EQUIVALENCE Statement

This statement is used to specify that two or more variable names in a program unit refer to the same storage location. This allows the names to be used interchangeably in the program unit. The general form of the statement is

```
EQUIVALENCE (list1),(list2),....
```

where each list contains a set of names of variables, arrays, array elements or character substrings, which are to be treated as equivalent. For example, the statement

```
EQUIVALENCE (A,B),(I,J,K)
```

causes the variable names A and B to refer to the same storage location and the variable names I, J and K to refer to the same storage location.

Equivalencing ·two array elements has the effect of equivalencing the other array elements in the appropriate way. For example, the statements

```
DIMENSION A(100),B(10,10)
EQUIVALENCE (A(1),B(1,1))
```

have the effect of making A(1) equivalent to B(1,1), A(2) equivalent to B(2,1) and so on, A(100) being equivalent to B(10,10).

The example just given is a sensible way of using equivalence between two arrays. However, it would not be incorrect to use the statement

        EQUIVALENCE (A(5),B(3,3))
In this case, A(1) is equivalent to B(2,9), A(2) to B(2,10), ...,
A(5) to B(3,3), ... and A(82) to B(10,10). Only some of the elements
of the arrays are equivalent and clearly great care must be
exercised. When array names rather than specific array elements are
equivalenced, the effect is the same as equivalencing the first
elements of the two arrays.

   Entities of type CHARACTER must not be equivalenced to entities of
any other type. Although FORTRAN 77 does not prohibit it, it is
strongly recommended that data types should not be mixed in an
equivalence list. There are restrictions on the use of EQUIVALENCE;
for example, the same storage location must not be equivalenced for
two different elements of the same array. Also, since complications
can arise when equivalencing items within COMMON BLOCKS, it is
recommended that this is avoided. Full details of these restrictions
may be found in the ANSI Standard.

10.4 ADDITIONAL CONTROL STATEMENTS

FORTRAN 77 defines a total of 16 control statements, most of which
were introduced in earlier chapters. The END statement was
introduced in chapter 2; the GOTO, BLOCK IF, ENDIF, ELSE, ELSEIF,
logical IF, DO, CONTINUE and STOP statements in chapter 4; and the
RETURN and CALL statements in chapter 7. The four remaining control
statements are the arithmetic IF, computed GOTO, assigned GOTO and
PAUSE statements. Of these, the only one to provide a useful
additional facility is the computed GOTO statement.

10.4.1 The Arithmetic IF Statement

The general form of this statement is
        IF (arithmetic expression) label1,label2,label3
The effect is that the statement whose label is "label1" is the next
statement to be obeyed by the program if the result of the arithmetic
expression is negative; the statement whose label is "label2" is
obeyed next if the result of the arithmetic expression is zero; and
the statement whose label is "label3" is obeyed next if the result of
the arithmetic expression is positive. It should be noted that any
two of the three labels can be the same, so that the statement
        IF (A-1.0) 11,11,12
is valid. The effect of this statement is that the statement
labelled 12 is the next to be obeyed if A-1.0 is positive (that is,
the value of A is greater than 1.0) and the statement labelled 11
otherwise. In fact, arithmetic IF statements are normally

constructed in this way if the arithmetic expression being tested is
real, since round-off errors make a test for zero unreliable.

   Arithmetic IF statements were a feature of early versions of
FORTRAN which are not recommended for modern programs, since their
use makes it difficult to structure a program properly.

10.4.2 The Computed GOTO Statement

The general form of this statement is

        GOTO (label1,label2,...,labeln),e

where "e" is an integer expression and "label1", "label2", ...,
"labeln" are the labels of executable statements in the program. The
effect of the computed GOTO statement is that the next statement to
be obeyed by the program is that whose label is "label1" if the value
of "e" is 1, that whose label is "label2" if the value of "e" is 2,
and so on. The same statement label may appear more than once in the
same computed GOTO statement. If the value of the integer expression
"e" is outside the range from 1 to "n", the statement following the
computed GOTO statement is obeyed next by the program. If the
programmer wishes, the comma following the closing bracket in a
computed GOTO statement may be omitted.

   As an example of the use of a computed GOTO statement, the main
program part of program EX73 (see section 7.3.5) may be rewritten as

```
          ..........
          READ *,EPS
      11  READ *,A,B,C
          CALL QUADEQ (A,B,C,EPS,R1,R2,INDIC)
          GOTO (12,13,14,15,16) INDIC
          PRINT *,´THE VALUE OF INDIC DOES NOT LIE BETWEEN 1 AND 5´
          STOP
      12  ROOT1=R1+SIGN(R2,R1)
          ROOT2=C/(A*ROOT1)
          PRINT 101,A,B,C,ROOT1,ROOT2
          GOTO 11
      13  PRINT 102,A,B,C,R1,R2,R1,R2
          GOTO 11
      14  PRINT 104,A,B,C,R1
          GOTO 11
      15  PRINT 103,A,B,C
          GOTO 11
      16  STOP
          ..........
```

Comparison of this with program EX73 shows that the computed GOTO
statement is neater in this case than a BLOCK IF statement.

10.4.3 The ASSIGN Statement and the Assigned GOTO Statement

The general form of the ASSIGN statement is

ASSIGN label TO i

where "i" is an integer variable. The effect is that the appropriate label, which must be that of an executable statement in the program, is assigned to the integer variable. It should be noted that this statement can only be used to assign labels; it cannot be used instead of a normal assignment statement as described in chapter 2.

The general form of the assigned GOTO statement is

GOTO i,(label1,label2,...,labeln)

where "i" is an integer variable which must have been assigned a value earlier in the program by means of an ASSIGN statement; and "label1", "label2", ..., "labeln" are the labels of executable statements in the program. The effect is that the statement identified by the statement label assigned to the integer variable is the next statement to be obeyed by the program. The list of labels in the brackets need not be present; if it is, the statement label assigned to the integer variable must be present in the list.

Since the computed GOTO statement is simpler to use, normally more efficient, and fulfils the same function as the assigned GOTO statement, it is strongly recommended that the assigned GOTO statement is not used.

10.4.4 The PAUSE Statement

The general form of the PAUSE statement is

PAUSE n

where "n", which need not be present, is a character constant of up to five digits. Execution of the PAUSE statement causes suspension of execution of the program. In modern terms, this does not make sense except in an interactive environment. The value of "n" is available during the period during which execution of the program is suspended. It allows the program to be restarted in a manner to be determined by the implementor.

The STOP statement, as described in chapter 4, can be extended in a similar way. Its general form is

STOP n

10.5 ADDITIONAL FEATURES OF PROGRAM UNITS

In chapter 7, most of the properties of subprograms were described. However, there are three additional features that will be described

in this section. Firstly, it is possible to use a very simple form
of function definition, known as a STATEMENT FUNCTION. Secondly, it
is possible to have alternative ENTRY points to a subprogram to cater
for different cases. Thirdly, it is also possible to have alternative
forms of the RETURN statement.

10.5.1 Statement Functions

A STATEMENT FUNCTION is a very simple form of function which is
defined within a program unit and which is only available for use
within that program unit.   It must be sufficiently simple for the
definition to be accomplished by a single statement.   The following
example illustrates the use of this feature of the language.

In the salesman problem introduced in section 3.5.4, a number of
distances were evaluated using Pythagoras´ formula

$$\sqrt{(X1-X2)^2 + (Y1-Y2)^2}$$

This formula could be programmed as a STATEMENT FUNCTION called
DSTNCE, and program EX36 modified to become:

```
      PROGRAM EX101
CCCC  SALESMAN PROBLEM USING A STATEMENT FUNCTION
CCCC  DEFINITION OF STATEMENT FUNCTION
      DSTNCE(X1,X2,Y1,Y2)=SQRT((X1-X2)**2+(Y1-Y2)**2)
      READ *,XH,YH,XA,YA,XB,YB,XC,YC
      DHA=DSTNCE(XH,XA,YH,YA)
      DHB=DSTNCE(XH,XB,YH,YB)
      . . . . . . . . . .
      END
```

The use of DSTNCE is no different to the use of a function subprogram
or an intrinsic function.   In its definition, the dummy arguments
X1,X2,Y1,Y2 are used and are replaced by the actual arguments when
the function is used.

The rules governing statement functions are as follows:
(i)   the function must be defined by a single statement,
(ii)   it is only available within the program unit in which it is
defined,
(iii) the general definition is of the form:
          function-name (argument-list) = expression
(iv)   "function-name" is the name of the statement function, created
in accordance with the rules for function subprogram names,
(v)   "argument-list" contains the dummy arguments used to calculate
the function value,

(vi) "expression" may contain references to constants (actual constants or the symbolic names of constants), variables (dummy arguments or the names of actual variables defined in the program unit), intrinsic functions, function subprograms and other statement functions which have been defined in previous statement function statements within the same program unit,

(vii) the value of "expression" is returned whenever the function is referenced,

(viii) the STATEMENT FUNCTION statement must occur after the specification statements and before the executable statements, as specified in appendix 3.

10.5.2 The ENTRY Statement

The ENTRY statement allows alternative entry points into a function or subroutine subprogram, in addition to the normal entry point which is the FUNCTION statement or SUBROUTINE statement. The skeleton form of a function with alternative entry points could be as follows

```
        FUNCTION name1 (argument-list1)
        ..........
        ENTRY name2 (argument-list2)
        ..........
        ENTRY name3 (argument-list3)
        ..........
        END
```

In this outline, "name1" is the normal name of the function which, when used in the calling program unit, causes entry at the function statement and "name2" and "name3" are alternative entry points to the function subprogram. When an alternative entry name is used in the calling program unit, the first executable statement after the appropriate entry statement associated with that name is obeyed. For obvious reasons, an ENTRY statement may not occur in the middle of a BLOCK IF statement or a DO loop. There need be no correspondence between the argument lists associated with the different names. However, when a name is used in the calling program unit, the actual argument list provided must correspond with the dummy argument list associated with that name.

This is useful when a subprogram is required to perform a number of slightly different tasks. If the difference is in the initialisation of some quantities and the main sequence of statements is the same for all tasks, alternative entry points may be used for initialising with a jump being made to the main sequence of statements.

As an example, consider a program which reads a set of names terminated by ZZZZ, and which uses a subroutine to sort them. In the sorting process, the positions of the names are not changed. Instead, an index vector, as described in section 8.4.1, is set by the subroutine to indicate the correct order. The subroutine has two entry points with names UP and DOWN. When UP is used, the ordering which results from the subroutine is alphabetic, while when DOWN is used, the ordering is reverse alphabetic. The sorting process is basically the same whichever order is required, the difference being achieved by setting appropriate initial values. The sorting process starts at the subroutine statement labelled 10, the statements before this being used to define the entry points and to set the initial values. It should be noted that, in the definition of DOWN, the dummy arguments and local variables are the same as in the definition of UP, so that the arrays A, M and INDEX need not be redefined.

The program is as follows

```
        PROGRAM EX102
CCCC    NAME SORTING PROGRAM
        PARAMETER (NDIM=100,LENGTH=12)
        CHARACTER*(LENGTH) NAMES(NDIM),NAME
        DIMENSION INDEX1(NDIM),INDEX2(NDIM)
        N=0
        DO 10 I=1,NDIM
            READ *,NAME
            IF (NAME.EQ.'ZZZZ') GOTO 15
            NAMES(I)=NAME
            N=I
     10 CONTINUE
     15 CALL UP(NAMES,N,INDEX1)
        CALL DOWN(NAMES,N,INDEX2)
        PRINT 100
        DO 20 I=1,N
            PRINT 101,NAMES(I),NAMES(INDEX2(I)),NAMES(INDEX1(I))
     20 CONTINUE
    100 FORMAT (1X,'ORIGINAL',4X,'REVERSE',5X,'ALPHABETIC'//)
    101 FORMAT (1X,3A)
        END
        SUBROUTINE UP(A,N,INDEX)
        CHARACTER A(*)*(*),M*50
        DIMENSION INDEX(*)
CCCC    SET INITIAL VALUES FOR ALPHABETIC SORTING
        N1=N
        I1=1
        I2=1
CCCC    JUMP TO SORTING SECTION
```

```
        GOTO 10
CCCC    ALTERNATIVE ENTRY POINT
        ENTRY DOWN(A,N,INDEX)
CCCC    SET INITIAL VALUES FOR REVERSE ALPHABETIC SORTING
        N1=1
        I1=N
        I2=-1
CCCC    MAIN SORTING INSTRUCTIONS
    10  DO 20 I=1,N
            INDEX(I)=I
    20  CONTINUE
        DO 40 I=I1,N1,I2
            I3=I
            M=A(INDEX(I))
            DO 30 J=I,N1,I2
                IF (M.GT.A(INDEX(J))) THEN
                    M=A(INDEX(J))
                    I3=J
                ENDIF
    30      CONTINUE
            J=INDEX(I)
            INDEX(I)=INDEX(I3)
            INDEX(I3)=J
    40  CONTINUE
        END
```

When this program was run, the output was

ORIGINAL	REVERSE	ALPHABETIC
SMITHERS	SMITHERS	ARCHIMEDES
JONES	JONES	BABBAGE
ARCHIMEDES	BABBAGE	JONES
BABBAGE	ARCHIMEDES	SMITHERS

10.5.3 Alternative Return Points from a Subroutine Subprogram

Under normal circumstances a RETURN or END statement in a subprogram returns control to the point at which the subprogram was called. However, it is possible to arrange to return to different points in the calling program unit from a subroutine, but not from a function.

In the definition of the subroutine, a number of dummy arguments (equal to the number of alternative return points) consisting of asterisks are specified. For example,

    SUBROUTINE FRED(A,B,C,*,*)

indicates that there will be two alternative return points for FRED.
When the subroutine is called, the actual arguments used in place of
the asterisks are of the form "* statement label". An example is

    CALL FRED(X,Y,X,*100,*150)

where the statements labelled 100 and 150 are the alternative return
points in the calling program unit.

   Within the subroutine, an alternative return is specified by a
RETURN statement of the form

    RETURN i

where "i" is an integer constant or integer expression which
indicates the return label that is to be used. In the example given,
the statement with label 100 is the return point if i=1, the
statement with label 150 is the return point if i=2, while any other
value of "i" causes a normal return to the point at which the
subroutine was called.

   It is questionable whether this feature is more useful than
confusing. It could be used in program EX73 (see section 7.3.5),
where the subroutine QUADEQ distinguishes between several different
cases and alternative returns might be made to the appropriate PRINT
statements for the printing of the results. However, as in program
EX73, it is always possible to use an argument as an indicator to
show which case has arisen and to take the appropriate action once a
standard return has been made.

10.6 ADDITIONAL FEATURES OF LIST-DIRECTED INPUT

List-directed input was introduced in chapter 2, when features
relating to numeric data were described. Aspects concerning the
input of character data were discussed in chapter 8. As some of the
less important facilities were omitted from these chapters, they are
included in this section.

10.6.1 ADDITIONAL SEPARATORS

In chapter 2, it was stated that one or more space characters can be
used to separate items on a data record. FORTRAN 77 allows two other
separators, the comma and the slash character.

   The comma, which can be preceded and followed on the data record by
space characters, has precisely the same effect as a space character.
Hence, if FRED is a character variable of length eight characters,
the result of the statement

    READ *,ALICE,IRENE,FRED,BRIAN

when used with the data record

   3.7,   7   ,´COMPUTER´,-7.0

is that ALICE, IRENE, FRED and BRIAN are given values 3.7, 7, COMPUTER and -7.0 respectively. Thus the effect is the same as if the data record had been

   3.7   7   ´COMPUTER´ -7.0

The slash character, which can be preceded and followed on the data record by space characters, terminates the execution of the list-directed READ statement. The values of any items in the list of the READ statement which have not been given values before the slash character on the data record is encountered will be unchanged. If the item was undefined before the READ statement was obeyed, it will remain undefined as a result of the statement. As an example, suppose that variables A, B and D have values 1.0, 2.0 and 3.0 respectively and that a variable C is undefined when the statement

       READ *,A,B,C,D

is obeyed. If the data record contains

   11.0,12.0/13.0,14.0

the result is that A and B are given values 11.0 and 12.0 respectively; that C remains undefined, and that the value of D remains at 3.0.

It should be noted that the space character, the comma and the slash character can appear in character constants on a data record in the same way as any other character. If A and B are character variables, each of length six characters, the statement

       READ *,A,B

when the data record contains

   ´ //,,´,´/,/,//´

results in A being given the value ^^//,, and B the value /,/,// where ^ represents a space character. The characters between the first two apostrophes form the value given to A and those between the third and fourth apostrophes form the value given to B. The third comma on the data record is the separator.

10.6.2 REPEAT SPECIFICATIONS

If an item of the form

   r*c

appears in the data which is to be read by a list-directed READ statement, the effect is as if "r" occurrences of the constant "c" had been present. As an example, suppose that E, F and G are character variables, each of length three characters. The effect of

       READ *,A,B,C,D,E,F,G,H

when the data record contains

    1.0,2*2.0,3.0,3*´CAT´,5.0
is that A, B, C, D, E, F, G and H are given values 1.0, 2.0, 2.0,
3.0, CAT, CAT, CAT and 5.0 respectively. It   should be   noted   that
this is the same as if the data record had contained
    1.0 2.0 2.0 3.0 ´CAT´ ´CAT´ ´CAT´ 5.0

10.6.3 NULL VALUES

A null value in the data to be read by a list-directed READ statement
is specified when there are no characters between two separators,
when no characters precede the first separator on a data record, or
when the constant "c" is omitted from the repeat specification. When
a null value is read, the value of the item in the list of the list-
directed READ statement is not altered. Hence, if the values of A,
B, C, D and E are 1.0, 2.0, 3.0, 4.0 and 5.0 respectively, the result
of the statement
        READ *,A,B,C,D,E
when used with the data record
    ,11.0,2*,,
is that the value of A is unchanged, B is given the value 11.0, the
values of C and D are unchanged, as is the value of E.

10.7 ADDITIONAL FORMAT EDIT DESCRIPTORS

Earlier parts of this book have contained descriptions of most of the
edit descriptors allowed by FORTRAN 77, each of which is used for a
particular task.   FORTRAN 77 allows   a   few   additional   edit
descriptors, but it should be noted that those defined earlier are
sufficient for most purposes.

10.7.1 The G-format Edit Descriptor

The G-format edit descriptor allows any type of non-integer numeric
data to be input or output. For medium-sized numbers, the output is
similar to F-format, but there is no possibility of asterisks being
output if the field width is not sufficient for the size of the
number. The usual form of this edit descriptor is
    Gw.d
where "w" is the field width and "d" is an integer which, together
with the magnitude of the number, determines the number of decimal
places to be output. On input, this edit descriptor operates in the
same way as the F-format edit descriptor, as described in section
6.7.2. On output, the size of the number being printed determines
the form of the output. For example, the edit descriptor

G10.3

will cause the following output.

number to be output	form of output
0.04	^0.400E−01
0.4	^0.400^^^^
4.0	^^4.00^^^^
40.0	^^40.0^^^^
400.0	^^400.^^^^
4000.0	^0.400E+04

In general when using Gw.d, numbers less than 0.1 or greater than $10**d$ are printed using the corresponding E-format edit descriptor, while numbers between 0.1 and $10**d$ are printed using a form of output which is similar to F-format, but which allows a total of "d" digits plus the decimal point, followed by four blank characters.

There is a more general form of this edit descriptor, namely

Gw.dEe

where "e" specifies the number of digits in the exponent part of the output. A similar extension,

Ew.dEe

is allowed for the E-format edit descriptor. Full details may be found in the ANSI Standard.

As output from the G-format edit descriptor is less tidy than that from the F-format or the E-format edit descriptors, it is recommended that these are used in preference to G-format.

10.7.2 The H-format Edit Descriptor

This edit descriptor offers an alternative method for the output of a character string. Its general form is

$nHh_1h_2h_3...h_n$

where "h_1", "h_2", ..., "h_n" represent "n" characters. The effect is the same as if the character string

$'h_1h_2h_3...h_n'$

appeared in a FORMAT statement. For example, both the statements

```
      PRINT 100,I,J
  100 FORMAT (14H DERBY COUNTY ,I1,
    1     19H MANCHESTER UNITED ,I1)
```

and the statements

```
      PRINT 100,I,J
  100 FORMAT (' DERBY COUNTY ',I1,
    1    ' MANCHESTER UNITED ',I1)
```

will, if the values of I and J are 3 and 1 respectively, cause the output of

DERBY COUNTY 3 MANCHESTER UNITED 1

It should be noted that this edit descriptor can only be used in
FORMAT statements for output. It is called a HOLLERITH STRING and
was a feature of earlier versions of FORTRAN. Its use is not
recommended in FORTRAN 77 because it involves counting characters,
which many people find difficult to do accurately.

10.7.3 The T-format, TL-format and TR-format Edit Descriptors

The T-format, TL-format and TR-format edit descriptors are concerned
with the positioning of the next character to be sent to or from a
record. They are rather more general than the X-format edit
descriptor described in chapter 6.

The T-format edit descriptor has the general form

Tn

where "n" is a positive integer. The effect is that the next
character to be sent to or from the record will be in position "n" of
the record. For example, the statements

        PRINT 100
    100 FORMAT (T10,´THREE´,T20,´BLIND´,T30,´MICE´)

cause the output of

    ^^^^^^^^THREE^^^^^BLIND^^^^^MICE

where ^ indicates a space character. It should be noted that the
first character in the record is the carriage control character, so
that the T of THREE appears in position nine of the output.
Similarly, the statements

        READ 100,I,J,K
    100 FORMAT (T3,I2,T7,I2,T4,I2)

where I, J and K are integer variables and the data record being read
is

    1234567890

will result in I being given the value 34, J the value 78 and K the
value 45.

The TL-format edit descriptor has the general form

TLn

where "n" is a positive integer. The effect is that the next
character to be sent to or from the record will be from position
"c-n+1", where "c" is the current position, unless "c-n+1" is not
positive, in which case the first character in the record will be
sent. For example, the statements

        READ 100,I,J,K
    100 FORMAT (T7,I2,TL4,I2,TL3,I2)

where I, J and K are integer variables and the data record is

    1234567890

will   result   in I being given the value 78, J the value 56 and K the
value 45.   Similarly, the statements

        PRINT 100
    100 FORMAT (T10,´THREE´,TL3,´BLIND´,TL2,´MICE´)

will result in the output

    ^^^^^^^^^THBLIMICE

Finally, the TR-format edit descriptor has the general form

    TRn

where "n" is a positive integer.   The effect is precisely the same as
the X-format edit descriptor nX.

10.7.4 The S-format, SP-format and SS-format Edit Descriptors

These edit descriptors can be used to control whether or not   a   plus
sign appears in numeric output.   They are ignored on input.   The ANSI
Standard leaves the implementor to decide   whether   or   not   positive
numeric   output   should be preceded by a plus sign.   Negative numeric
output must, of course, always be preceded by a minus sign.

    The   SP-format   and SS-format edit descriptors allow the programmer
to override the convention that the implementor has   used.   The   SP-
format   edit   descriptor   in a FORMAT statement requires all positive
numeric output after the SP has appeared and which is   output   using
that   FORMAT   statement to be preceded by a plus sign.   The SS-format
edit descriptor requires that   all   positive   numeric   output   which
appears   after the SS in a format statement should not be preceded by
a plus sign.   The S-format edit descriptor is used to return   to   the
convention   used   by   the   implementor.   Note   that   this   is   done
automatically at the close of the FORMAT statement.

10.7.5 The P-format Edit Descriptor

The general form of this edit descriptor is

    nP

where the integer "n" is a scale factor.   On   input,   the   result   of
using the scale factor with F-format, E-format, D-format and G-format
edit descriptors is that, provided the number on the data record does
not have an exponent, the number stored will be 10^{-n} times the number
on the data record.   For example, the statements

        READ 100,A
    100 FORMAT (2P,F10.0)

when the data record is

    0.7831

result   in   A   being   given the value 0.007831.   If the number on the data record has an exponent, the scale factor has no effect. For example, if the data record above had been

   7.831E-1

then A would have been given the value 0.7831.

On output, the scale factor has no effect when used with an F-format edit descriptor. With E-format and D-format edit descriptors, the real number part of the output is multiplied by 10^n and the exponent part is reduced by "n". For example, the statements

        PRINT 100,A
   100 FORMAT (1P,E13.6)

will, if the value of A is 78.31, result in

   ^7.831000E+01

being output. With the G-format edit descriptor, the scale factor has no effect if the number would not have been printed with an exponent if the scale factor were not present and has a similar effect to its use with an E-format edit descriptor otherwise. Because of the confusion which is likely to result from this feature of FORTRAN 77, it is strongly recommended that scale factors are not used.

10.7.6 Other Format Specifiers

In chapters 2 and 6, two of the possible FORMAT IDENTIFIERS were described. These are the asterisk that appears in list-directed input and output statements as described in chapter 2, and the integer that appears in formatted READ, PRINT and WRITE statements to represent the label of the FORMAT statement which governs the form of the input or output. Other format identifiers allowed include an integer variable that has been assigned the statement label of a FORMAT statement, as described in section 10.4.3; a character constant consisting of suitable edit descriptors; and a character variable whose value is a string of suitable edit descriptors.

As an example, consider the statements

        PRINT 100,I,A
   100 FORMAT (´ X´,I1,´ = ´,F10.4)

It was described in chapter 6 that these produce the output

   X3 =   3.1416

if I has the value 3 and A the value 3.14159.

The same output is produced by the statements

        ASSIGN 100 TO K
        PRINT K,I,A
   100 FORMAT (´ X´,I1,´ = ´,F10.4)

This method is not recommended in most cases, since it requires an additional statement compared to the method described in chapter 6.

The statement
        PRINT ´(´´ X´´,I1,´´ = ´´,F10.4)´,I,A
will also produce the same output, the format identifier in this case
being the character string
        ´(´´ X´´,I1,´´ = ´´,F10.4)´
It should be noted that in this case, the format specifier is a
character constant, so that the single apostrophes that would
normally appear in the edit descriptors have to be replaced by pairs
of apostrophes, as described in section 2.2. It is not recommended
that this form is used because, although the number of statements is
reduced by there being no FORMAT statement, the PRINT statement
itself is considerably more complicated.

Finally, if F has been declared to be of type CHARACTER, the
statements
        F=´(´´ X´´,I1,´´ = ´´,F10.4)´
        PRINT F,I,A
will also produce the same result. In this case, the format
specifier is the character variable F. This form of format specifier
is not recommended for general use, as it is normally more
complicated than the method recommended in chapter 6. It should be
noted that in this case, the character assignment statement must have
been obeyed in the program before the PRINT statement is executed.

10.8 THE INQUIRE STATEMENT

As mentioned in chapter 9, the properties of a file can be determined
by the INQUIRE statement. For example, the statement
        INQUIRE (FILE=´MYFILE´,EXIST=LOGIC)
checks for the existence of a file named MYFILE. LOGIC is the name
of a LOGICAL variable which is set to .TRUE. if MYFILE is accessible
to the program. If MYFILE is not accessible to the program, LOGIC
will be given a value of .FALSE.

It may be that the types of access permitted to a file are not
known and the program must first test to see if a desired mode of
access is permitted. This can be done with a statement such as
        INQUIRE (FILE=´MYFILE´,DIRECT=ISDIR)
which causes the CHARACTER variable ISDIR to be given a value ´YES´
if MYFILE includes direct access in its permitted modes of access,
and a value ´NO´ if it does not. Sometimes the processor may not be
able to determine the answer, in which case a value of ´UNKNOWN´ is
returned.

The name of the file connected to unit "n" can also be determined
by an INQUIRE statement. As an example, consider
        INQUIRE (UNIT=10,NAME=FNAME)

The CHARACTER variable FNAME is given a value equal to   the   name   of
the   file   connected   to unit 10, assuming that there is a named file
connected to that unit.

From   these   examples,   it   can   be seen that there are two ways of
making inquiries. One is to INQUIRE by   name   and   the   other   is   to
INQUIRE by unit.

10.8.1   INQUIRE by Name

To   obtain   information concerning a named file, the INQUIRE statement
in the form
          INQUIRE (FILE=filename, inquire-list)
is used, where "inquire-list" is a list of inquiries being   made   and
"filename"   is   a   character   expression   whose   value is a file name
acceptable to the system.   Blank characters which   appear   after   the
last   non-blank   character in "filename" are discounted.   The inquire
list can be a combination of any of the sixteen specifiers   given   in
section   10.8.3.   Seldom,   if   ever,   will   all sixteen specifiers be
required. The programmer selects the relevant subset   and   omits   the
rest.

A common situation is   the   need   to   keep   two   generations   of   a
sequential   file,   a   "father" and a "son". When the file is updated
the latest version (the son) is used. If the processing is successful
the newly created file becomes the latest version (the "son") and the
previous "son" becomes the "father". The   previous   "father"   is   no
longer   required   and   can   be   deleted.   Should   the   processing   be
unsuccessful, the newly-created file   is   not   required   and   can   be
deleted.   All   the housekeeping for this situation can be carried out
within a FORTRAN 77 program.   To do this, the CHARACTER variables F1,
F2   and   F3   are set to the names of three files to be used. Since at
any time there is only one "father" and one "son", only   two   of   the
files will exist.   The statements
          INQUIRE (FILE=F1,EXIST=LF1)
          INQUIRE (FILE=F2,EXIST=LF2)
          INQUIRE (FILE=F3,EXIST=LF3)
where   LF1,   LF2 and LF3 are LOGICAL variables, determine which files
exist.   These have their associated LOGICAL variables set to   .TRUE.,
the   other   LOGICAL   variable being set to .FALSE.   If the file names
are used in a cyclic order, one of   three   possible   situations   will
exist.   These are
   (i)   F1 is the "father" and F2 is the "son" with F3 not in use,
   (ii)   F2 is the "father" and F3 is the "son" with F1 not in use,
   (iii) F3 is the "father" and F1 is the "son" with F2   not   in   use.
Assuming no errors occur during the processing, if case (i) exists at

the start of the processing, case (ii) will exist   at   the   end.   If
case   (ii) exists at the start, case (iii) will exist at the end.   If
case (iii) exists at the start, case (i) will exist at the end.

   To   decide   which   files   should   be   used   for   input   and   output
initially, the conditional statement

```
      IF (LF1 .AND. LF2) THEN
         INFILE=F2
         OUTFIL=F3
      ELSEIF (LF2 .AND. LF3) THEN
         INFILE=F3
         OUTFIL=F1
      ELSEIF (LF3 .AND. LF1) THEN
         INFILE=F1
         OUTFIL=F2
      ELSE
         CALL SETUP
      ENDIF
```

should   follow   the above three INQUIRE statements.   Here, SETUP is a
subroutine which sets up the original files correctly.   The result of
the   statement   is   that INFILE will contain the name of the "father"
and OUTFIL the name of the "son".   When the program   terminates,   one
of   the   files   must   be   deleted.   If the program terminates after a
successful update, the unused file is deleted   as   it   would   be   the
grandfather; while if the program terminates with an error, the newly
created file must be deleted. To   delete   the   unused   file   requires
opening   and   closing that file using the parameter STATUS=DELETE, as
was described in chapter 9.   If unit   5   was   used   for   output,   the
statement for deleting the appropriate file is

```
      IF (.NOT. ERROR) THEN
         CLOSE (5)
         IF (LF1 .AND. LF2) THEN
            OPEN (5,FILE=F1)
         ELSEIF (LF2 .AND. LF3) THEN
            OPEN (5,FILE=F2)
         ELSE
            OPEN (5,FILE=F3)
         ENDIF
      ENDIF
      CLOSE (5,STATUS='DELETE')
```

10.8.2 INQUIRE by Unit

This is the same as INQUIRE by file except that the   unit   number   is
quoted   instead   of the file name.   The general form of the statement

is now
            INQUIRE (UNIT=n,inquire-list)
where "n" is an integer expression defining the unit number and
"inquire-list" is as described in the next section.

10.8.3 Specifiers for the INQUIRE Statement

The examples in section 10.8.1 demonstrated that the INQUIRE
statement can be used with relatively few specifiers. However, as
programmers´ use of files becomes more sophisticated, their need for
more information grows. It is assumed that by the time programmers
need this extra information, they will have had sufficient experience
to judge for themselves what information is relevant.   All that is
given here is a list of the type of information that can be obtained
and the way to obtain this information.
   (i)   DETERMINING THE STATUS OF A FILE
The specifier for this is exactly the same as used in the OPEN
statement, that is
    IOSTAT=ios
where "ios" is an integer variable indicating the input/output status
of the file. If the value is zero, all is well; but if it is non-
zero, some potential error has occurred. A value of −1 indicates that
the endfile condition has been detected, while values greater than
zero indicate processor-dependent errors.
   (ii)   CHECKING THAT A FILE EXISTS
This facility can only be used with INQUIRE by file. The relevant
specifier is
    EXIST=logic
where "logic" is a logical variable set to .TRUE. if the file is
accessible to the program for data transfer, and to .FALSE. if not.
   (iii) CHECKING THAT A FILE IS OPEN
This can be used to check whether or not a file is connected to a
particular unit or whether a particular file has been opened. The
specifier is written
    OPENED=isopen
where "isopen" is a logical variable. When used with INQUIRE by file,
"isopen" is set to .TRUE. if the file indicated in the call is
connected to a unit; otherwise "isopen" is set to .FALSE. Used with
INQUIRE by unit, the value of "isopen" is set to .TRUE. if the
specified unit is connected to a file and to .FALSE. if it is not.
   (iv)   CHECKING THE UNIT NUMBER
The number of the unit currently connected to a file can be
determined by an INQUIRE by file using the specifier
    NUMBER=num

where "num" is an integer variable set to the value of the unit number of the unit connected to the specified file. If no unit is connected to the specified file, "num" is <u>not</u> defined.

   (v)   CHECKING FOR SCRATCH FILES

To check whether or not a named file is connected to the unit specified in a call of INQUIRE by unit, the specifier

     NAMED=isname

is used. If a named file is connected to the specified unit, "isname" is set to .TRUE., otherwise "isname" is set to .FALSE.

   (vi)   CHECKING THE NAME OF A FILE

To check the name of the file connected to a specified unit, the specifier

     NAME=fname

where "fname" is a character variable, whose value is the name of the file connected to the unit specified if the file has a name. If the file does not have a name, the character variable is undefined.

   (vii) CHECKING THE ACCESS MODE OF A FILE

To determine the mode of access set up between a file and a unit, the specifier

     ACCESS=mode

is used. The character variable "mode" is set to the value ´SEQUENTIAL´ or ´DIRECT´ if a connection exists. If there is no connection, the value of "mode" is undefined.

   To check whether or not a file can be connected for sequential access, the specifier

     SEQUENTIAL=isseq

can be used. In this case the character variable "isseq" is set to ´YES´ if sequential access is included in the permitted access methods for the file and to ´NO´ if is not. Sometimes it is not possible for the system to determine the answer. On these occasions, "isseq" is set to ´UNKNOWN´. The specifier

     DIRECT=isdir

can be used in a similar way to check for direct access.

   (viii) CHECKING FOR FORMATTED FILES

To determine whether or not a file is connected for FORMATTED input or output, the specifier

     FORM=format

can be used. The character variable "format" is given the value ´FORMATTED´ if the file is connected for formatted use, and ´UNFORMATTED´ if it is connected for unformatted use. If there is no connection, the value of "format" is undefined.

   To determine whether records in a file can be formatted, the specifier

     FORMATTED=isform

is used. The character variable "isform" is set to 'YES' if FORMATTED is included in the allowed forms for the file; to 'NO' if it is not; and to 'UNKNOWN' if the processor is unable to determine the answer. The specifier

    UNFORMATTED=isunfm

can be used in the same way. This time the character variable "isunfm" is set to 'YES' if UNFORMATTED is included in the allowed forms for the file and to 'NO' if it is not included. Again, if the processor is unable to determine the answer, the variable is set to 'UNKNOWN'.

(ix)   CHECKING THE RECORD LENGTH

The length of records on a file connected for direct access can be determined with the aid of the specifier

    RECL=length

where "length" is an integer variable. The value of "length" is set to the length of the record measured in the appropriate units. Should the file not be connected for direct access, the value of "length" is undefined.

(x)   CHECKING THE FILE POSITION

The position of the next record on a direct access file can be determined using the specifier

    NEXTREC=next

where "next" is an integer variable that is assigned the number of the next record on the direct access file specified. If the file is not connected for direct access or the position of the file cannot be determined because of a previous error, "next" is undefined.

(xi)   CHECKING BLANKS

To determine whether or not blanks are treated as zeros in numeric fields, the specifier

    BLANK=isnull

can be used. The character variable "isnull" will be set to 'NULL' if null blank control is in effect and to 'ZERO' if zero blank control is in effect. If no file is connected or the file is connected for unformatted input/output, "isnull" becomes undefined.

(xii)   DEALING WITH ERRORS

The INQUIRE, OPEN, CLOSE, READ, WRITE, BACKSPACE, ENDFILE and REWIND statements all have

    ERR=s

specifiers, where "s" is the label of the next statement obeyed if an error occurs. This enables the program to be designed so that an error in any of these statements does not cause a failure but results in a jump to the part of the program which takes remedial action.

Only those specifiers that are necessary should be quoted when the INQUIRE statement is used.

APPENDIX 1
INTRINSIC FUNCTIONS

It was explained in section 3.4 that many of the standard mathematical functions are provided as part of FORTRAN 77 and are known as INTRINSIC FUNCTIONS. Some of the more commonly used ones were considered there and a complete list of intrinsic functions is given in this appendix.

Many of the intrinsic functions possess two names, a SPECIFIC name and a GENERIC name. The reason for this is that there are often several functions which perform the same operation, but require different types of argument. For example, ALOG is the specific name of the intrinsic function which finds the logarithm of a real number, DLOG is the specific name of the function which finds the logarithm of a double precision number and CLOG is the specific name of the function which finds the logarithm of a complex number. When these specific names are used, the arguments must be of the specified type or a failure will occur. However, the generic name LOG may be used in place of any of the three specific names and the type of answer produced will be determined by the type of argument provided. In general, the type of value produced is the same as that of the argument. Thus, using generic names avoids the need to remember a number of slightly different specific names for similar functions.

Two important points need to be noted. Firstly, when an intrinsic function is used as an argument of a subprogram, the specific name rather than the generic name must be used, as described in section 7.5.2. Secondly, when external functions were discussed in section 7.2.2 it was stated that the function name determines the type of value produced, either by the normal type convention or by appearing in a TYPE statement. This is also true for the specific names of intrinsic functions. Thus, for example, ALOG starts with an A and returns a real value. However it is not true for generic names, since the same name can return different types of value depending upon the type of argument.

The following table lists the intrinsic functions. The notes following the table are referred to, where appropriate, and the symbol # is used to denote an intrinsic function which may not be used as the actual argument of a subprogram, as described in note 20.

Function Purpose	Definition	Number of Arguments	Generic Name	Specific Name	Type of Argument	Type of Function
Type Conversion	Conversion to integer - see note 1	1	INT	—	Integer	Integer
				# INT	Real	Integer
				# IFIX	Real	Integer
				# IDINT	Double	Integer
				—	Complex	Integer
	Conversion to real - see note 2	1	REAL	# REAL	Integer	Real
				# FLOAT	Integer	Real
				—	Real	Real
				# SNGL	Double	Real
				—	Complex	Real
	Conversion to double - see note 3	1	#DBLE	—	Integer	Double
				—	Real	Double
				—	Double	Double
				—	Complex	Double
	Conversion to complex - see note 4	1 or 2	#CMPLX	—	Integer	Complex
				—	Real	Complex
				—	Double	Complex
				—	Complex	Complex
	Conversion integer/ character - see note 5	1	—	# ICHAR	Character	Integer
		1	—	# CHAR	Integer	Character
Truncation	int(x) - see note 1	1	AINT	AINT	Real	Real
				DINT	Double	Double
Nearest whole number	- see note 6	1	ANINT	ANINT	Real	Real
				DNINT	Double	Double
Nearest integer	- see note 6	1	NINT	NINT	Real	Integer
				IDNINT	Double	Integer
Absolute value	|x|	1	ABS	IABS	Integer	Integer
				ABS	Real	Real
				DABS	Double	Double
	- see note 7			CABS	Complex	Real
Remaind- ering	- see note 8	2	MOD	MOD	Integer	Integer
				AMOD	Real	Real
				DMOD	Double	Double

Function Purpose	Definition	Number of Arguments	Generic Name	Specific Name	Type of Argument	Type of Function
Transfer sign	– see note 9	2	SIGN	ISIGN	Integer	Integer
				SIGN	Real	Real
				DSIGN	Double	Double
Positive difference	–see note 10	2	DIM	IDIM	Integer	Integer
				DIM	Real	Real
				DDIM	Double	Double
Double precision product	x1*x2	2	–	DPROD	Real	Double
Choosing largest value	max(x1,x2, x3,...) –see note 11	≥2	#MAX	# MAX0	Integer	Integer
				# AMAX1	Real	Real
				# DMAX1	Double	Double
			–	# AMAX0	Integer	Real
				# MAX1	Real	Integer
Choosing smallest value	min(x1,x2, x3,...) –see note 11	≥2	#MIN	# MIN0	Integer	Integer
				# AMIN1	Real	Real
				# DMIN1	Double	Double
			–	# AMIN0	Integer	Real
				# MIN1	Real	Integer
Length	–see note 12	1	–	LEN	Character	Integer
Index of a substring	–see note 13	2	–	INDEX	Character	Integer
Imaginary part	Im(x+iy)=y	1	–	AIMAG	Complex	Complex
Complex Conjugate	$\bar{z}=x-iy$	1	–	CONJ	Complex	Complex
Square root	$+\sqrt{x}$ –see note 14	1	SQRT	SQRT	Real	Real
				DSQRT	Double	Double
				CSQRT	Complex	Complex
Exponential	e^x	1	EXP	EXP	Real	Real
				DEXP	Double	Double
				CEXP	Complex	Complex
Natural Logarithm	$\log_e x$ –see note 15	1	LOG	ALOG	Real	Real
				DLOG	Double	Double
				CLOG	Complex	Complex
Common Logarithm	$\log_{10} x$ –see note 15	1	LOG10	ALOG10	Real	Real
				DLOG10	Double	Double
Sine	sin x –see note 16	1	SIN	SIN	Real	Real
				DSIN	Double	Double
				CSIN	Complex	Complex

Function Purpose	Definition	Number of Arguments	Generic Name	Specific Name	Type of Argument	Type of Function
Cosine	cos x -see note 16	1	COS	COS DCOS CCOS	Real Double Complex	Real Double Complex
Tangent	tan x -see note 16	1	TAN	TAN DTAN	Real Double	Real Double
Arcsine	arcsin x -see note 17	1	ASIN	ASIN DASIN	Real Double	Real Double
Arccosine	arccos x -see note 17	1	ACOS	ACOS DACOS	Real Double	Real Double
Arctangent	arctan x -see note 17	1	ATAN	ATAN DATAN	Real Double	Real Double
	arctan(x1/x2) -see note 18	2	ATAN2	ATAN2 DATAN2	Real Double	Real Double
Hyperbolic sine	sinh x	1	SINH	SINH DSINH	Real Double	Real Double
Hyperbolic cosine	cosh x	1	COSH	COSH DCOSH	Real Double	Real Double
Hyperbolic tangent	tanh x	1	TANH	TANH DTANH	Real Double	Real Double
String Comparison	-see note 19	2 2 2 2	—	# LGE # LGT # LLE # LLT	Character Character Character Character	Logical Logical Logical Logical

The following notes were referred to in the above table.

1. INT(X) is obtained by truncating X to an integer. When X is complex, the real part of X is truncated. AINT(X) truncates X to an integer and converts the result back to the same type as X. The Standard recommends that the specific names IFIX and IDINT should not be used, as they are included only for compatibility with FORTRAN 66.

2. REAL(X) is obtained by converting X to real form. When X is complex, the real part of the complex number is taken. The Standard recommends that the specific names FLOAT and SNGL should not be used, as they are included only for compatibility with FORTRAN 66.

3. DBLE(X) is obtained by converting X to double precision. If X is complex, the real part is converted to double precision.

4. CMPLX may have one or two arguments. If there is only one argument, it may be of type integer, real, double precision or complex. If there are two arguments, they must both be of the same type and may be integer, real or double precision.

When X is complex, CMPLX(X) has the value X. When X is integer,

real or double precision, CMPLX(X) is the complex number whose real
part is REAL(X) and whose imaginary part is zero.

CMPLX(X1,X2) is the complex number whose real part is REAL(X1) and
whose imaginary part is REAL(X2).

5. As explained in chapter 8, all characters have a position in a
collating sequence.   ICHAR(X) returns the integer which indicates the
position of X in the collating sequence.   CHAR(I) returns the
character in the I-th position in the collating sequence. The first
character in the sequence has position 0 and the last has position
n-1, where "n" is the number of characters in the collating sequence.

6. ANINT(X) rounds X to the nearest integer and converts this
integer back to the same type as X. NINT(X) rounds X to the nearest
integer.

7. If X is of type integer, real or double precision, ABS(X) is
the magnitude of X.   If X is a complex quantity of the form x+iy,
then ABS(X) = SQRT(x**2+y**2)

8. MOD(X1,X2) is the remainder when X1 is divided by X2, that is
    MOD(X1,X2) = X1 - INT(X1/X2)*X2.
Both arguments must be of the same type and the result is of the same
type as the arguments.

9. SIGN(X1,X2) = ABS(X1) if X2>0
    SIGN(X1,X2) = -ABS(X1) if X2<0
If the value of X1 is zero, the result is zero, which is neither
positive nor negative.

10. DIM(X1,X2) = X1-X2 if X1>X2
     DIM(X1,X2) = 0   if X1<X2

11. MAX and MIN may both have any number of arguments in excess of
one. The Standard strongly advises against the use of AMAX0, MAX1,
AMIN0 and MIN1, which are functions that return values of a different
type to the arguments. Instead it recommends the use of a type
conversion function after the use of MAX or MIN. For example,
REAL(MAX(I,J,K)) should be used in place of AMAX0(I,J,K).

12. LEN(c) produces the length of the character expression "c".

13. INDEX(c1,c2) returns the starting position of the first
occurrence of string "c2" in string "c1". If string "c2" does not
occur in "c1", the value zero is returned. The first position in the
string "c1" is numbered 1, in contrast to CHAR and ICHAR where the
first position is numbered 0, see note 5.

14. The argument for SQRT and DSQRT must be non-negative.
CSQRT(X) yields the principal value, with the real part non-negative.
When the real part of the result is zero, the imaginary part is non-
negative.

15. Real or double precision arguments for any of the logarithm
functions must be positive.   The argument for CLOG must not be

(0.0,0.0). The range of the imaginary part of the result of CLOG lies in the range $-\pi <$ imaginary part $\leq +\pi$. The imaginary part of the result is $+\pi$ only when the real part of the argument is negative and the imaginary part of the argument is zero.

16. All angles must be expressed in radians. There is no restriction on the range of argument.

17. The argument of ASIN and ACOS must lie in the range $(-1,1)$. The result of ASIN and ATAN is an angle in radians which lies in the range $(-\pi/2,\pi/2)$. The result of ACOS is an angle in radians lying in the range $(0,\pi)$. These are the PRINCIPAL VALUES. In mathematics, the functions arcsin, arccos and arctan are also written $\sin^{-1}$, $\cos^{-1}$ and $\tan^{-1}$ respectively.

18. The result of ATAN2(X1,X2) is an angle in radians lying in the range $(-\pi,+\pi)$ and indicates the quadrant in which the point (X1,X2) lies. The arguments X1 and X2 must not both be zero, but X2 may be zero on its own.

19. The American National Standards Institute has defined a collating sequence (ordering sequence) known as the American Standard Code for Information Interchange (ASCII) collating sequence. The characters in the sequence are in the order:

blank $ ' ( ) * + , - . / 0 1 2 3 4 5 6 7 8 9 : =

A B C D E F G H I J K L M N O P Q R S T U V W X Y Z

LGE(c1,c2) compares the two character strings "c1" and "c2" using the ASCII collating sequence. It returns the value TRUE if c1=c2 or if "c1" follows "c2", otherwise it returns the value FALSE.

LGT(c1,c2) returns the value TRUE if "c1" follows "c2", otherwise it returns the value FALSE.

LLE(c1,c2) returns the value TRUE if c1=c2 or if "c1" precedes "c2", otherwise it returns the value false.

LLT(c1,c2) returns the value TRUE if "c1" precedes "c2", otherwise it returns the value FALSE.

If "c1" and "c2" are of unequal length, the shorter string is extended by inserting blanks on the right-hand end to make its length equal to that of the longer string. If either "c1" or "c2" contains a character which is not in the ASCII character set, the result is dependent on the particular compiler.

20. It was stated in section 7.5.2 that certain intrinsic functions may not be used as actual arguments in a subprogram. The following intrinsic functions are in this category and they are marked with the symbol # in the table:

INT, IFIX, IDINT, FLOAT, SNGL, REAL, DBLE, CMPLX, ICHAR, CHAR, LGE, LGT, LLE, LLT, MAX, MAX0, AMAX1, DMAX1, AMAX0, MAX1, MIN, MIN0, AMIN1, DMIN1, AMIN0, MIN1.

APPENDIX 2
ARRAYS AND CHARACTER VARIABLES

In this appendix, a more detailed examination is made of the method used to access array elements in the computer store and the mechanism involved in the use of arrays and character variables as arguments of subprograms.

A2.1 THE STORAGE OF ARRAY ELEMENTS

Associated with an array name is the address at which the first element of the array is stored. All elements of the array are arranged in a sequence in the store and the position of a particular element in this sequence is determined by its SUBSCRIPT VALUE. Details of how to calculate the subscript value are given later.

The array declaration is made in a TYPE, DIMENSION or COMMON statement. It is of the general form:

array name (L1:U1,L2:U2,...,L7:U7)

where L_i, U_i are the lower and upper bounds of the i-th dimension. A maximum of 7 dimensions are allowed in FORTRAN 77. The SIZE OF THE DIMENSION I is the value D_i, where

$$D_i = U_i - L_i + 1$$

and is the number of different elements in that dimension. The SIZE of an n-dimensional array is the total number of elements in the array and is equal to the product of the sizes of all the n dimensions, that is, $D_1*D_2*...*D_n$. As an example, consider

DIMENSION X(100),Y(0:10,5)

Here, X is a one-dimensional array, the size of the first dimension is 100 and the size of the array is also 100. Y is a two-dimensional array, the size of the first dimension is 11, the size of the second dimension is 5 and the size of the whole array is 55.

The elements of an array are ordered and stored in a sequence which is determined by the subscript value of each element. These subscript values range from 1 (the first element) to the value of the size of the array (the last element). The subscript value is calculated from the subscripts of the element and the dimensional parameters of the array. The rules for the calculation are given in the following table:

Declaration	n	Dimension Sizes	Subscript	Subscript Value
(L1:U1)	1	$D1=U1-L1+1$	(S1)	$1+(S1-L1)$
(L1:U1,L2:U2)	2	$D1=U1-L1+1$ $D2=U2-L2+1$	(S1,S2)	$1+(S1-L1)$ $+(S2-L2)*D1$
(L1:U1,L2:U2,L3:U3)	3	$D1=U1-L1+1$ $D2=U2-L2+1$ $D3=U3-L3+1$	(S1,S2,S3)	$1+(S1-L1)$ $+(S2-L2)*D1$ $+(S3-L3)*D1*D2$
:	:	:	:	:
(L1:U1,....,L7:U7)	7	$D1=U1-L1+1$ $D2=U2-L2+1$ $D3=U3-L3+1$ .... $D7=U7-L7+1$	(S1,...,S7)	$1+(S1-L1)$ $+(S2-L2)*D1$ $+(S3-L3)*D1*D2$ .... $+(S7-L7)*D1*..*D6$

The following points should be noted

(i)   If a lower limit is not specified for any dimension, it is taken to be 1.

(ii)   In calculating a subscript value, the upper limit of the last dimension (Un) is never used. It is for this reason that it may be replaced by an asterisk (*) in the dimension statement of a dummy array in a subprogram.

The following examples illustrate the order in which elements are stored:

        DIMENSION X(0:4)

The array X is of size 5 with elements stored in the order X(0), X(1), X(2), X(3), X(4).

        DIMENSION Y(3,-1:2)

The array Y is of size 12 with elements stored in the order Y(1,-1), Y(2,-1), Y(3,-1), Y(1,0), Y(2,0), Y(3,0), Y(1,1), Y(2,1), Y(3,1), Y(1,2), Y(2,2), Y(3,2). It should be noted that the lower limit of the first dimension is 1 by default.

        DIMENSION Z(-1:3,2,0:2)

The array Z is of size 30 with elements stored in the order

Z(-1,1,0)	Z(0,1,0)	Z(1,1,0)	Z(2,1,0)	Z(3,1,0)	Z(-1,2,0)
Z(0,2,0)	Z(1,2,0)	Z(2,2,0)	Z(3,2,0)	Z(-1,1,1)	Z(0,1,1)
Z(1,1,1)	Z(2,1,1)	Z(3,1,1)	Z(-1,2,1)	Z(0,2,1)	Z(1,2,1)
Z(2,2,1)	Z(3,2,1)	Z(-1,1,2)	Z(0,1,2)	Z(1,1,2)	Z(2,1,2)
Z(3,1,2)	Z(-1,2,2)	Z(0,2,2)	Z(1,2,2)	Z(2,2,2)	Z(3,2,2)

In all cases, the first subscript varies most rapidly and the last subscript varies most slowly. This arrangement is known as COLUMN MAJOR ORDERING. It can be seen that the address of any element of the array can be obtained from the starting address of the array and the subscript value of the element. Clearly this process is fairly involved so that in general it takes longer to locate an array element in the store than a simple variable. It is for this reason that arrays should only be used where necessary and the number of dimensions should be kept to a minimum. If the same array element is to be used several times, it is common practice to access the array element once and to store its value in a temporary simple variable location. Thereafter, the simple variable is used in place of the array element, thus making the program a little more efficient.

Whenever an array name, without an implied DO loop, appears in a READ statement, the order in which the array elements are allocated values is the order in which the elements are arranged in the store, as described above. The same order is implied when an array name, without an implied DO loop, appears in a PRINT or WRITE statement.

A2.2 ARRAYS USED AS ARGUMENTS OF SUBPROGRAMS

Having described the process involved in the location of a particular array element in the store, it is possible to describe the mechanism involved in using arrays as arguments of subprograms. In section 7.4.3, the function SUMMAT was defined in outline as

```
FUNCTION SUMMAT(A,M,N,LL1,LU1,LL2)
DIMENSION A(LL1:LU1,LL2:*)
..........
END
```

Here, A is the name of a dummy array and other arguments are used to bring information about the size of the actual array. The information carried across to the subprogram in association with the actual array name used is the address in the main store at which the array starts. Every time a dummy array element is referred to in the subprogram, its subscript value is calculated from the dimensional information in the subprogram. This value is then used, in conjunction with the starting address, to calculate the address of

the actual array element that is to be used. In this way the
association between dummy array elements and actual array elements is
established and, in this case, dummy array elements and actual array
elements with the same subscript values are associated.

This is the normal way in which actual and dummy arrays are used in
programs. However, FORTRAN 77 is much more flexible than this.   For
instance, it is possible to use an ARRAY ELEMENT as the actual
argument in place of the array name. In this case, the address of
the array element is used as the starting address and association
between dummy and actual array elements is established on this basis.
However, the size of the dummy array must not exceed the number of
remaining elements in the actual array. This means that the size of
the dummy array must not exceed the size of the actual array, minus
the subscript value of the array element used as argument, plus one.
For a one-dimensional dummy array with upper bound specified by *,
this is automatically taken into account and the assumed upper limit
is adjusted so that the size of the dummy array is equal to the
number of remaining elements in the actual array. The same is true
for n-dimensional arrays (n>1) provided that the product of the sizes
of the first (n-1) dimensions of the dummy array does not exceed the
number of remaining elements in the actual array. For example, in
the following outline program

```
PROGRAM EXA21
DIMENSION A(100)
..........
CALL SUB(A(10),...)
..........
END
SUBROUTINE SUB(X,...)
DIMENSION X(*)
..........
END
```

the actual argument provided in the call of SUB is not the name of
the array A but the name of the array element A(10). In the
subprogram, the dummy array X is used and the association then
established is X(1) with A(10); X(2) with A(11) and so on.   Clearly
this means that X(91) is associated with A(100) and because the upper
bound of X is specified by *, X(91) is the last element in the dummy
array. If the DIMENSION statement in the subroutine were changed to
                DIMENSION X(100)
a failure would occur with the call of SUB given, because the size of
the dummy array X would exceed the number of remaining elements in

the actual array A, which is 91.

It is also permissible for the dummy array to be of different dimension to the actual array. Thus a program of the form

```
PROGRAM EXA22
DIMENSION A(5,10)
..........
CALL SUB(A,50,...)
..........
END
SUBROUTINE SUB(X,N,...)
DIMENSION X(N)
..........
END
```

produces the association X(1) with A(1,1), X(2) with A(2,1),..., X(K) with A(I,J) where K=I+5*(J-1).

In program EXA22, the actual array A and the dummy array X both have the same number of elements. Although this might appear sensible, it is not a requirement of FORTRAN 77. In principle, the array X could be of any size provided it does not exceed the size of the actual array (or remaining part) that is used.

It is clear that when using these special features of array handling, great care has to be exercised to guard against picking up incorrect array values or having dummy arrays that are too large.

A2.3 CHARACTER VARIABLES AS ARGUMENTS OF SUBPROGRAMS

This topic was first considered in section 8.7, where a brief description was given. A more detailed account of the mechanism is given here where the two types of character variable, the simple character variable and the character array, are considered separately.

A2.3.1 Simple Character Variables as Arguments

A dummy argument which is a simple variable of type CHARACTER may only be associated with an actual argument that is a character constant, character variable, character substring, character array element or character expression.

The length of a dummy character argument must be specified in a subprogram by either *c or *(*) in a CHARACTER statement, where "c" must be a non-zero unsigned integer constant or a positive integer constant expression enclosed in parentheses. If, when the length is specified by *c, the actual character argument has length greater than "c" then only the first "c" characters from the left hand end are associated with the dummy argument. When the length of the dummy argument is specified by (*), the length of the dummy argument is automatically set equal to the length of the actual character argument used.

The association set up between dummy character arguments and actual character arguments that are character constants, character variables, character substrings and character array elements is straight-forward and only subject to the length considerations mentioned above. In the case of a character substring, the length is the length of the substring. For a character expression used as an actual argument, none of the operands may be a character variable whose length has been specified by using (*). The length of the actual argument is the sum of the lengths of the operands that have been concatenated.

A2.3.2 Character Arrays as Arguments

A character array may be thought of in two ways; either as a set of array elements, each containing a character string of a specified length, or as a set of character storage locations, each identified by the array element to which it belongs and its position within the array element. The size of a character array (as for a numeric array) is the number of array elements. It is also convenient to define the CHARACTER SIZE of an array as the number of character storage units in the array. This is the product of the number of elements by the character length of each element.

In the call of a subprogram, a dummy character array argument may only be associated with an actual argument which is the name of a character array, a character array element or a character array substring. As with numeric arrays, the actual argument indicates the address at which the association between the actual array and the dummy array commences. Thus, if the actual argument is a character array name, the address of the first element of the array (in fact the address of the first character storage unit) is taken to be the starting address of the association. Similarly, if the actual argument is an array element or substring, the address of the first character storage unit of the array element or substring is taken to be the starting address of the association.

The situation is complicated by the fact that FORTRAN 77 does not insist that the dimensions of the dummy and actual arrays are the same, as considered previously in section A2.2, or that the lengths of the dummy and actual array elements are equal. All that is required is that the character size of the dummy array must not exceed the number of remaining character storage units in the actual array, measured from the address of the start of the association to the end of the actual array.

The length of the elements of the dummy character array must be specified by either *c or *(*) in a CHARACTER statement in the subprogram, as for a simple character argument. When the length specification is (*), the length assumed depends upon the form of actual argument. If the actual argument is a character array name or array element, the assumed length is that of the array element. However, if the actual argument is an array substring, the length assumed is that of the substring.

In a similar way to numeric arrays, the bounds of the dummy array must be specified in either the CHARACTER statement or in a DIMENSION statement. The size of an assumed size array, that is one whose upper bound of the last dimension is specified by *, is calculated as

$$INT((s-t+1)/c)$$

where "s" is the character size of the actual array, "t" is the character storage unit at which the association starts (numbered from the left hand end from the start of the array) and "c" is the character length of the dummy array elements. Obviously for an n-dimensional array with $n>1$, the product of the sizes of the first (n-1) dimensions must not exceed this value, otherwise the dummy array is too large.

The following skeleton program outline illustrates most of the points mentioned above

```
PROGRAM EXA23
CHARACTER X(5)*3
..........
CALL SUB(X(2)(2:3),...)
..........
END
SUBROUTINE SUB(Y,...)
CHARACTER Y(2,*)*(*)
..........
END
```

The character array in the calling program unit is X, which is one-dimensional and of size 5, character length 3 and character size 15. The dummy character array Y is two-dimensional, of assumed size because the upper limit of the second dimension specified by *, and has its character length also assumed, being specified by (*).

The actual argument in the call of SUB is the substring X(2)(2:3)

and since this is of length two characters it sets the character
length of the dummy array to c=2.   Since X(2)(2:3) starts at
character storage unit 5 in X this makes t=5 and the character size
of X is s=15.   Thus, the assumed size of Y is

$$INT((s-t+1)/c) = INT((15-5+1)/2) = 5$$

so that Y only contains the five elements Y(1,1), Y(2,1), Y(1,2),
Y(2,2), Y(1,3).   The association is shown in the following diagram:

X(1)				X(2)		X(3)			X(4)			X(5)		
A	B	C	D	E	F	G	H	I	J	K	L	M	N	O

array X

X(2)(2:3)

Y(1,1)		Y(2,1)		Y(1,2)		Y(2,2)		Y(1,3)	
E	F	G	H	I	J	K	L	M	N

array Y

Thus if X contained the character strings shown, then as a result of
the association Y(1,1)=´EF´, Y(2,1)=´GH´,   Y(1,2)=´IJ´,   Y(2,2)=´KL´,
Y(1,3)=´MN´ and the characters A,   B,   C,   D,   and O in X are not
associated with elements of Y at all.

APPENDIX 3

THE ORDER AND CONSTRUCTION OF FORTRAN 77 STATEMENTS

All FORTRAN 77 statements are classified as either EXECUTABLE STATEMENTS or NON-EXECUTABLE STATEMENTS. Within each of these broad categories there are subdivisions, as indicated below

EXECUTABLE STATEMENTS

1. Assignment Statements:
   Arithmetic, Logical, Character, Statement Label (ASSIGN).
2. Control Statements:
   Block IF, ELSEIF, ELSE, ENDIF,
   Arithmetic IF, Logical IF,
   Unconditional GOTO, Computed GOTO, Assigned GOTO,
   DO, CONTINUE,
   STOP, END, CALL, RETURN, PAUSE.
3. Input/Output/File Statements:
   READ, PRINT, WRITE, OPEN, CLOSE,
   INQUIRE, BACKSPACE, ENDFILE, REWIND.

NON-EXECUTABLE STATEMENTS

4. Specification Statements:
   IMPLICIT, PARAMETER,
   Type Statements (REAL, INTEGER, LOGICAL, CHARACTER, COMPLEX,
                    DOUBLE PRECISION),
   DIMENSION, COMMON,
   INTRINSIC, EXTERNAL,
   SAVE,
   EQUIVALENCE.
5. Program Unit Statements:
   PROGRAM, FUNCTION, SUBROUTINE, BLOCK DATA, ENTRY.
6. DATA Statements.

7. FORMAT Statements.

8. Statement Function Statements.

9. Comment Statements.

ORDER OF STATEMENTS IN A PROGRAM UNIT.

In general, non-executable statements should be placed before
executable statements. The detailed rules are illustrated in the
following table, which is given in the ANSI manual.

	PROGRAM, FUNCTION, SUBROUTINE OR BLOCK DATA STATEMENTS		
COMMENT	FORMAT AND ENTRY STATEMENTS	PARAMETER STATEMENTS	IMPLICIT STATEMENTS
			OTHER SPECIFICATION STATEMENTS
STATEMENTS		DATA STATEMENTS	STATEMENT FUNCTION STATEMENTS
			EXECUTABLE STATEMENTS
END STATEMENT			

In this table, vertical lines separate types of statement that may
be interspersed, and horizontal lines separate types of statement
that may not be interspersed.

The following are examples of this interpretation:

(i)   Comment Statements may occur anywhere in the program unit,
except after an END statement.

(ii) The first statement, other than a comment, must be a PROGRAM,
FUNCTION, SUBROUTINE, or BLOCK DATA statement, as appropriate.

(iii) The last statement in a program unit must be an END statement.

(iv) FORMAT and ENTRY statements may occur anywhere between
statements mentioned in (ii) and (iii) above.

(v)   IMPLICIT statements must occur before any other specification
statements, with the exception of PARAMETER statements, with which
they may be interspersed.

(vi) DATA statements must occur after all specification statements, but may be interspersed with executable statements.

CONSTRUCTION OF ASSIGNMENT STATEMENTS

(a)   variable-name = expression
(b)   ASSIGN label TO variable-name
   In (a), "variable-name" can be replaced by the name of an array element or the name of a substring.

THE CONSTRUCTION OF CONTROL STATEMENTS

(a)   IF (logical-expression) THEN
(b)   ELSEIF (logical-expression) THEN
(c)   ELSE
(d)   ENDIF
(e)   IF (expression) label,label,label
(f)   IF (logical-expression) executable-statement
(g)   GOTO label
(h)   GOTO (label,label,...), integer-expression
(i)   GOTO variable-name, (label,label,...)
(j)   DO label, variable = expression,expression,expression
(k)   CONTINUE
(l)   STOP character-constant
(m)   END
(n)   PAUSE character-constant
(o)   CALL subroutine-name (arguments)
(p)   RETURN integer-expression
   In (e) and (j), the expressions must be real, integer or double precision arithmetic expressions.
   In (f), the executable statement must not be a block IF statement, a logical IF statement, an ELSEIF statement, an ELSE statement, an ENDIF statement, a DO statement or an END statement.
   In (h), at least one label must be present, and the comma following the closing bracket is optional.
   In (i), the comma following "variable-name" is optional. Each label can be omitted: if there are no labels, the brackets are also omitted.
   In (j), the comma following the label is optional. The expressions must be arithmetic expressions. If the third expression is not present, a value of 1 is assumed for it.
   The character constant in (l) and (n) can be replaced by up to five digits, or it can be omitted altogether.
   The arguments in (o) need not be present, in which case the brackets are optional.

CONSTRUCTION OF DATA TRANSFER AND AUXILIARY DATA TRANSFER STATEMENTS

(a)   READ format-identifier, input-list
  or READ (UNIT=unit-identifier, FMT=format-identifier,
         REC=integer-expression, END=label, ERR=label,
         IOSTAT=integer-variable) input-list

(b)   WRITE (UNIT=unit-identifier, FMT=format-identifier,
         REC=integer-expression, ERR=label,
         IOSTAT=integer-variable) output-list

(c)   PRINT format-identifier, output-list

(d)   OPEN (UNIT=unit-identifier, ERR=label,
         FILE=character-expression, STATUS=character-expression,
         ACCESS=character-expression, FORM=character-expression,
         RECL=integer-expression, BLANK=character-expression,
         IOSTAT=integer-variable)

(e)   CLOSE (UNIT=unit-identifier, ERR=label,
         STATUS=character-expression, IOSTAT=integer-variable)

(f)   INQUIRE (UNIT=unit-identifier, FILE=character-expression,
         IOSTAT=integer-variable, EXIST=logical-variable,
         OPENED=logical-variable, NUMBER=integer-variable,
         NAMED=character-variable, NAME=character-variable,
         ACCESS=character-variable, SEQUENTIAL=character-variable,
         DIRECT=character-variable, FORM=character-variable,
         FORMATTED=character-variable, ERR=label,
         RECL=integer-variable, NEXTREC=integer-variable,
         UNFORMATTED=character-variable, BLANK=character-variable)

(g)   BACKSPACE (UNIT=unit-identifier, ERR=label,
         IOSTAT=integer-variable)

(h)   ENDFILE (UNIT=unit-identifier, ERR=label,
         IOSTAT=integer-variable)

(i)   REWIND (UNIT=unit-identifier, ERR=label,
         IOSTAT=integer-variable)

In (a), (b) and (c), the input/output lists consist of expressions, array names and input/output do lists separated by commas. An input/output do list has the form

        (input-output-list, variable-name = arithmetic-expression,
           arithmetic-expression, arithmetic-expression)

The third arithmetic expression may be omitted, in which case a value 1 is assumed.

In (b) and (c), output-list need not be present.

An array element can replace any variable in the above definitions.

In every statement, "UNIT=" can be omitted, in which case the unit identifier must come first.

In the READ and WRITE statements, "FMT=" can be omitted, in which case the format identifier must come second.

A unit identifier must be an asterisk or be of type integer or character. It can be an integer expression, a variable name, an array name, an array element name or a substring name.

A format identifier must be an asterisk, a label, an integer or character variable name, an integer or character array name or a character expression.

CONSTRUCTION OF SPECIFICATION STATEMENTS

(a)   IMPLICIT type (letter-letter, letter-letter, ...),
         type (letter-letter, letter-letter, ...), ...

(b)   PARAMETER (constant-name=constant-expression,
         constant-name=constant-expression, ...)

(c)   REAL variable-name, variable-name, ...

(d)   INTEGER variable-name, variable-name, ...

(e)   LOGICAL variable-name, variable-name, ...

(f)   COMPLEX variable-name, variable-name, ...

(g)   DOUBLE PRECISION variable-name, variable-name, ...

(h)   CHARACTER*length variable-name*length,
         variable-name*length, ...

(i)   DIMENSION array-declarator, array-declarator, ...

(j)   COMMON /block-name/ variable-name, variable-name, ...,
         /blockname/ variable-name, variable-name, ..., ...

(k)   INTRINSIC function-name, function-name, ...

(l)   EXTERNAL function-name, function-name, ...

(m)   SAVE variable-name, variable-name, ...

(n)   EQUIVALENCE (variable-name, variable-name, ...),
         (variable-name, variable-name, ...), ...

In (a), "type" can be REAL, INTEGER, LOGICAL, COMPLEX, DOUBLE PRECISION and CHARACTER*length, where "*length" can be omitted.

In (c), (d), (e), (f), (g) and (h), "variable-name" can be replaced by a constant name, an array name, a function name or an array declarator.

In (a) and (h), "length" can be an asterisk, a non-zero unsigned integer constant or "(integer-constant-expression)".

In both (a) (see the first note) and (h), "length" can be omitted.

In (i), an array-declarator has the form
      array-name(integer-expression:integer-expression,
         integer-expression:integer-expression, ...)
There can be up to seven occurrences of "integer-expression:integer-expression", none of which can contain an array element name or a reference to a function. The first integer expression and the colon

can be omitted and the second replaced by an asterisk.

In (j), any variable name can be replaced by an array name or an array declarator. The comma immediately before "/block-name/" is optional. One occurrence of "/block-name/" can be omitted.

In (k), each function name must be that of an intrinsic function.

In (1), no function name must be that of an intrinsic function or a statement function. Any function name can be replaced by a subroutine name or a block data subprogram name.

In (m), any variable name can be replaced by an array name or by "/common-block-name/".

In (n), any variable name can be replaced by an array element name, an array name or a substring value.

CONSTRUCTION OF PROGRAM UNIT STATEMENTS

(a)   PROGRAM program-name
(b)   type FUNCTION function-name (arguments)
(c)   SUBROUTINE subroutine-name (arguments)
(d)   ENTRY subprogram-name (arguments)
(e)   BLOCK DATA subprogram-name

In (b), the brackets must be present. The "type" can be REAL, INTEGER, LOGICAL, COMPLEX, DOUBLE PRECISION or CHARACTER*length, where "*length" can be omitted.

In (b), (c) and (d), the arguments can be variable names, array names, array names, subprogram names or (except in the case of a function) asterisks, each being separated from the next by a comma.

In (e), "subprogram-name" can be omitted.

CONSTRUCTION OF DATA STATEMENTS

            DATA variable-name, variable-name, ... / constant,
                  constant, ... /, variable-name, variable-name, ... /
                  constant, constant, ... /, ...

Any variable name can be replaced by an array element name, an array name, a substring name or a data implied do list. Any constant can be replaced by a constant name. Groups of constants can be replaced by "i*constant", where "i" represents a non-zero unsigned integer constant or a constant name. The commas following the slash characters are optional. The form of a data implied do list is

            (array-element-name, array-element-name, ..., variable-name
                  = int-con-exp, int-con-exp, int-con-exp)

where "int-con-exp" represents an integer constant expression. Any array element name can be replaced by a data implied do list. The third expression can be omitted, the default value being 1.

CONSTRUCTION OF FORMAT STATEMENTS

FORMAT (format specification)

The format specification consists of a number of edit descriptors separated by commas. The edit descriptors allowed by FORTRAN 77 are

Iw	Iw.m			(integer)
Fw.d	Ew.d	Gw.d	Ew.dEe	Gw.dEe	(real)
Dw.d				(double precision)
kP				(scale factor)
A	Aw	´...´	nH...	(characters)
Lw				(logical)
Tc	TLc	TRc	nX	(position)
S	SP	SS		(sign)
BN	BZ			(blanks)
/				(new record)
:				(terminate format control)

An apostrophe in a character string is signified by ´´.

Sequences of edit descriptors may be repeated using repeat edit descriptors, which are unsigned non-zero integer constants.

CONSTRUCTION OF STATEMENT FUNCTIONS

function-name (variable-name, variable-name, ...) = expression

There need be no variable names within the brackets, but the brackets themselves must be present.

CONSTRUCTION OF COMMENT STATEMENTS

A comment statement has a C or an asterisk in position 1 of the line.

CONSTRUCTION OF NAMES

Names of variables, constants, arrays, common blocks, programs, block data subprograms, functions and subroutines consist of up to six letters and digits, starting with a letter. Unless changed by an IMPLICIT statement or a type statement, variables, constants, arrays and functions whose names start with I, J, K, L, M or N are of type integer; while those starting with any other letter are real.

Array element names have the form

array-name (integer-expression, integer-expression, ...)

There can be up to seven integer expressions.

Substring names have the form

character-variable-name (integer-expression:integer-expression)

The character variable name can be replaced by an array element name. Either integer expression can be omitted, in which case the endmost character positions are assumed.

CONSTRUCTION OF EXPRESSIONS

integer expressions
(a)   integer-variable arithmetic-operator integer-variable
arithmetic expressions
(b)   arithmetic-variable arithmetic-operator arithmetic-variable
character expressions
(c)   character-variable //   character-variable
logical expressions
(d)   .NOT. logical-variable
(e)   logical-variable logical-operator logical-variable
relational expressions
(f)   arithmetic-expression relational-operator arithmetic-expression
(g)   character-expression relational-operator character-expression
    In each case, the corresponding constant expression is obtained by replacing the appropriate variable by a constant, a constant name or another constant expression.
    In (a) and (b), the arithmetic operators are +, -, *, / and **.
    In (a), any integer variable can be replaced by an integer constant, an integer constant name, an integer array element name, or by a reference to an integer function.
    In (b), any arithmetic variable can be replaced by a constant, a constant name, an array element name or by a reference to a function. Arithmetic implies real, integer, double precision or complex.
    In (c), the character variables can be replaced by character constants, character constant names, character array element names, substring names, references to character functions or by "(character expression)".
    In (d) and (e), the logical variables can be replaced by logical constants (.TRUE. and .FALSE.), logical constant names, logical array element names, references to logical functions, relational expressions or "(logical-expression)".
    In (e), the logical operators are .AND., .OR., .EQV. and .NEQV.
    In (f) and (g), the relational operators are .LT., .GT., .LE., .GE., .EQ. and .NE.

CONSTRUCTION OF LABELS

A label is one, two, three, four or five digits, at least one of which is non-zero.

APPENDIX 4

A COMPARISON OF FORTRAN 66
AND FORTRAN 77

For most practical purposes, FORTRAN 66 is a subset of FORTRAN 77, but in a few cases FORTRAN 77 forbids features that are allowed by FORTRAN 66. This appendix compares the two Standards, giving the most important of the restrictions and an overview of the extensions. A complete list of the incompatibilities between the two Standards is to be found in appendix A of the 1977 ANSI Standard.

CHARACTER SET

The FORTRAN 77 character set contains two additional characters, the apostrophe and the colon, compared to that of FORTRAN 66. However, it should be noted that the apostrophe featured in most implementations of FORTRAN prior to 1977.

LABELS

Labels are treated in the same way by the two Standards.

NAMES

Names are constructed in the same way in the two Standards.

EXPRESSIONS

Character expressions were not part of FORTRAN 66, although a limited amount of character handling was allowed, as is described later in this appendix.

Logical expressions are the same in the two Standards, except that the logical operators .EQV. and .NEQV. are not part of FORTRAN 66.

Arithmetic expressions have been extended by FORTRAN 77 in three main directions. These are
(1) Mixed mode arithmetic was not permitted in the 1966 Standard, although most implementations allowed it. It is permitted by the 1977 Standard. All combinations of numeric quantities may appear in an arithmetic expression except that double precision quantities must

not be mixed with complex quantities.

(ii) A**B**C was not allowed by FORTRAN 66, whereas FORTRAN 77 defines it as A**(B**C).

(iii) The number of intrinsic functions has been extended.

In fact, FORTRAN 66 defined BASIC EXTERNAL FUNCTIONS, which could be used in EXTERNAL statements, and INTRINSIC FUNCTIONS, which could not. In FORTRAN 77, however, the basic external functions have been absorbed into the group of intrinsic functions and additional intrinsic functions have been added. In addition, the concept of generic and specific names, which was not part of FORTRAN 66, has been introduced.

The basic external functions defined by FORTRAN 66 were

EXP	DEXP	CEXP	ALOG	DLOG	CLOG	ALOG10
DLOG10	SIN	DSIN	CSIN	COS	DCOS	CCOS
TANH	SQRT	DSQRT	CSQRT	ATAN	DATAN	ATAN2
DATAN2	DMOD	CABS				

The intrinsic functions defined by FORTRAN 66 were

ABS	IABS	DABS	AINT	INT	IDINT	AMOD
MOD	AMAX0	AMAX1	MAX0	MAX1	DMAX1	AMIN0
AMIN1	MIN0	MIN1	DMIN1	FLOAT	IFIX	SIGN
ISIGN	DSIGN	DIM	IDIM	SNGL	REAL	AIMAG
DBLE	CMPLX	CONJG				

The additional intrinsic functions defined by FORTRAN 77 are

ICHAR	CHAR	DINT	ANINT	DNINT	NINT	IDNINT
DDIM	DPROD	TAN	DTAN	ASIN	DASIN	ACOS
DACOS	SINH	DSINH	COSH	DCOSH	DTANH	LGE
LGT	LLE	LLT	MAX	MIN	LOG	LOG10
INDEX	LEN					

In FORTRAN 66, only seven forms of integer expression were allowed as array subscripts. These were

$$K \quad V \quad V+K \quad V-K \quad K*V \quad K*V+K1 \quad K*V-K1$$

where K and K1 represent integer constants and V an integer variable. This restriction is not part of FORTRAN 77, which allows any integer expression as a subscript.

ASSIGNMENT STATEMENTS

These are implemented as in FORTRAN 66 except that the restriction that complex expressions may only be assigned to complex variables has been lifted and that character assignment statements are not part of the 1966 Standard.

CONTROL STATEMENTS

The arithmetic IF, logical IF, unconditional GOTO, CONTINUE, PAUSE and CALL statements are implemented in the same way by the two

Standards.

The BLOCK IF, ELSEIF, ELSE and ENDIF statements did not form part of FORTRAN 66, although a number of compilers allowed constructions akin to these statements.

The conditional GOTO statement is implemented by FORTRAN 77 in the same way as by FORTRAN 66 except that, in the new Standard, control passes to the next statement if the control variable is out of range. FORTRAN 66 did not define what was to happen in this case.

The assigned GOTO statement is allowed by FORTRAN 77 to have no label list. This was not allowed by FORTRAN 66.

In FORTRAN 77, the END statement is executable, whereas it was non-executable in the old Standard.

FORTRAN 66 required every main program to have at least one STOP statement and every subprogram to have at least one RETURN statement. This is no longer necessary. In addition, the alternate RETURN statement was not part of FORTRAN 66.

The DO statement has been both enhanced and restricted by the new Standard. The enhancements are

(i) Real and double precision DO variables are allowed by FORTRAN 77. FORTRAN 66 only allowed integer DO variables.

(ii) Integer, real and double precision variables are allowed as parameters in DO statements by FORTRAN 77. In the old Standard, only integer variables and constants were allowed.

(iii) In FORTRAN 66, the values of parameters were limited to positive integers. There is no such restriction in FORTRAN 77.

(iv) In FORTRAN 66, array variables were not allowed as parameters. FORTRAN 77 has no such restriction.

(v) The old Standard did not allow parameters to be changed in the course of a DO loop. In the new Standard, the number of times that a DO loop is to be executed is set at the start of the loop and the parameters can be changed by the execution of the loop.

(vi) The terminal statement of a DO loop must not be another DO statement, an arithmetic or logical IF statement, a GOTO statement, a RETURN statement, an END statement, or a STOP statement according to FORTRAN 66. In FORTRAN 77, a DO loop must not be terminated by any of the above statements, and in addition BLOCK IF, ELSEIF, ELSE and ENDIF statements must not be used.

(vii) When control left a DO loop in FORTRAN 66, the DO variable was undefined, although most implementations did not adhere strictly to this requirement. In FORTRAN 77, the DO variable retains the last value assigned to it when control leaves the DO loop, as described in section 4.2.2.

The restriction imposed by FORTRAN 77 on the DO statement is that it is no longer permitted to re-enter a DO loop. This construction, which is called the extended range of a DO loop, is bad programming practice. FORTRAN 66 did not explicitly prohibit it, with the result that most FORTRAN compilers allowed it.

The other change to the DO statement is that FORTRAN 66 required a DO loop to be executed at least once. In FORTRAN 77, the statements in the loop are not executed if the increment is positive and the initial value of the DO variable is greater than the final value (or vice versa if the increment is negative).

DATA TRANSFER STATEMENTS

As no direct access file handling was specified by FORTRAN 66, the only files permitted were sequential.

The only data transfer statements allowed by the old Standard were limited forms of the READ, WRITE, BACKSPACE, ENDFILE and REWIND statements. The PRINT, OPEN, CLOSE and INQUIRE statements were therefore not present in FORTRAN 66, although many implementations included a PRINT statement. List-directed READ, WRITE and PRINT statements were likewise not part of the 1966 Standard, although very few implementations did not allow some form of "free format".

The specifiers allowed as parameters for the READ, WRITE, statements in FORTRAN 66 were limited to a unit identifier and a format identifier. Many implementations also permitted END= or ERR= specifiers (or their equivalents).

The specifiers allowed in connection with the BACKSPACE, ENDFILE and REWIND statements in the 1966 Standard was limited to the unit identifier.

SPECIFICATION STATEMENTS

The IMPLICIT, PARAMETER, CHARACTER, INTRINSIC and SAVE statements were not defined by FORTRAN 66, although the IMPLICIT statement was available on most implementations.

The EXTERNAL statement is defined in the same way in the two Standards.

The EQUIVALENCE statement is slightly more restrictive in FORTRAN 77 in that it cannot be used with an array element which has a different number of subscripts from that defined in the DIMENSION (or equivalent) statement.

The REAL, INTEGER, LOGICAL, COMPLEX, DOUBLE PRECISION and COMMON statements are unchanged in FORTRAN 77 except when they are used to dimension arrays. In this case the extensions are the same as those for the DIMENSION statement.

The DIMENSION statement in FORTRAN 66 only allowed integer constants or (in subprograms) integer variables to be used as subscripts. No assumed size array declarators or integer expressions were allowed. Only three subscripts were allowed, and the lower bound for every subscript was 1.

PROGRAM UNIT STATEMENTS

The PROGRAM and ENTRY statements did not form part of the old Standard, which also required a FUNCTION to have at least one argument.

The other program unit statements are implemented in the same way by the two Standards.

DATA STATEMENTS

Array elements had to be assigned values individually in FORTRAN 66. This means that implied DO loops were not permitted. Likewise, the use of an unsubscripted array name to mean the entire array was also not permitted.

Although character variables did not form part of FORTRAN 66, it was permitted to assign character strings as values for variables in a DATA statement provided (according to the Standard) H-format was used to define the character string. Variables of any type could be used to hold the character string, but the number of characters held by a variable was machine-dependent.

FORMAT STATEMENTS

Although FORMAT statements themselves are constructed in the same way according to the two Standards, a number of FORTRAN 77 edit descriptors were not part of the earlier Standard. These are the colon, BN-format, BZ-format, S-format, SS-format, SP-format, T-format, TL-format and TR-format edit descriptors, although the T-format edit descriptor was available in many earlier implementations.

In addition, FORTRAN 66 did not permit character strings to be bounded by apostrophes, although this was used so widely that it became a de facto Standard.

A number of extensions were made by FORTRAN 77 to existing edit descriptors. Among these were the extension to the I-format descriptor which permits the form Iw.m and the extensions to the E-format, G-format and D-format edit descriptors which permit the forms Ew.dEe, Gw.dEe and Dw.dEe respectively.

Another extension allowed by FORTRAN 77 is that the A-format edit descriptor now permits an A by itself. FORTRAN 66 required a digit after the A.

One alteration in the defaults laid down by the two Standards should be noted. According to the 1966 Standard, blank characters in a numeric field were to be read as zeros. In FORTRAN 77, the default is that blank characters are null. Hence it is as if the default setting were BZ in FORTRAN 66 and BN in FORTRAN 77.

STATEMENT FUNCTIONS

These are implemented in the same way by the two Standards except that FORTRAN 66 required there to be at least one argument for the statement function and it did not allow array elements to be used.

COMMENT STATEMENTS

FORTRAN 66 only allowed a C in position 1 of a program line to signify a comment. In FORTRAN 77, a C or an asterisk in position 1 signifies a comment.

CHARACTER HANDLING

The 1966 Standard did not define character variables. However, it allowed Hollerith strings such as 3HJIM to be stored in a single storage unit which could be referenced using a normal variable name. Assignment statements were not allowed, although character data could be read from data records using an A-format edit descriptor or it could be assigned to variables by means of a DATA statement. FORTRAN 77 still retains this facility except that Hollerith strings are not allowed in DATA statements. Character constants such as ´ME´ must be used instead.

Another character handling facility allowed by FORTRAN 66 was that Hollerith strings in FORMAT statements could be altered at runtime. As an example of how this was done, consider

```
      WRITE (2,100)
      READ (1,100)
      WRITE (2,100)
  100 FORMAT (17H THREE BLIND MICE)
```

When used with a data record containing

```
    SEE HOW THEY RUN
```

the output was

```
  THREE BLIND MICE
  SEE HOW THEY RUN
```

This is not allowed by the 1977 ANSI Standard, although it is probable that most FORTRAN 77 compilers will permit it.

INDEX